# Global Politics

# Global Politics

## An Introduction

*Edited by*

*Charlotte Bretherton*
*and*
*Geoffrey Ponton*

 BLACKWELL
*Publishers*

Copyright © Blackwell Publishers 1996
Selection and editional matter copyright © Charlotte Bretherton and Geoffrey Ponton 1996

First published 1996

2 4 6 8 10 9 7 5 3 1

Blackwell Publishers Ltd
108 Cowley Road
Oxford OX4 1JF
UK

Blackwell Publishers Inc.
238 Main Street
Cambridge, Massachusetts 02142
USA

*British Library Cataloguing in Publication Data*

A CIP catalogue record for this book is avaiable from the British Library.

*Library of Congress Cataloging-in-Publication Data*

Global politics: an introduction/edited by Charlotte Bretherton and Geoffrey Ponton.
    p.    cm.
  Includes bibliographical references and index.
   ISBM 0-631-19564-5. – ISBM 0-631-19565-3 (pbk.)
   1. World politics–1989  2. Geopolitics.  I. Bretherton,
Charlotte.  II. Ponton, Geoffrey.
  D860.G65  1996
  909.82'9–dc20                                95-15097
                                                    CIP

Typeset in 11 on 13 pt Plantin
by Best-set Typesetter Ltd., Hong Kong
Printed and bound in Great Britain by Hartnolls Limited, Bodmin, Cornwall

This book is printed on acid-free paper

# Contents

# Figures

# Tables

# The Contributors

The contributors are lecturers at the School of Social Science, Liverpool John Moores University – with the exception of Colin Parkins, who is a Tutor-Counsellor for the Open University in Barcelona and was a student with Charlotte Bretherton at the (then) Liverpool Polytechnic in the late 1970s.

A range of disciplinary backgrounds is represented by the authors: Charlotte Bretherton and John Vogler teach and research in the field of International Relations, Mike Mannin in Comparative Politics and Geoffrey Ponton in Russian Politics. Chris Mulhearn is an Economist and Colin Parkins's focus is upon Development Studies.

# Introduction: Global Politics in the 1990s

## Charlotte Bretherton

*The global village. The new world order. The peace dividend. These are all buzzwords of the 1990s that reflected an optimistic outlook for the dawning of the next century. Each idea brought a sense that finally we could progress from the dysfunction caused by failing to understand that we are one family.*

*Unfortunately, it has become obvious that the corner turned did not lead to a smooth road on which racism, nationalism and a plethora of insular, myopic attitudes were put behind us. In fact it seems that we have entered a period where many of the demons of the Cold War era – whether economic, environmental or social – still loom like an ominous cloud on the horizon.*

Elizabeth Dowdeswell, Executive Director, United Nations Environment Programme, May 1994

Elizabeth Dowdeswell's words express feelings of disappointment and frustration common to liberal internationalists in the mid-1990s. The end of the Cold War brought hopes for enhanced international co-operation and a fresh commitment to strengthening the role of international organizations which would, in turn, facilitate attempts to address a range of global issues. Prominent among these issues are the concerns of the present authors – the perennial problems of economic inequality and social injustice and of armed conflict, and the newer issues of environmental change and degradation.

The reformist hopes expressed by Elizabeth Dowdeswell differ from the triumphalism of other commentators, for whom the end of the Cold War appeared to demonstrate the superiority of western values and belief systems. This was to herald not only the final achievement of capitalism's global reach but also the global extension of liberal democratic political institutions. The result of the globalization of these 'virtuous' systems would be a relatively peaceful and prosperous new world order (Fukuyama 1989; Kober 1990). By the mid-1990s, however, triumphalists had reason to share with reformists feelings of disappointment and uncertainty.

Inevitably, the implications of the ending of the Cold War have been perceived somewhat differently by historical pessimists. Thus we are reminded by realist commentators that post-war periods, whether after 1815, 1918, 1945 or 1989, have been characterized by the emergence of 'entirely natural', but misguided, periods of optimism that 'the future will be less perilous than the past' (Gray 1994:31). On the contrary, it is claimed, the future is likely to resemble the past; except that it will be even more dangerous. Here argument has focused, for example, on the presence of nuclear weapons without the stabilizing effect of institutionalized conflict during the Cold War, suggesting to one commentator that 'limited and carefully managed nuclear pro-liferation' is 'the best hope for avoiding war in post-Cold War Europe' (Mearsheimer 1990:54).

In a just a few paragraphs we have moved a long way – from notions of a closely interconnected 'global village' to fears that Europe will once again be riven by interstate warfare. These very different visions do not apply, as one might suppose, to different planets; they provide rather crude caricatures of two broad approaches to analysis of global politics. We shall consider these approaches, liberal pluralism and realism, among other analytical perspectives. But first let us explain what we mean by global politics.

Use of the term 'global' implies an ideological and methodological orientation based on conscious rejection of the term international. In consequence, what may appear to be a mere semantic nicety becomes a statement of the authors' position. This involves an attempt to move away from the traditional, realist approach to international politics, with its focus upon interstate relations and issues of diplomacy and security, in order to encompass both a more inclusive agenda and a range of non-state actors. These aims might be accomplished through adoption of a pluralist, 'world society' approach such as that developed by John Burton (1972).

However, we have been concerned, also, to describe and analyse the patterns of inequality which are inherent in global politics; between North and South, between women and men, and between different races and cultures. In consequence we have moved beyond the behavi-oural approach of liberal pluralism to consider the political and econ-omic structures which shape and constrain behaviour. This means that our enquiries have been directed towards different levels of analysis; it does not imply reliance upon a single theoretical perspective.

The above comments notwithstanding, we believe that the notion of global politics is itself problematic. Hence a major concern, and unify-ing theme, of this book is assessment of the extent to which it is appropriate to speak of global politics at all. In addressing this question we focus upon two areas: the implications of the ending of the Cold War and analysis of the processes implied by the concept of globalization. A differing emphasis on these two areas is reflected in the two parts of the book; both, however, focus upon globalization as central to any notion of global politics.

## Globalization

The concept of globalization is frequently employed but seldom clearly defined. To be useful, therefore, the concept requires more careful specification; in particular there is a need to demonstrate that globalization refers to a new, distinct phase in world politics. This is by no means self-evident, nor is the idea uncontested: indeed the notion of globalization stands in contradiction to the cyclical approach implied by the 'back to the future' arguments referred to above. Nor, as the history of imperialism shows, is geographical extensiveness itself a new phenomenon. What meaning, then, is conveyed by the concept of globalization?

To have utility, the concept must involve more than the geographical extension of a range of phenomena and issues – for which the term 'worldwide' would suffice. Thus globalization suggests a significant intensification of global connectedness and a consciousness of that intensification, with a corresponding diminution in the significance of territorial boundaries and state structures. Clearly, assessment of so broad and abstract a concept is a difficult task. Nevertheless, if we are to investigate the possibility that globalization refers to qualitatively different global processes and relationships than have existed heretofore, it is necessary to tease out factors which might constitute a new phase in world politics. Aspects of the globalization thesis which we see as central, interlinked and overlapping, are separated, below, for the purpose of analysis:

the enabling role of technological change
the development of a global economy
political globalization
the globalization of ideas.

### *Technological change*

While we see technological development as primarily an enabling rather than a determining factor, such development is necessary to all other aspects of globalization. From the invention of the wheel to the creation of the Internet, technological innovation has facilitated communication between people. Similarly, however, developments in weapons technology have ensured that conflicts which divide people may be prosecuted with ever more lethal effect. Technology, therefore, is supportive both of conflict and cooperation, and the direction of its influence is not necessarily towards the global. In addition, technological developments have been subject to evolution over time, albeit with greatly accelerated growth following the Industrial Revolution. We are seeking more recent changes of great significance. Here the principal candidate is the rapid development of new technologies since the Second World War – particularly, but by no means exclusively, in the field of communications.

The ability to exploit the potential of geo-stationary orbit and the electro-magnetic spectrum, coupled with the development and application of micro-electronics, has produced systems of communication which are both instantaneous in effect and global in scope. Moreover the cost of such systems has declined significantly over the past twenty-five years,[1] while new developments such as use of broadband fibre-optics have greatly expanded capacity, permitting massive increases in the volume of communications. Time–space compression is central to the globalization thesis, underlying many other aspects of globalization. Thus, for example, new communications technologies have facilitated the development of global production strategies and the integration of financial markets, and were essential to the intensification of the operations of transnational capital, particularly in relation to service activities, discussed in the final section of chapter seven.

New communications technologies have also enabled political issues and events to be discussed worldwide in 'real-time', both facilitating the dissemination of ideas and contributing to perceptions of global interconnectedness. Here the potential of a global information infrastructure has been urged by United States Vice President Al Gore, whose discussion of the virtues of information superhighways is positively liturgical:

> These highways – or, more accurately, networks of distributed intelligence – will allow us to share information, to connect, and to communicate as a global community. From these connections we will derive robust and sustainable economic progress, strong democracies, better solutions to global and local environmental challenges, improved health care, and ultimately – a greater sense of shared stewardship of our shared planet (Gore 1994:4).

At present, however, such dreams are far from realization. In practice, while the spread of new communications technologies is global in scope, there is a significant telecommunications gap between developed and developing countries; indeed there are huge disparities in access even to a basic telephone. The extent to which modern communications have penetrated domestic societies remains very uneven, and in developing countries in particular their availability tends to be restricted to major urban areas (Winsbury 1994).

The existence of technological gaps – between urban and rural areas, between regions and, most significantly, between industrialized and less developed countries (LDCs) – reminds us that access to new technologies is far from global. Demands from the Group of 77 bloc of LDCs for a New World information and communications order involving 'equity in orbit' have not been met, while the North–South technology gap remains a constant source of tension during international negotiations on a range of issues from trade policy to environmental protection. The strengthening of rights to ownership of technological knowledge (intellectual property) during the GATT (General Agreement on Tariffs and Trade) Uruguay Round provides fresh evidence of impediments to globalization of new technologies: Ali Mazrui (1990:4) may be right in arguing that 'International stratification is more about know-how than about income'.

New technologies have also contributed to the development of a range of new problems deemed to require global solutions – from nuclear weapons proliferation to the ability, again acquired only since the end of the Second World War, to commercially exploit the resources of the deep sea-bed. Thus, in areas such as the oceans and space, where new technologies have facilitated exploitation of resources beyond the jurisdiction of states, new problems of global governance arise. These issues are explored in chapter eight, where the concept of the 'global commons' is employed to highlight the scope of ecological interdependence. Here again, the role of technology has been significant. Clearly it is associated with the unintended environmental consequences of industrial processes, but this is not a new phenomenon. What is new, however, is the development of techniques such as remote sensing which have enabled us to perceive, for the first time, that aspects of environmental change are both essentially interconnected and global in scope.

In a variety of ways, then, technology plays an important role in processes of globalization; indeed it is necessary to such processes. Nevertheless its impacts are both uneven and mixed. Thus technology can enhance the ability of states to control or repress their citizens, while simultaneously contributing to the reduction of government autonomy in the economic sphere. New communications technologies, however, are inherently transnational. They facilitate direct, worldwide links between individuals and groups, presenting considerable challenges to state sovereignty. Nevertheless, while they are used to enhance global cooperation, they may equally serve to emphasize cultural divisions. Ultimately, economic and political considerations influence the choice and spread of technologies; the ownership of knowledge, as argued in chapter two, is an increasingly important aspect of structural power.

## Economic globalization

Much discussion of globalization has focused upon the extent to which it is appropriate to speak of a global economy. The growth of international trade in the nineteenth century and of transnational production in the twentieth have been associated with the gradual expansion of capitalism. An important impetus towards economic globalization was provided by the 1944 post-war settlement, which specifically aimed to prevent governments from following policies of economic nationalism. Thus the post-war Bretton Woods system and, subsequently also the General Agreement on Tariffs and Trade (GATT), established international institutions intended to supervise economic liberalization. During the Cold War, of course, the scope of these institutions was limited to the capitalist world. The end of the Cold War, however, has provided further impetus to globalization of the capitalist economy through introduction of market measures into most of the centrally planned economies of the former communist bloc. Similarly, the structural adjustment requirements of the International Monetary Fund (IMF) and the World Bank over the past fifteen years have increased both the openness and the outward orientation of the economies of most developing countries.

Economic globalization, however, implies more than the extensive reach of capital; it implies the existence of a unified global economy which has a dynamic beyond the interaction of separate domestic economies. Here arguments rest upon two principal processes: the globalization of production and the globalization of finance. Both relate to the evolving strategies of large business corporations and are substantially founded, as we have argued, upon technological innovation and the ownership of knowledge.

It is estimated that more than half of the world's goods and services are now produced according to strategies which involve planning, design, production and marketing on a global scale (Stopford and Strange 1991:4). Such strategies are adopted not simply in the interests of profit maximization but as a necessary response to a changing balance of production costs. Thus, for each unit of production, changes in design and technology enabled firms, in the decade 1974–84, to make savings of up to 40 per cent on raw materials and to substantially reduce the proportion of total costs absorbed by labour (ibid.). In addition, the cost of communications and transport has fallen significantly. The cost of research and development, however, has escalated, reflecting the enormous cost of keeping abreast of technological change. This increases the imperatives both to spread the cost of research and development by extending the scope of production, and to increase market concentration through mergers or a variety of more or less formal links between firms operating in the same sector. For examples of market concentration we need look no further than the automobile and aircraft industries. The resulting global strategies have been facilitated by trade liberalization and financial deregulation over the past twenty years.

Significant as these changes may be, they do not represent the whole picture. Global production strategies coexist with traditional international trade and with localized production. Nor are all regions of the world equally involved in the global economy. The simultaneous production of the *Financial Times* newspaper in London, New York, Frankfurt and Tokyo reminds us, perhaps, that major cities in the developed world are particularly well integrated. A rather different relationship to the global economy is revealed when we consider the number of pairs of (female) hands, from different parts of the less developed world, which have worked upon a single garment we may buy (Enloe 1989). Finally, it is evident that some of the regions of the world – notably Sub-Saharan Africa – are at best tenuously linked to global production processes; indeed the most evident link with the global economy of many of the world's poorest countries is through indebtedness.

Perhaps even more than new forms of production, financial globalization, involving transactions in money, equities and credit, has been emphasized as an agent of globalization – through its role in financing global production and as a distinct form of economic activity. The growth of global networks of banks and finance corporations has been encouraged both by financial deregulation since the mid-1970s and by the availability of cheap, reliable and instant means of communication. Growth of the finance sector over the past twenty years has been rapid, and much emphasis has been placed upon the value of financial transactions, estimated in 1992 at US $1 trillion daily – fifty times greater in value than the flow of goods and exceeding the reserves of the major central banks (Myerson 1992:8).

Such statistics imply that the role of finance corporations is becoming more significant to global politics than that of governments. Indeed one commentator has concluded that the size, scope and unregulated nature of the financial sector heralds the 'end of geography', that is the demize of the territorial state (O'Brien 1992). However, the impacts of financial globalization upon governmental decision-making are likely to vary considerably with the strength of the domestic economy and, once again, to vary according to region.

These issues are systematically explored in chapter seven, which assesses the notions of economic and financial globalization in terms both of extensiveness and degree of market integration. Here again there is emphasis upon the instability and unevenness of these processes. This theme is very evident, also, in chapter three, which examines North–South relations. It is inevitable that any discussion of these issues will include analysis of the manner in which the countries of the South are linked into the global economy, whether through production, trade, aid or debt.

## Political globalization

Political globalization refers to a growing tendency for issues to be perceived as global in scope, and hence requiring global solutions; and to the development of international organizations and global institutions which attempt to address such issues. More tentatively, the concept also suggests the development of a global civil society, in which local groups and grassroots organizations from all parts of the world interact both directly and through the United Nations system. Some evidence of this is found in chapter three, which discusses the emergence of community-based development initiatives linking municipalities in the North and South, while chapter eight explores the claim of radical political ecologists that grassroots movements provide the only hope of safeguarding the planet. In addition chapter nine explores the notion of cosmopolitan democracy and chapter ten discusses the role of human rights organizations in linking individuals to global political processes. These examples notwithstanding, it is difficult to find substantial evidence of the development of a global civil society: it must be concluded that it is, at best, embryonic.

The growth of formal international organizations is not difficult to chart, however. In 1909 there were in existence 37 intergovernmental organizations (IGOs) and 176 international non-governmental organizations (NGOs). By 1993 these had increased in number to 286 and 4,696 respectively, while the scope of their operations had expanded considerably, and continues to do so (Willetts 1995). In addition to these formal organizations there exist a range of more or less explicit understandings and collaborative procedures – some based upon treaty law, others upon custom and practice – which shape expectations of behaviour in relation to global issues. Understanding of global politics requires that attention be paid to these global institutions, or regimes, as well as to the operation of formal organizations – an issue which is taken up in chapter eight in relation to global environmental change.

The issues to be considered as constituting the agenda of global politics can be divided into three broad categories:

Issues which have traditionally been considered the responsibility of individual states (and jealously guarded as aspects of state sovereignty) but are increasingly seen in terms of collective responsibility, whether this be regional or universal. Here we include military security and human rights.

Issues which are transboundary or worldwide in scope or effect, where international cooperation is widely practised and/or seen as desirable. These include international terrorism; drug-related crime; control of infectious diseases; transport and communications and transborder pollution.

Issues which are global in scope and require global cooperation if they are to be effectively addressed. Here we include issues associated with the global economy; with development; population movements; and management of the global commons, as well as the more specific problems of stratospheric ozone depletion and climate change.

The issues included in the second category above are not discussed in depth in the chapters which follow. They are areas where international cooperation has traditionally been practised, albeit not without controversy, and hence do not provide a test for theses of globalization.

Attention will focus, however, on the category one issues of security and human rights, where shifting perceptions of salience and responsibility, associated in part with the ending of the Cold War, fundamentally challenge traditional approaches to interstate relations. These issues are discussed in chapters six and ten.

The broad and complex issues referred to in the third category above inevitably receive attention in several chapters. Issues associated with economic inequality, debt, development and the environment are closely interlinked; they also impinge directly upon questions of human rights and democracy. In addition chapter eight focuses upon those environmental issues where global interconnections are particularly apparent. Here, global environmental change provides the archetypal example of a global issue or, more properly, set of issues. The notion of environmental change introduces complex sets of issue linkages (for example between carbon dioxide emissions and deforestation) which necessitate a global approach to resource allocation and use. In addition global environmental change links consumption patterns in the North and women's reproductive rights in the South, potentially affecting the everyday lives of all the earth's people.

### Globalization of ideas

Dissemination of ideas is a further, important aspect of the globalization thesis. Here interest focuses on two areas: first, the extent to which ideas concerning social, economic and political relationships have become global in scope; and, second, the potential emergence of a cosmopolitan culture.

Of particular influence with regard to the first of these areas has been the broad set of ideas associated with the concept of modernization. Essentially a product of western thought, the notion of modernization posits stages of development whereby, through evolution or revolution, traditional societies become modern. These ideas are extremely pervasive, providing a framework for evaluation of the development of different societies, and ultimately peoples, based on norms suffused with cultural biases.

Ideas associated with modernization have also had considerable practical impact. They have underlain the policies of development agencies, producing alien forms of maldevelopment insensitive to the needs of local people and destructive of fragile ecosystems (Shiva 1989). They have encouraged many thousands of women who lack adequate resources to feed their babies on formula milk in the belief that breastfeeding is unmodern. They have fostered the belief that cultural westernization is a prerequisite for technological modernization; and, above all, they have served to legitimize patterns of domination and exploitation.[2]

Global as their impact may be, the ideologies of modernization are not new; indeed they are an essential aspect of colonialism dating back to the eighteenth century. In consequence the pervasive impact of these ideologies is a prerequisite for, rather than an aspect of, the globalization of ideas. It is to the post-Second World War period that we look for further evidence.

Much of the period following the Second World War was dominated by two highly significant sets of events; the Cold War and the dissolution of the European empires. While fundamental divisions were created between East and West, the Cold War became a global phenomenon. In an effort to extend their spheres of interest, attempts were made both by the United States and the Soviet Union to influence the domestic and foreign policies of states worldwide. Hence the Cold War and the decolonization process became intertwined as the superpowers of the First and Second Worlds competed to influence the development, and gain the allegiance, of Third World states.

The post-1945 period, then, saw the globalization of the state as a form of political organization (in 1945 there were just 51 members of the United Nations, by the end of 1994 there were 185); and the globalization of the idea that the state was owed the allegiance of its peoples. Beyond this general principle, ideas concerning the form and development of the state in newly independent countries became an aspect of Cold War competition between two modernizing ideologies – Marxism and liberalism. In practice this competition had tended to remain at the level of rhetoric; superpower support was extended to governments on the basis of their strategic significance rather than their domestic political arrangements. However the ending of the Cold War, in ending this global contest of ideas, has provoked considerable debate concerning the prospects for democracy, not only in the former eastern bloc but in the various regions of the Third World also (Held 1993).

In the post-Cold War period, rhetoric has been accompanied by action. Thus debt management, aid or trade agreements have increasingly included – at the insistence of western governments and intergovernmental economic organizations – conditionality clauses designed to encourage, or indeed impose, the introduction of liberal economic and political arrangements. In consequence questions are raised concerning the potential globalization of liberal democratic ideas and forms of governance.

These issues are taken up in chapter two in relation to the Third World and in chapter four in relation to the successor states of the Soviet Union. However chapter nine deals specifically with issues of democracy and democratization, examining the prospects for and pressures upon liberal democratic forms of government in the contexts of Italy in the West, of the former eastern bloc countries and the various regions of the Third World. Even more than was the case with economic globalization, the spread of ideas concerning liberal democracy is found to be uncertain and problematic. Moreover, it is suggested that liberal democratic forms are subject to adaptation in different contexts to accommodate distinctive cultural norms and traditions. This is an important point, suggesting that globalization is not necessarily synonymous with westernization; but rather that the potential exists for the emergence of a variety of hybrid political forms. This notion resonates with ideas about the development of a cosmopolitan culture.

The potential for the emergence of a hybrid, cosmopolitan culture is a function of the generally enhanced communications opportunities of the modern age, intensified by the development and spread of new technologies in recent years. Involving an eclectic mixture of ethnic themes and images which links young people, in particular, across physical and cultural boundaries, the notion of an emerging cosmopolitanism presents a counter-argument to more traditional claims of increasing western cultural domination. While such arguments remind us that we are not yet inhabiting McWorld, they tend to be based upon rather impressionistic evidence. Here some interesting trends are revealed by analysis of the content of television broadcasting on a global basis.

Support for the notion of increasing cosmopolitanism is provided by the increasing scope and popularity of television productions emanating from Third World countries. Export of programmes from Latin America, for example, has spread far beyond Spanish or Portuguese speaking countries and the United States. Foremost among the Latin American exporters is the Brazilian company, TV Globo, which sells programmes to more than 100 countries including China and Russia and much of eastern Europe, where they are hugely popular. Significantly, assumptions concerning the unrivalled popularity, worldwide, of American soap operas are not borne out. Indeed, contrary evidence can be found which suggests insularity rather than cosmopolitanism. For example, a global television news survey carried out in 1992 found that most countries or regions of the world were overwhelmingly concerned with their own news. It was concluded that 'Local concerns predominate . . . It seems that there are many worlds on this one earth – and that mostly they stay next door, minding their own business' (Chapman 1992:33).

It is evident that the dissemination of ideas, whether they reflect western or cosmopolitan values, does not imply their acceptance; indeed reaction to new ideas can range from complete assimilation to outright rejection. Arguably the 1979 Iranian Revolution represented the latter response to westernization. We have subsequently witnessed the growth of religious fundamentalism in various regions of the world and, since the end of the Cold War, a resurgence of ethno-cultural particularism which involves, in part, a reaction against globalization. This suggests, not the emergence of a cosmopolitan culture, but political fragmentation in the face of economic globalization – an issue discussed in chapter five which examines contemporary sources of military conflict.

## Summary

Globalization is depicted as a set of overlapping processes that are neither inexorable nor irreversible; the impact of which varies in intensity and is highly differentiated in effect. Simply put – globalization is an uncertain process which affects some people more than others; it also produces winners and losers.

If the concept is to have utility it must be demonstrated that it has a meaning which is distinct from older concepts such as westernization. We have argued that globalization is particularly associated with technological and political developments since the Second World War. Although this might indicate merely an intensification of a long-term process rather than a new phase of global politics, the existence of such a phase is suggested by the emergence of globally oriented grassroots movements which utilize advanced communications technologies. This embryonic global politics can be seen in a number of areas but is associated, in particular, with the assumptions of environmentalists that such a global politics is necessary to the survival of the planet. Thus the apparently simplistic slogan 'think global, act local' is a manifestation of a new politics which has proved capable of challenging governments, business corporations and intergovernmental economic organizations such as the World Bank.[3] Despite some successes, however, there are many impediments to effective global cooperation between environmental groups – not least the unequal access to resources and differences in focus which divide groups based in the North from Third World grassroots organizations whose concerns are frequently both local and immediate. Such difficulties can be generalized to other policy areas.

We consider globalization to be a concept worthy of investigation which is none the less beset with difficulties. We have attempted to analyse and assess the various aspects of globalization through a combination of empirical and theoretical approaches.

## Approaches to Analysis of Global Politics

Given the scope and complexity of our subject matter it is inevitable that some phenomena will be emphasized at the expense of others, and that many will be omitted altogether. Analytical perspectives are useful in helping us to ensure that these omissions are not random, provided we are aware that the criteria for selecting what is significant, and hence worthy of study, are based upon gendered, culturally specific and ideologically biased judgements about how the world is or should be ordered. In an attempt to overcome this difficulty it is helpful to consider a number of different perspectives which provide competing, but not necessarily mutually exclusive, explanations of global politics; and in particular to range beyond the two traditional approaches – realism and liberal pluralism.

Realism derives from the conservative tradition, focusing upon what might broadly be termed the practice of statecraft. Its title suggests the pretension that its principles accord closely with the realities of life in a harsh environment, where states are endlessly engaged in competition for power. Thus its protagonists value prudence over morality and seek consciously to distance themselves from what is considered to be the naive idealism of many liberals. While realism has ancient roots, its contemporary form, neo-realism, is associated with the post-Second World War period. Nevertheless neo-realists continue to focus primarily upon interstate relations, exploring what is identified as the central problematic – the maintenance of order in an international system which is ungoverned, and hence anarchical. The principal innovation of neo-realism is the introduction of a structural perspective based upon the power capabilities of states: chapter two discusses these issues in some detail.

Liberal analyses encompass a variety of approaches whose principles tend to be less well specified than those of realism. Nevertheless liberals share assumptions, rooted in the Kantian tradition, concerning the possibility of a stable world order based upon common adherence to the rule of law. Contemporary liberal pluralists also adopt, as their name implies, a relatively inclusive approach to analysis. Understanding of global politics, it is argued, requires that attention be focused not only on the decisions of foreign policy elites but also on the activities of social movements, business corporations and international organizations. In addition, the significance of transnational links is emphasized – between fractions of state bureaucracies, sub-national units of government, subsidiaries of large corporations and networks of pressure and interest groups. Consequently, for liberal pluralists, global politics reflects processes of bargaining within states and across state boundaries, with the result that the agenda is broadened to include a range of financial, economic and welfare issues in addition to traditional preoccupations with state security.

The broader scope of liberal pluralist analysis might suggest that this perspective, in encompassing many of our stated concerns, is our preferred approach. This is not necessarily the case, however. We are critical of both realist and liberal pluralist approaches to analysis – neither alone nor in combination do they satisfactorily account for the phenomena that concern us. However our principal criticism of these two approaches to analysis is that their very dominance is a reflection of the interests of dominant groups. Realism concerns itself almost exclusively with the behaviour of powerful states. Liberal pluralism, while apparently broad in scope, nevertheless operates more subtle forms of marginalization and exclusion. Thus, by failing adequately to conceptualize the mechanisms of domination and exploitation which characterize aspects of contemporary North–South relations, or to recognize the processes which conceal women's role in global politics, pluralist analysis effectively excludes some three-quarters of the earth's population.

In addition to these traditional approaches there is a range of critical analyses of global politics. Here Robert Cox makes a useful distinction between problem-solving and critical theories (Cox 1983). Both neo-realism and pluralism are examples of the problem-solving approach, which

> ... takes the world as it finds it, with the prevailing social and power relationships and the institutions into which they are organised, as the given framework for action. The general aim of problem-solving is to make these relationships and institutions work ... (Cox 1983:165).

Critical analyses of global politics include a range of structuralist and feminist perspectives which, despite their considerable differences, share an approach that is

... critical in the sense that it stands apart from the prevailing order of the world and asks how that order came about ... does not take institutions and social and power relations for granted but calls them into question ... is directed towards an appraisal of the very framework for action, or problematic, which problem-solving theory accepts as its parameters (ibid.).

In order to show how various analytical approaches may be applied to the issues with which we are concerned, we have separated questions of structure from considerations of actorness in global politics. Ultimately, however, it is the interaction between these levels with which we are concerned.

### The level of structure

Several perspectives focus on, and give primacy to, the structural level. Below we briefly discuss two examples of structural analysis – the neo-realist conceptualization of structure as patterns of interstate relations; and Susan Strange's model of structure in terms of global patterns of socio-economic relations – these and other structural approaches are discussed more fully in chapter two.

Neo-realists largely follow the approach developed by Kenneth Waltz (1979). The structure of the interstate system is defined in terms of its organizing principle (anarchy), the distribution of capabilities (military power) and the extent of functional differentiation (or division of labour) between its units. Since the units – states – are not regarded as participating in a division of labour, neo-realist analysis focuses on power balancing in conditions of anarchy or, more recently, 'polarity'. With some nostalgia for the 'stark simplicities and comforting symmetry' of Cold War bipolarity (Waltz 1993:44), neo-realists are currently charting the dangerous waters of multipolarity; or perhaps unipolarity. As the dominant approach to analysis of international relations, neo-realism requires examination. Nevertheless, on many of the dimensions of globalization we consider significant, this perspective remains silent.

An approach to structure which is both more inclusive in content, and global in scope, is provided by Susan Strange (1988; 1991). Strange constructs a flexible model comprising four overlapping structures – security, production, finance and knowledge. In this model, structural power derives from the extent to which access to the four structures is overlapping. This provides the potential to conceptualize shifts in power which is sometimes lacking in structural analyses. It also allows us to move beyond the neo-realist emphasis upon military capability, involved in the security structure. Significantly, it provides for inclusion of two aspects we consider to be central to the notion of globalization; the finance structure and the knowledge structure. Thus business corporations having access to the finance and knowledge structures may be more powerful than states whose power is based upon traditional industries and conventional military capabilities.

In addition to the discussion of structural analysis in chapter two, the structural level is addressed in chapter three, which analyses the structures and processes underlying contemporary North–South relations, and chapter seven which describes and analyses the structure of the global economy.

## Actors in global politics

As is already apparent, identification of significant actors is a further issue which illustrates differences between analytical perspectives. These differences centre upon the questions of inclusiveness and relative significance, focusing in particular upon the role of states.

Realism is alone in its almost exclusive concentration on states, which are conceptualized as unitary actors engaged in rational calculations of risk as they interact in conditions of anarchy. This reification of the state leads to a high level of generalization. While other actors may participate in global politics, states remain of central importance.

Susan Strange's structural approach proposes a limited mixed actor model in which states and firms interact with markets and technology. This model has the advantage of clearly identifying the actors considered to be significant and, by including markets and technology, encompassing important aspects of globalization. Nevertheless we are not convinced that reification of markets and technology is necessarily more helpful than reification of states.

Liberal pluralists, inevitably, adopt a pluralistic view of decision-making, both within states and at the global level. This is associated with a complex 'cobweb' model of global politics which is highly inclusive (Burton 1972). This approach allows us to discuss a wide range of actors and to conceptualize links between the local and global levels. However, the pluralist dissociation of the behaviour of actors from the structures of power makes it difficult to identify those actors whose preferences routinely influence policy outcomes. In consequence it might appear that an international Scouts Jamboree and a meeting of the Intellectual Property Association were of equal importance.

Significant, also, is the failure of pluralist analysis to identify the exclusionary effects of the operation of structural power. In consequence, this apparently highly inclusive approach has shared with the narrowly focused perspective of realism an inability to conceptualize the role of women in global politics. In recent years, however, the application of gender analysis to global politics has increased understanding of the social processes which underlie political and economic relationships, providing a framework which enables us to conceptualize links between individuals, state and corporate actors, and global structures. Thus Cynthia Enloe's analysis of the social gender relations underlying both the creation of the Cold War and its ending, exemplifies a truly global approach to global politics (Enloe 1988; 1993).

These issues are dealt with differently in the chapters which follow. Although nowhere is there an entirely state-centric approach, the degree of inclusiveness varies both with the perspective of individual authors, the level of analysis addressed and the particular issues under consideration.

Chapters six and eight focus primarily on the global level. Chapter eight examines the record of and potential for cooperation between states and other actors across a range of environmental issues. A number of factors specific to the environmental agenda are discussed, including the links between environment and development encapsulated in the concept of sustainability. Chapter six discusses the concept of security, focusing upon attempts to construct a broad approach to security and examining the potential for intergovernmental cooperation, through the United Nations, in addressing the complex challenges of a broadly defined security agenda. Here, again, linkages are evident between global issues – of security, environment, development and democracy.

Chapters four and nine direct attention to the level of the state, focusing upon processes of economic and political change within states and the influence of external factors on governmental policy-making. Thus chapter nine examines the concept of democracy and processes of democratization in several different contexts, including a case study highlighting contemporary problems of democracy in Italy, in order to test western liberal triumphalism on home ground. Chapter four focuses upon the disintegration of the Soviet Union and assesses the prospects for peaceful transition and development in each of the successor states. In addition the relationship between Russia and other successor states is discussed, together with the difficulties faced by Russian policy-makers in formulating a coherent approach to external relations.

Chapters five and ten focus upon links between different levels of analysis. Potential sources of armed conflict are examined in chapter five. Here a distinction is made between interstate conflict and intercommunal conflict, and sources of conflict at the structural, state and societal levels are examined. Thus discussion ranges from problems of resource scarcity and the potentially destabilizing effects of population movement, to issues of cultural identity associated with ethnicity or religion. Finally chapter ten, in discussing human rights issues, explicitly links the individual and the global levels and addresses directly the question of women's exclusion from global politics.

## Major Themes and Organization of the Book

The division of the book into two parts, which focus on the end of the Cold War and globalization respectively, is an organizational device which reflects only a difference in emphasis. Most chapters examine the impact of the ending of the Cold War and, unsurprisingly, many find this to have been significant. In particular, of course, the disintegration of the Soviet Union, and of the eastern bloc, has resulted in considerable political instability in that region. This has been associated with a resurgence of identity politics based primarily upon ethnicity. Here, at least in the medium term, the potential for political fragmentation militates against notions of globalization. In other areas, however, the end of the Cold War has brought prospects of more fruitful intergovernmental cooperation in addressing security and development issues. An exception here relates to the environment, where intergovernmental cooperation was relatively unimpeded by Cold War politics and the end of the Cold War, in consequence, has had little impact.

All of the chapters contribute, in different ways, to discussion of globalization, although this is more explicitly the focus of Part II. In each case, while some evidence is found to support the globalization thesis, reservations are expressed about the unevenness and fragility of the processes of globalization. In particular chapters seven and nine, in discussing, respectively, the global economy and democratization, express grave concerns about the prospects for inclusion of Sub-Saharan Africa in any such processes. These concerns are echoed in chapter three on North–South relations and in discussion of the potential for armed conflict in chapter five. These pessimistic conclusions are ameliorated only in small part by intimations of an embryonic global politics linking individuals and communities worldwide in defence of human rights and the environment.

The organization within each part of the book broadly reflects the different levels of analysis addressed. Thus each part begins with a chapter or chapters focusing upon the overarching structures and moves on to examine issues at the level of the state, aspects of interstate relations, and global political issues. Thus the book progresses from consideration of approaches to structural analysis in chapter two, to examination of the basis for and content of individual human rights in chapter ten – a truly global compass.

## Notes

1 This reduction in cost is exemplified by the fact that in the 1960s the cost of an Intelsat telephone circuit connecting one point of the earth's surface to any other was 60,000 US dollars; by the early 1990s it was only 9,000 dollars – a reduction of 85%.

2 The relationship between cultural values and attitudes towards technological innovation in different contexts is discussed in some detail by Ali Mazrui (1990). His discussion of the cultural foundations of power links cultural factors with technological development and the ownership of knowledge.

3 Numerous examples can be found of environmental groups' influence on government and corporate policy, particularly in areas affecting animal rights. A lesser known but potentially significant example is the success of environmental organizations in persuading the World Bank to withdraw funding from the Narmada River project in India because of its damaging environmental impacts.

# Part I

# After the Cold War:
## The Traditional Agenda
## Revisited

# 2

# The Structures of Global Politics

## John Vogler

The events of 1989–91 are already being associated with 'structural change' as profound as that which followed events in Paris, two hundred years before. Yet use of the term 'structural' may often signify little more than that the observer feels the changes to be important. 'Structure' is both an overworked and under-defined concept. One purpose of this chapter is to consider its uses in international relations. They have been quite diverse reflecting, as they do, the focus of interest and the assumptions of the analyst. A consideration of the various structures that we may perceive in the world system, and the possible relationships between them, serves as a necessary preliminary to the other task of this chapter, which is to consider those structural changes associated with the ending of the Cold War.

The everyday meaning of the term 'structure' is readily apparent. The structure of a building or some other artefact is its main framework; it also denotes the way in which the various constituent parts fit together. In communications systems, structure can usefully be seen as the fixed 'pipework', 'wiring' or 'tracks' along which materials or messages flow back and forth. The structure of the London Underground system is represented by the familiar stylized map in which different coloured 'lines' join its many stations. The fixed structure of a telecommunications system or a national power grid could be similarly portrayed. These examples are of manufactured structures, consciously organized by human agency. Structures may also be perceived in the natural world – as with molecular structure in chemistry. In this instance 'structure' denotes the arrangement of atoms in a molecule. Such a structure is, of course, not an artefact but a set of patterns or regularities which we observe and then systematize.

Except where structures are consciously designed (as in a formal organization) the analogy with the scientist's observation of patterns in the natural world also holds good for many aspects of social life. Thus, in societies: '. . . all distinctive forms of association have discernible structures which permit analysis in terms of their elements and the ways in which these operate together as a single whole' (Bullock and Stallybrass 1977:608). Many significant social structures arise as a consequence of a myriad of human interactions which both constitute and reinforce them. For example, market structures occur, not because they were planned; but as the consequence of large numbers of individuals or firms interacting in the pursuit of their own material interests.

Why do structures matter in the study of society in general and international relations in particular? The answer is that they serve to constrain and channel behaviour and to prescribe the choices open to actors. A banal example is provided by the structure of transport systems. If the system is structured in a certain way with roads between certain points, it will matter little that individuals may wish to travel by train or by different routes; their behaviour will effectively be constrained. In the same way the inhabitants of a less developed country (LDC) in the world economic structure may have very few choices as to what they can consume and produce. Furthermore, reference to the structure within which economic or political relationships occur can explain why the intentions of individual actors are not reflected in outcomes at the level of the system. In international politics realists have assumed that state actors strive to become more powerful than their neighbours. The outcome, when a number of states pursue this end within the structure of a 'balance of power' system, is usually a rough equilibrium between them.

In the social sciences there have been wide variations of opinion as to the significance of structures as determinants of human behaviour. This 'agent–structure debate' has recently been rehearsed in the international relations literature (Wendt 1987; Dessler 1989; Buzan, Jones and Little 1993:102–13), although it has always been implicit in theoretical debates between Marxists and liberals or between traditional realists who tend to emphasize the characteristics of state actors, and neo-realist structuralists. The latter may be regarded as structuralists because of their belief that human activity (in this case the behaviour of state governments) is ineluctably shaped by structural forces. On the other side of this argument the essential significance of human agency and 'free will' are asserted in opposition to the 'mechanistic determinism' of structuralist thinkers. Although 'structure and agency' provide a neat dichotomy, such simplicity may be misleading. Scholars rarely go to extremes and most include some elements of both structure and human agency in their work. None the less, there is a clear division between those who attribute overriding importance to structure and those who do not.

In the study of international relations neo-realists along with Marxists and other structuralists are located in the former camp. They all advance structural explanations, but there is a marked difference in the kind of international or global structure to which they attribute significance. Without arguing that structures are simply patterns and regularities that we arbitrarily impose on reality, it is the case that analysts will select and study different structures according to their different purposes and interests. Above all they will be guided by their ontological assumptions. These are the basic irreducible assertions about the nature of existence that lie behind any theory.

In international relations, realists have a particular ontology comprising beliefs about the central importance of power, wealth and status-seeking among state actors. Accordingly, their focus will be upon the 'power structure' that arises from the pattern of interstate relations. Their main concern, discussed in the next section of this chapter, is the way in which a particular configuration of power structure is associated with order and stability. The end of the Cold War and the collapse of the Soviet Union obviously brought about the most fundamental rearrangement in the power structure and realists continue to debate the likely shape of the new structure and its implications for order and security.

It is difficult to discuss the power structure in isolation from the underlying economic structure of the global system. Questions of the changing economic and technical bases of 'great power' status and the underlying forces that drive structural change have long preoccupied students of world history and appear in particularly acute form in the last decades of the twentieth century. For neo-realists there has also been a more immediate concern, dating back to the 1970s, with structural dominance and leadership (hegemony) in the world economy. Paradoxically the United States appeared to achieve unchallenged political and military primacy at the end of a decade in which many academic commentators had bewailed its loss of economic hegemony.

Neo-realist arguments about power balances and hegemony between states do not exhaust the potential of structural thinking in international relations – although they have tended to dominate the field. The third section of this chapter considers some of the alternatives which go beyond state-centric assumptions. Marxists and other structuralists have an altogether different idea of what constitutes the structure of the world system.[1] This reflects their concern with the material bases of historical change and an analysis in which classes and the ownership of the means of production hold centre stage. Structures, from this viewpoint, are composed of patterns of economic inequality, dominance and dependence. A concentration on such structures sheds an altogether different light upon recent change in the global system which indicates, amongst other things, a different problematic of inequality and injustice as opposed to realist concern with preservation of order. It may also provide an alternative way of thinking about power in structural rather than purely relational terms.

## Power Structure

Realism, with its emphasis on international relations as 'power politics' continues to dominate the academic study of the international system just as it also forms an important part of the intellectual equipment of policy-makers. There was always a structural element in realist thought in that writers such as Carr (1939) and Morgenthau (1967) emphasized the significance of the anarchic character of the system and the configuration of relations between the major powers as a determinant of state behaviour. Yet alongside this there was often a philosophical pessimism about man's inherently evil and power-seeking nature, on occasion modified by references to 'national character' (Morgenthau 1967:122–7).

It is neo-realism, and most significantly Kenneth Waltz's *Theory of International Politics* (1979) that provides us with a genuinely structural theory of international politics. Waltz, like Morgenthau before him, is concerned to establish the autonomy of the political sphere and his concept of system is of the international political system, composed of state units. Waltz's debt to economic theorizing is also clearly expressed:

> International-political systems, like economic markets, are formed by the coaction of self-regarding units. International structures are defined in terms of the primary political units of an era, be they city states, empires, or nations. Structures emerge from the coexistence of states. No state intends to participate in the formation of a structure by which it and others will be constrained. International political systems, like economic markets are individualist in origin, spontaneously generated and unintended. In both systems structures are formed by the coaction of their units (Waltz 1979:91).

Thus, structure, defined as the relationship between state units, both arises from and determines their interaction. Waltz's theory of international politics is a structural rather than what he describes as a 'reductionist' theory because it locates explanation at the level of structure (Waltz 1979:ch. 2). The structure of political systems, both international and domestic, is defined in terms of three characteristics: '. . . first by the principle according to which they are organized or ordered, second by the differentiation of units and the specification of their functions, and third by the distribution of capabilities across the system' (Waltz 1979:88).

The *organizing principle* of the international political structure is anarchy as opposed to the hierarchy one might expect to find in domestic systems. This has a very important consequence for the second element of structure which is the *differentiation* of the units. Whereas, in domestic societies, sociologists are mainly concerned with the ways in which the various units in the structure exhibit different characteristics and functions, no such differentiation occurs in the international system. The logic of anarchy and the absence of an ordered hierarchy means that each unit must compete with its counterparts and fulfil equivalent functions, leading ineluctably to a situation in which they all resemble each other. The most controversial and minimalist part of Waltz's theory follows directly from this assumption. If all the units are essentially similar there is no need to consider their characteristics or differences when discussing system change. Thus, in Waltz's memorable phrase, differentiation, the second part of the definition of structure, simply 'drops out' of consideration.

This leaves the third defining element of structure which is the *distribution of capabilities* across units. A distinction may be made between this changeable aspect of structure and what has been called 'deep structure' – Waltz's organizing principle of anarchy. The two are, in the last analysis, logically related because if one unit were to amass such power in relation to the others that it could completely subordinate them, an anarchic structure would be replaced by a hierarchical one.

Discussion of attempts by various states to achieve such a dominant position embroider the pages of European history, but whether in the case of sixteenth-century Spain, or France in the seventeenth and eighteenth centuries, anarchy always prevailed and the essential structure of the system was maintained. The ways in which this was achieved, the shifting configurations of capability and political and military power and their relationship to the incidence of large-scale war and international order (not always the same thing), have been the central preoccupation both of academic realism and the writing of diplomatic history.

The conventional way of referring to the distribution of capabilities across the units of the system has been the 'balance of power'. There are few terms which have been as heavily used, both in academic studies and practical statecraft. Yet, as Inis Claude's (1962) classic study demonstrates, there are few which have caused such confusion or have been subject to so many variations of meaning. Recent discussion in international relations has concentrated upon the implications (in terms of peace, order and stability) of particular distributions of power, or to put it another way, the relative power position of the major state units. In European history a 'balance of power system' can be identified, displaying a dynamic equilibrating principle, wherein, through shifting alliances, the major units always tended towards an approximate equality in power. (Waltz asserts that balance of power politics prevails where 'two and only two requirements are met: that the order be anarchic and that it be populated by units wishing to survive' [1979:121]). This manifestly did not avoid warfare, but it did maintain the deep structure of the system and, over long periods, the integrity of the major states.

Europe's 'classical balance' logically required at least three and preferably five or more major actors. An international structure exhibiting this type of distribution might have been observable in the Europe of the eighteenth and nineteenth centuries, but the events of the early twentieth dramatically altered the relative distribution of capabilities. By the early years of the Cold War a 'bipolar' structure was evident in which the United States and the Soviet Union commanded capabilities which were so far in excess of those possessed by any other units in the system that they were regarded as the only 'superpowers'. As the 'long peace' of the Cold War extended through the 1960s and 1970s realist analysts, including Waltz, came to appreciate the stability and order conferred by a bipolar structure in contradistinction to the diplomatic and military minuet played out by the old European 'powers'. There were dissenting voices arguing, not so much that bipolarity failed to provide order, but that the economic re-emergence of Japan and Western Europe and the entry of China into world politics, rendered inaccurate the notion of a capability distribution with two poles. Inevitably, the concept (unknown to physics) of 'multipolarity' was coined.

## The Polarity of the post-Cold War System

The precipitate abdication of superpower status by the Soviet Union left confusion in its wake. It was particularly troubling for neo-realist theorists of international structure who, in common with almost everybody else, had exhibited a depressing inability to predict the events of 1989–91. Robert Jervis summed up the dilemma of those attempting to come to terms with an unfamiliar international landscape where, although the crippled USSR remained the only state that could present a military challenge to the USA, the latter's economic rivals were also its close allies:

> This configuration is so odd that we cannot easily determine the system's polarity. Is it unipolar because the United States is so much stronger than the nearest competitor, bipolar because of the distribution of mili-

tary resources, tripolar because of an emerging united Europe, or multipolar because of the general dispersion of power? (Jervis 1991/2:42)

Almost inadvertently the America of Bush and Clinton seemed to have achieved the kind of unparalleled military and political primacy that realist writers once described as the unattainable goal of great powers. Where Louis XIV, Napoleon, Kaiser Wilhelm II and Adolf Hitler had failed they had succeeded. As ever, the arguments in academic journals intersected real policy debates in Washington. The leaked Defense Planning Guidance for Fiscal Years 1994–9 attempted a post-Cold War redirection of US national security strategy which explicitly endorsed the benefits of primacy and set national goals in terms of maintaining 'the mechanisms for deterring potential competitors from even aspiring to a larger regional or global role'.[2] In the public domain Huntington (1993:83) concluded that US primacy mattered because without it there would be a world with 'more violence and disorder and less democracy and economic growth'. The claim was far-reaching indeed: 'The sustained international primacy of the United States is central to the welfare and security of Americans and to the future of freedom, democracy, open economies, and international order' (ibid.).

This conclusion ran counter to a nagging neo-realist doubt about the sustainability of a dominant position in the power structure. According to Layne's (1993) Waltzian analysis of the 'unipolar illusion', both historical examples (the short-lived dominance of France 1660–1714 and of Britain 1860–1910) and structural principles indicate the impossibility of sustained primacy. Projections of the end of primacy notwithstanding, there was also some uncertainty as to whether primacy was, in any case, currently enjoyed by the United States. Writing in 1991 Waltz himself claimed in answer to his own question 'How does the weakened condition of Russia affect the structure of international politics?' that 'bipolarity endures' (Waltz 1993:52). This was because no other great power had yet emerged and Russia retained the military capability to 'take care of itself'. However, later in the same article he predicted the imminent disappearance of bipolarity in favour of a multipolar system (ibid.:73).[3] If primacy existed in the early 1990s it sometimes came in a strange guise. President Bush was able to lead a successful coalition against Iraq in 1991 but thereafter the promised 'new world order' under US tutelage seemed to recede. The prolonged wrangling over the GATT Uruguay Round hardly demonstrated effortless control and US military intervention under UN auspices in Somalia ended in chaos, disillusionment and withdrawal. This fed an increasingly isolationist trend in American public opinion reflected in an unwillingness to deploy the military assets of a superpower to assist the solution of a range of conflicts dotted around the world. America's allies might have cause to reflect that 'primacy', in terms of unequalled capabilities, was meaningless in practical terms without the political will to use them.

The question of the utility of primacy or the implications of bi- or multipolarity for international stability have been central to the post-Cold War debate. There is, after all, little other than scholastic interest in neo-realist structural analysis unless it says something about the causes of war and the conditions of peace and order. The classic realist position was that order was only obtainable through a balance of power. In effect this meant the avoidance of single power dominance, the preservation of the organizing principle of anarchy and the distribution of capabilities across a number of 'great power' actors. Asserting that balance of power processes or particular power configurations were conducive to international order defined as peace, or more accurately the absence of large-scale conflict, was much more problematic. Limited war, especially in the period of Europe's 'classical balance' in the eighteenth century could be seen as an essential part of the balancing process – indeed the only reliable way of ascertaining whether diplomatic activity had created an actual power equilibrium. In the twentieth century, the catastrophic consequences of large-scale war have encouraged consideration of the balance of power as a war prevention mechanism.

Opinions have differed as to the efficacy of multipolar or bipolar structures. Obviously the classical balance was multipolar, but Waltz, Mearsheimer (1990) and others have argued, on the basis of the Cold War experience, that bipolarity provided the key to international stability and peace. The logical corollary to this is that multipolarity or in the short term the 'challenged primacy' of the United States is conducive to instability and conflict. This is an important implicit, and frequently explicit, theme in the post-Cold War debate.

In practice the end of bipolarity may not have the serious consequences that some have predicted. Waltz, as a number of his critics have pointed out (e.g., Lebow 1994) has moved from reliance upon the stability-producing role of a structural property – bipolarity, to an emphasis on a unit level characteristic – the possession of nuclear weapons. It was these weapons that 'produced an underlying stillness at the center of international politics' during the Cold War (Waltz 1993:54). This opens up questions of the desirability of proliferation and the emergence of what used to be described as a 'unit veto' system in which all the major players have nuclear capability. It is, to repeat, clearly a move away from a structural explanation of peace and stability and falls into the same category as other 'unit attribute' theories (such as the popular idea that democracies do not wage war on each other) previously derided by 'structural' neo-realists.

Structural neo-realism clearly finds itself in some disarray in the aftermath of the Cold War. The fundamental problem is not the relationship between various power structural configurations and stability but an inability to decide upon and describe accurately how the international power structure is constituted in the first place. The difficulty is neatly summarized in the quotation from Jervis given above which reveals a simultaneous ability to envisage uni-, bi-, tri- and multipolar structures. Confusion arises because there is no uniform measure of power, thus the structure may appear bipolar in terms of military assets but will take on a different configuration if other capabilities are taken into account. The problem of defining and measuring the constituents of national power (or more accurately capability) is not new. Morgenthau (1967:106−43) lists a range of 'elements' including geographical position, natural resource and technological endowments, industrial/military capability and finally the intangibles of national morale and character and the quality of government and diplomacy. Given the centrality of 'the distribution of capabilities' to structural realism, a failure to measure them accurately or even to approach agreement on how they might be defined represents something of an impediment to adequate theory. This is recognized even by those who are generally in sympathy with the neo-realist approach.[4] Waltz himself insists on the aggregation of various components of national capability: 'The economic, military and other capabilities of states cannot be sectored and separately weighed'. There are difficulties but 'historically one finds general agreement about who the great powers of the period were' and 'common sense' will resolve the problem of counting the number of great powers (Waltz 1979:131).

Whereas it may once have been possible to erect an aggregate category of 'great power' involving economic resources, political cohesion and military strength, with some expectation that the main actors in the system could be accommodated within it, the problems of characterizing the post-Cold War structure suggest that this is no longer the case. Reckoning up the military statistics in the IISS (International Institute of Strategic Studies) annual *The Military Balance* would still make Russia a very great power, placing Japan and Germany in positions of relative structural insignificance. A similar exercise with the economic 'pecking order' established by ranking the national figures for total GDP given in the annual World Bank *Development Report* would have the opposite consequence. Adding other factors such as social coherence, morale and growth rates would further complicate matters. Only the United States can plausibly be presented as a great power on most possible dimensions and even in this case, as the 'loss of hegemony' debate of the 1970s and 80s demonstrated, there may be some doubts as to her continuing economic dominance.

**Table 2.1** Relative military and economic capability of nine major states

| | Economic rank | GDP (1992) + | GNP per cap (1992) | Armed forces active personnel | Active divs | Combat aircraft* | Principal surface ships | Subs | Nuclear capability |
|---|---|---|---|---|---|---|---|---|---|
| USA | 1 | $5,920,199 | $23,240 | 1,650,500 | 15 | 5,371 | 137 | 104 | YES |
| Japan | 2 | $3,670,979 | $28,190 | 237,000 | 13 | 540 | 62 | 22 | NO |
| Germany | 3 | $1,789,261 | $23,030 | 367,300 | 8 | 611 | 12 | 40 | NO |
| France | 4 | $1,319,883 | $22,260 | 409,600 | 5 | 868 | 43 | 18 | YES |
| UK | 5 | $903,126 | $17,790 | 254,000 | 2 | 586 | 38 | 20 | YES |
| China | 6 | $506,075 | $470 | 2,930,000 | 93 | 5,845 | 55 | 50 | YES |
| Russia | 7 | $387,476 | $2,510 | 1,714,000 | 106 | 3,342 | 161 | 185 | YES |
| Brazil | 8 | $360,405 | $2,770 | 336,000 | 8 | 272 | 21 | 4 | NO |
| India | 9 | $214,598 | $310 | 1,265,000 | 37 | 864 | 25 | 15 | YES |

* Does not include helicopters

+ In billions of US$

*Source:* for GDP and GNP per capita, World Bank (1994) *World Development Report 1994*, New York: Oxford University Press; *Source:* for military statistics, International Institute of Strategic Studies (1994), *The Military Balance 1994–95*, London: Brasseys.

Many of the interesting questions relating to change and the future power structure of the system actually require that the distribution of military and political capabilities be correlated with the prevailing international economic structure. The rate and direction of changes in this structure are very significant, even for realist analysts whose focus is upon the political sphere, because they provide the underlying motor for shifts in the power structure. More day-to-day considerations, related to the outcome of particular negotiations and conflicts of interest, also require consideration of separate structures. Keohane and Nye (1977) pointed out the 'non-fungibility' of conventional power resources under the new conditions of complex interdependence, and noted that the outcome of specific negotiations could not be predicted from the 'overall power structure'. The lack of consistency between the international political, military and economic structures was by then readily apparent across a range of issues and negotiations beyond the strictly bipolar strategic confrontation between the USA and Soviet Union.

## Economic Structures and the Correlation of Wealth and Power

Realists have usually asserted the primacy and indeed the autonomy of the political sphere. Yet international economic structure could never sensibly be divorced from analyses of the distribution of power capabilities. In its crudest form the international economic structure may be regarded in much the same way as the realist's power structure. That is to say it is formed by the productive capabilities of states and their economic interactions. At any one time there are greater and lesser economic powers for which relative gross domestic product figures provide a convenient indicator. A cursory view of recent economic history would reveal a structure dominated by the enormous relative wealth and productive capacity of the United States in the 1940s and 50s to be followed by the emergence or re-emergence of alternative economic poles starting with Germany and Western Europe from the 1960s. European economic recovery was paralleled and in some ways exceeded by Japan while in the most recent period attention has turned to the spectacular growth rates of the other Asian economies the newly industrializing countries (NICs) and now China itself. These trends are analysed in detail by Chris Mulhearn in the first part of chapter seven.

As we have already seen the mismatch between this international economic structure, with its apparent 'multipolarity', and the military/political bipolarity of the Cold War and the apparent 'unipolarity' of its aftermath has led to more than a little difficulty in conceptualizing the overall structure of the international system. During the Cold War it was possible at least to think about the structures separately, because one of the consequences of US policy (which made no such separation between economic and strategic elements) was to isolate the Soviet bloc from involvement in the rest of the world economy and its institutions. A primary objective of Gorbachev's ill-fated policy of the late 1980s was to bring this 'unnatural' and enforced separation to an end before the productivity and competitiveness of the moribund Comecon economies[5] slipped even further and irretrievably behind that of their capitalist counterparts.

Issues concerning the management of the international economy, from which the communist states were largely excluded, have formed much of the substance of modern international relations. While the older realist textbooks stressed the primacy of the traditional 'high politics' of foreign policy, the actuality was plainly at odds with such a conception. Summit meetings between the leaders of the principal western industrialized states (formalized since 1976 as the Group of Seven) have an explicitly economic content, although it has become almost impossible to disentangle it from the politics. Discussions of the levels of interest rates fixed by the national central banks loomed as large, if not larger, on the agenda than the more orthodox fare of statecraft. Academic commentators spoke of the end of the traditional 'Westphalia' model of foreign policy in which economic interests were supposedly subordinated to political and strategic objectives (Morse 1976)[6] or the 'dissolution of the issue hierarchy' under the new conditions of complex economic interdependence which existed between modern industrial societies (Keohane and Nye 1977). In these circumstances, national positions in the international economic structure were regarded as an important determinant of the outcome of key negotiations relating to monetary affairs or the GATT trade regime. On a grander scale economic order and prosperity were related to structural configurations and, specifically, to the phenomenon of American economic hegemony.

For hundreds of years prior to these events, mercantilist thinkers had conceptualized the relationship between positions in the international economic and military/political structures. The latter was predominant when it came to determining the outcome of immediate conflicts of interest, but, in the long term, it was also understood that wealth and economic capability must underpin state power. Shifts in the political structure of the international system might be the result of chance, military (in)competence or geographical position, but the most persistent underlying relationship was between essentially material factors and political and military capability. At its crudest, relative wealth would, in the long run, determine relative power. It was in this respect that international economic and political structures were conjoined. In the words of the most recent exponent of this view, there is a continuing: 'process of rise and fall among the Great Powers – of differentials in growth rates and technological change, leading to shifts in the global economic balances, which in turn gradually impinge upon the political and military balances . . .' (Kennedy 1988:xx).

In Kennedy's argument, which spans international history from 1500 to the present day, there is a lag between the achievement of a high position in the international economic structure and the attainment of great power status. Once achieved, there is a tendency to 'imperial overstretch' where political and military responsibilities are successively acquired and subsequently serve to diminish and then outrun the productive capabilities and wealth upon which they were originally based. This clearly happened to the British and French empires. In its turn, the collapse of the Soviet Union could be regarded as a spectacular instance of 'overstretch': a near inevitable consequence of attempting to compete militarily and politically with adversaries possessing perhaps four times as much economic strength.

The popularity of Kennedy's book was founded on its implications for the USA rather than the Soviet position in the international power structure. The implication of Kennedy's historical thesis (which chimes with the predictions of orthodox realism) is that even at its zenith there are clear indications that US military and political dominance is unlikely to endure, although Kennedy is careful to avoid dogmatic determinism. The underlying forces for change are already at work: they reveal themselves in gap that has been opening up, since the 1960s, between America's relative economic and political positions. To put this another way, the post-Cold War unipolar political and military structure cannot ultimately persist in opposition to the multipolar economic structure that is already in place.

Arguably, the emerging economic structure as represented in trade and related negotiations is tripolar. The US has consolidated its continental position through the creation in 1994 of NAFTA. The North American Free Trade Area already includes Canada and Mexico and is designed to be extended eventually to the rest of Latin America. In part it was a response to a perceived 'fortress Europe'. The European Community/Union's single market with its common external tariff constitutes the largest single trading bloc in the world and is already drawing much of the old Comecon bloc into its orbit. In Pacific Asia, the location of the world's most dynamic economies, the ties are much weaker but there is significant potential for the creation of a very powerful bloc, uniting Japan and the NICs with the vast markets and productive capacity of China.

## Hegemony and its Loss

The Kennedy thesis should be seen in the context of a long-running debate in the United States over 'loss of hegemony'. Although in the

1970s it was fed by disquiet over deterioration in the bipolar strategic relationship with the USSR – the loss of the Vietnam war and the apparent advances in the Soviet military position – the main academic debate centred upon the US position in the international economic structure. The 'hegemony' at issue related to economic dominance. This was to ascribe a particular meaning to a term the usages of which closely parallel the various conceptions of international or global structure rehearsed in this chapter. The original Greek *hegemonia* merely meant authority or leadership. Both in the practice and study of European diplomatic history 'hegemony' denoted something of central importance to realist discussions of the power structure, well expressed in A. J. P. Taylor's classic work *The Struggle for Mastery in Europe 1848–1918*:

> Men have not always acquiesced in the perpetual quadrille of the Balance of Power. They have often wished that the music would stop and that they could sit out the dance without maintaining a ceaseless watch on each other. They have sought for some universal authority which would overshadow the individual states and deprive them of sovereignty. The simplest 'solution' for anarchy, as Hobbes held, is that one Power should subdue all the rest. This solution has proposed itself in Europe again and again. Philip II of Spain and Louis XIV perhaps grasped at the hegemony of Europe: the great Napoleon certainly did so (Taylor 1954:xix).

To avoid confusion, this usage has not been followed here. The previous discussion was couched in terms of great power dominance or more precisely the pursuit or achievement of 'primacy' in a power structure that might then be described as unipolar. As we shall see below, the Gramscian use of the concept of hegemony in neo-Marxist discussions of structure is both unavoidable and much more complex. It involves not only class rule and the control of the means of production but a broader sway over ideas and institutions operating more through the consent of the oppressed than their direct coercion. Whereas orthodox Marxists referred to a basic structure of economic relationships and a dependent 'superstructure' of ideas; in Gramscian conceptions of hegemony the two are conjoined (Cox 1983).

For American scholars such as Keohane (1984) 'loss of hegemony' meant the loss of the dominant economic position enjoyed by the USA in the international economic structure at the ending of the Second World War. While Waltz associated bipolarity with strategic stability, neo-realists with an interest in international political economy associated the orderly cooperative arrangements for the management of the international economy, formalized at Bretton Woods in 1944, with the exercise of unparalleled US hegemony. In its simplest and most potent form this theory of 'hegemonic stability' (Kindelberger 1981) related cooperation to the existence of material economic hegemony. A country occupying a hegemonic position would have access to crucial raw materials, control over the major sources of capital and would enjoy comparative advantage in goods of high added value. Most crucially 'it would be stronger on these dimensions, taken as a whole, than any other country' (Keohane 1984:33–4). The theory of hegemonic stability was a truly structural (or systemic) theory when it took no account of intervening 'unit level' variables such as the willingness of governments and publics, finding themselves in an economically dominant position, to take up the burdens (and rather mixed blessings) of hegemonic leadership. A great deal of academic effort was expended on inconclusive efforts to test the theory.

Hegemonic stability theory was used retrospectively to account for the twenty years of economic growth, associated with cooperative management of the free world international political economy, that followed the Second World War and most specifically the creation of US led institutions from Bretton Woods onwards. The problem was that the essentially unipolar economic structure of the post-war world shifted very rapidly. The relative (but not the absolute) US position eroded dramatically from around a 50 per cent share of world GDP in 1945 to 27 per cent at the end of the 1980s (See chapter seven). The neo-realist 'hegemonic stability thesis' asserted, of course, that hegemonic leadership was the only way in which international cooperation in the management of the international economy (especially in the monetary area) could be initiated and maintained. It was the 'hegemon's dilemma' that successful management and the economic growth that it encouraged led inevitably to the revival and growth of other national economies which would challenge the hegemon and constitute a multipolar system. At this point 'after hegemony' international economic order would break down as evidenced by the collapse in 1971 of the old fixed parity monetary system anchored to the dollar (considered in detail on pp. 174–6, chapter seven). This, then, was a neo-realist structural theory of international cooperation. It has led, amongst other things, to a persistent and sometimes rather abstruse debate between liberal institutionalists and neo-realists as to the essential pre-requisites for the building and maintenance of international regimes.

From the other side of the Atlantic, Susan Strange made an important contribution by arguing that loss of economic hegemony was in fact a myth. Despite the developments in Europe and Pacific Asia, the relative GDP figures and the manifest erosion of the US manufacturing base, American hegemony persisted (Strange 1987). Her argument is significant to our purpose because it rests on a structural analysis; and one which bridges the conventional divide between political/military and economic spheres. There are, according to Strange, four essential structures. The first is the security structure and, as states tend to monopolize the use of force and the provision of security, this is in essence the international structure perceived by realists. The second, analogous to the conventional (and also the Marxist) view of structure, denotes production arrangements. The two additional structures represent a significant departure. The financial structure is defined as 'the sum of all the arrangements governing the availability of credit plus all the factors determining the terms on which currencies are exchanged for one another' (Strange 1988:88). Finally, and of accelerating importance in the contemporary world system, is the knowledge structure. This involves patterns of belief, but it also denotes the relative possession of technical knowledge and information of all types. The four structures are interdependent and Strange depicts them as four sides of a pyramid. Thus, the functioning of financial markets is dependent upon the knowledge structure and financial structures are a determinant of production. If hegemony is defined as a dominant structural position, the United States in Strange's view can still claim this position in all four. This is self-evident in the security structure and may be asserted without too much difficulty in the financial and knowledge structures.

Much of the argument about loss of hegemony depends upon a loss of relative position in the production structure. Even here, Strange argues, the United States is still predominant despite the draining away of actual industrial production from its shores:

> a perusal of any list of the top 100, 500, or 1,000 corporations producing for a world market will quickly bear out the contention that the decision-making power over the world's production structure still lies, not in Europe or Japan, but in the United States. Of the leading 300 enterprises in the world, 142 are US based (Strange 1987:568).

The supposed failure of the USA in the 1970s and 1980s to sustain orderly international economic regimes was, then, not so much one of loss of hegemony, but an irresponsible and inconstant failure to exercise it. The record since then has not demonstrated a continued failure of multilateral collaboration. The creation of the World Trade Organization to strengthen and supplant the GATT in 1995 provides a good example of the vitality of multilateral economic collaboration. To argue that this represents an exercise of US hegemonic leadership seems far-fetched but it should not be forgotten that in terms of the international economic structure, as Chris Mulhearn shows in chapter seven, the sheer scale of the North American economy puts it way ahead of its competitors.

## Global Structures

The final section of this chapter asks the question, what kinds of structure would be perceived by a student of a global rather than an international system? The various descriptions of structure discussed above have assumed a world of interacting sovereign states and national economies. The focus has been upon the relative position of essentially similar units and on the interconnection between their rankings in the military/political and economic structures. This form of structural analysis frequently takes no account whatsoever of the vast majority of the units (185 or more) in the system. In oligopolistic economic and political systems, according to Waltz (1979) it is enough to consider the relationship of a handful of the most powerful and wealthy units and structural analysis can thereby exhibit quite striking parsimony (some would say oversimplification).

Conventional structural analysis in international relations differs in quite fundamental ways from its counterparts in the sociology or political science of individual societies or national political systems. Sociologists emphasize stratified social structures where the units of analysis are differentiated by function. There is a division of labour and members of the society will be to some extent interdependent even if relationships are often highly asymmetrical. An equivalent differentiation is explicitly denied by neo-realists who inhabit a world of similar state units of varying capability. Once we begin to envisage a system which is global rather than international, our conception of structure is likely to change very radically. The units of the system will not be 'billiard ball' states but can be corporations, overlapping ethnic groups, classes or even individuals. We are essentially dealing with what John Burton (1972) and his associates have called a 'world society' which can be subjected to the same type of structural analysis, based upon functional differentiation, as any of its social subsystems.

There is, in fact, a long tradition of analysis in this vein to which mainstream international relations has been relatively impervious. Marxist theories of imperialism associated the aggressive behaviour of state governments with requirements of capital. The most influential early work of this kind was Lenin's *Imperialism the Highest Stage of Capitalism* (1965), written in 1916, which endeavoured to explain the First World War as the outcome of rival imperialisms driven by the demands of finance capital for higher returns. The historical evidence does not bear such an interpretation and a significant point about Lenin's argument was that, although the focus was upon capitalism and class rather than state interests, the underlying structure of the system was still perceived in terms of competition between national capitalisms. War was the product of the 'law of uneven development' in which the new capitalist imperialism of Germany challenged the established imperialists, Britain and France. Lenin explicitly rejected the ideas of Kautsky who argued that a consolidated, unified and transnational capitalist structure, which he termed 'ultraimperialism' would come to dominate.

In opposition to the orthodox study of imperialism, a number of scholars in the Marxist tradition employed historical research to argue that the development of capitalism should be regarded as an integrated worldwide rather than an essentially national phenomenon. Braudel (1981–4) painted a vast canvas of the development of early modern Europe in this fashion and Wallerstein's (1974) 'modern world system' had its origins in the sixteenth and seventeenth centuries. In this view, the structure of the system is based upon the functional differentiation of production. There were dominant centres, peripheries and semi-peripheries. Thus, well before the recent concern with transnational financial and production structures and the economic globalization thesis, structural models of global capitalism existed. An understanding of the essentially exploitative structure of the world economic system informed the 'dependency' theories that became politically significant in the 1970s.

Thinking in terms of economic dependency structures led to a particular interpretation of the extreme inequality (discussed in detail by Colin Parkins in chapter three) that characterized the post-1945 international economic system and the arguments about the way in which post-colonial economies could best achieve development – often defined as industrialization. Less developed countries had not achieved industrialization, not because they had not yet grown to maturity or achieved economic 'take-off', but because they were an essential part of a functionally differentiated economic structure. Their subordination was the obverse side of European and American 'development'. Describing economic relationships in terms of the dependency of the ex-colonial periphery upon a dominant industrialized centre provided the rationale for Southern demands for the restructuring of the international economy along more equitable lines – the programme for a new international economic order. This was actively, but ultimately unsuccessfully, pursued by a majority of countries within the United Nations General Assembly during the 1970s. Pressed to its logical conclusion dependency theory suggested that the only solution to the problem of underdevelopment was to break free from the post-colonial economic structures through a complete severance of relations.

Galtung's (1971) 'structural theory of imperialism' provides a good example of structuralist analysis of the world system, which although owing some debt to Marxism, departs from it in certain fundamental respects. His definition of imperialism is of a 'system that splits up collectivities and relates some of the parts to each other in relations of *harmony of interest* and other parts in relations of *disharmony of interest* or *conflict of interest*' (Galtung 1971:82). Harmony or disharmony is measured in terms of relative 'living condition'. Viewing the world in this way reveals a structure where there are centre and periphery countries; the developed world with high living standards and the less developed with low. Significantly, however, Galtung also takes account of the inequalities within countries. There are clearly centres and peripheries within both centre and periphery countries and whereas there is a harmony of interest between the centres of centre nations and centres of periphery nations, no such harmony exists between the deprived peripheral regions of developed nations and the often absolutely destitute hinterlands of the periphery nations. This centre–periphery structure is a consequence of the way in which the world economy functions. Those at the bottom of the production process are exploited by those at the top. It also rests on similarly lop-sided political, military and cultural relationships, often formed in colonial times.

Galtung's insight that, when societies are locked together in a range of unequal relationships, it is insufficient to outline a structure that merely contains rich and poor or centre and periphery countries, becomes more relevant as economic and cultural globalization proceeds. The point was made bluntly by a disillusioned ex-official of the United Nations Conference on Trade and Development when he argued that there was no such thing as rich and poor countries, only rich people and poor people: 'There is a strong community of interest between the rich people of the rich countries and the rich people of the poor countries. The governments of poor countries are virtually all controlled by rich people who have more in common with rich people who control . . . corporations than they have with their own poverty-stricken countrymen' (Ramsay 1984:393).

The stratification of the global system is, therefore, not just a rank order of developed and less developed states. Galtung argues that essentially imperialist centre–periphery structures are always evident and do not specifically derive from the development of monopoly capitalism. This represents a fundamental difference with orthodox Marxist writers who, although they may arrive at similar conclusions about the contemporary system, would regard Galtung's analysis as 'ahistorical'. None the less, Galtung has asserted that the structure is not static and that centres do shift, such a movement being discernible in the growing centrality of the dynamic economies of the Asian Pacific Rim (Galtung 1981). It will be necessary, in pursuing this form of analysis, to move well beyond structural models of the relationship of national economies and their component centres and peripheries. The existence of transnational production, capital and cultural structures is a central tenet of the globalization thesis and some writers, drawing their inspiration from Gramsci, have begun to theorize about a new era in global politics in which:

> it may be more appropriate to begin to speak of a more globally integrated set of structures . . . Whilst these structures have, at least until the late 1980s, been configured by the dialectical struggles between pre-capitalist, capitalist and communist socio-economic systems, recent evidence of changes in Eastern and Central Europe, the USSR and China as well as in countries like Vietnam, suggest that capitalism is once again spreading as the predominant form of socio-economic organisation not only across states, but within states, as marketisation and commoditisation deepens its social and geographical reach. (Gill 1993:6)

The foregoing discussion has focused on the socio-economic stratification of the system. Closely allied to this is the structure of interaction (this recalls one of our initial definitions of structure in terms of electronic circuits and transport routes). The structures under consideration here will be the paths along which people, goods, money and above all information flow. Contemplating the global system in this way will reveal a very striking centre–periphery pattern. Global airline routes for example, provide dense high-volume connections between the centres of the northern hemisphere, across the Atlantic, within Western Europe and across to Japan, Australia and the fast developing Pacific Rim countries. North–South connections, between Europe and Africa will tend to connect Northern centres with ex-colonial capitals. In the western hemisphere Miami airport serves as the 'hub' of Latin American air transport. However, there is severe underdevelopment or even a complete absence of South–South communications. Thus it is frequently necessary to fly between Latin American cities via Miami or between African cities via London or Paris. This pattern is repeated within countries, peripheries are connected to the capital but not with each other. Consider, for example, the Welsh rail and road network which, while failing to connect North, South and Mid-Wales provides good connections for each to English cities.

Telecommunications provide the essential infrastructure of globalization. A telecommunications map of the world would once again display a very marked centre–periphery structure. Intelsat (The International Satellite Telecommunications Organization) provided from the 1970s a global system with very high traffic levels across the Atlantic and between developed centres.[7] Intelsat's virtual monopoly of international switched satellite telephony (now challenged by commercial intruders) allowed it for many years to 'cross subsidize' basic international connections in the South. Thus, the centres of the periphery, with their national gateway satellite antennae, were part of the global network. Yet, there were often virtually no modern

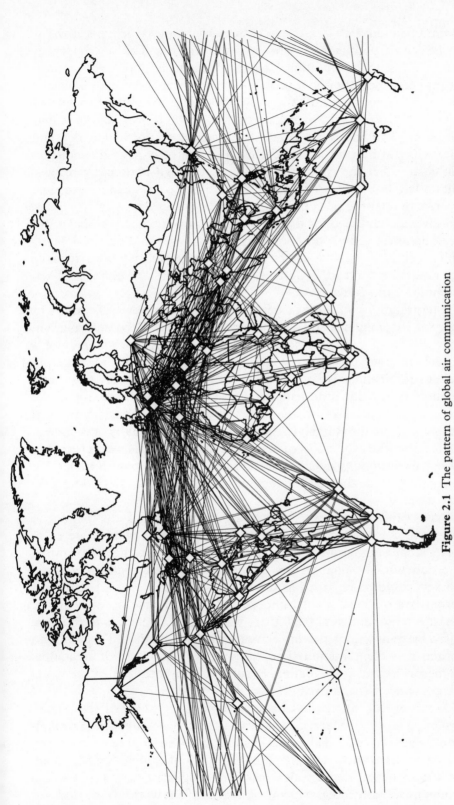

**Figure 2.1** The pattern of global air communication

Adapted from *ABC Air Travel Atlas*, Reed International, 1992. (Liverpool John Moores University, Cartographic Unit, 1995)

communications between these centres and the overwhelming majority of their own populations. This was the 'missing link' of the International Telecommunication Union's Maitland Report (1984) and its oft-quoted observation that there were more telephones in Tokyo than in the entire continent of Africa. Future maps of the world telecommunications and broadcasting system will, in all probability, be different again. The enormous contrast between the information rich and poor will still be evident but the exploitation of current technologies will ensure that the routing of messages through national 'gateways' will no longer be required (although state authorities can be expected to strive to retain some control and an ability to levy charges). Plans are already well advanced for the commercial introduction of global cellular telephones (based on constellations of low earth orbit satellites) which will allow instant direct communication to and from virtually any points on the earth's surface without recourse to established telecommunications networks.[8]

Interpretations of the meaning of such structures will vary. For analysts of dominance and dependence the maps of global information, financial or air transport structures will be interpreted as part of a 'feudal' interaction system (Galtung 1971) that served to underpin global stratification. By isolating members of the periphery from their neighbours, it made it difficult for them to challenge the dominance of the centre. Policies of '*divide et impera*' had been based upon such structures from the Roman to the British empire. Similarly, it is argued, the fact that the economies of many southern countries were created to serve the commodity needs of northern centres and not to complement each other, made the development of viable South–South trading links very difficult.

Such centre–periphery structures, the residue of the period of European colonialism, are still much in evidence. Yet there are complex changes in the rise and decline of centres and in the globalization of production and finance. It is a long time since Pacific Rim financial markets could be regarded as the Far Eastern (the term is significant) peripheries of the City of London, the Paris Bourse or Wall Street. Perhaps most fundamentally, there will be new challenges to the state posed by transactions flowing across formal boundaries. This is not an entirely new phenomenon. The legitimacy of the Soviet Union and its Comecon partners was definitely subverted by the flow of televisual images and other information from West to East.

Much of this change has been so rapid that it has, as yet, eluded structural analysis. Marxists will focus upon the global reach of capitalism, hegemony and dialectical challenges to hegemony. For others, liberal commentators for example, transnational global structures are carriers of liberal democratic ideas providing the essential bases of a more functionally integrated and interdependent world where undesirable national barriers to travel, commerce and the free exchange of ideas will be eroded.

## Structural Power

Most accounts of political activity stress behaviourial or relational power, interpreted as the ability to control the actions of others and produce intended outcomes. In domestic political systems, where there is an established government, control may be exercised by direct coercion of the populace by the organs of the state, but it is much more likely to assume the more legitimate forms of authority first analysed by Max Weber. In the realist vision of international relations such forms of control cannot exist amongst sovereign states – there is instead a 'Hobbesian' anarchy (it will be recalled that for Waltz this is the superordinate organizing principle of international structure). Power is conceptualized in terms of the essentially coercive relationships between rival states. It is ultimately dependent upon the ability to threaten or actually use military force, which is in turn related to economic strength and capability. Realist conceptions of the power structure provide a rather simplified outline of the framework within which such struggles are conducted. Most significantly they attempt to predict outcomes in terms of conflict or stability. Thus the debate about the implications of 'primacy' or particular 'power balances' is really about relative coercive power and the possibilities of international order – which is in turn often defined as the avoidance of large-scale direct violence between states. The arguments in realist political economy concerning 'hegemonic stability' are somewhat different. They concern the ability of the hegemon, not so much to coerce other states directly, but to write and maintain the rules of the game. This yields a different and more insidious form of 'structural power'.

There has long been an awareness in the political science literature that relational power alone, as employed in standard pluralist models of the political system, provided inadequate answers to Lasswell's famous question; 'who gets what, when and how?'. In 1962 Bachrach and Baratz proposed that there were in fact two faces of power. One related to observable conflicts and relational power between different actors, while the other 'second face' of power denoted the conflicts that never openly emerged and the system's tendency to exclude certain issues from the political agenda, leaving some groups marginalized and unrepresented. In a radical extension to this line of enquiry, Lukes (1974) proposed a 'third face of power' in which social structure itself determined the political agenda and essentially prevented the underprivileged from obtaining outcomes favourable to their interests and even, perhaps, from being able to appreciate what their interests might require.

Similar arguments for a structural view of power were advanced by Galtung (1971). The most effective form of imperialism is one that deploys 'structural power' where the colonized people accept the ideology of their masters and are in any case prevented by the 'feudal interaction structure' from combining against the centre. Structural power does not require an agent to do anything or coerce anybody, it simply ensures that outcomes favour those located in the dominant part of the structure. Galtung (1969) has also advanced a complementary conception of structural as opposed to overt or direct violence. While direct violence includes warfare, structural violence, like structural power inheres in the structure of the system and may be measured by the extent to which the life-chances of individuals are diminished by disease, poverty or malnutrition which arise, for example, from exploitative structures of economic exchange. Taking such a structural view gives a different perspective on security, especially in the developing world: 'There are 20 soldiers for every doctor in the developing world, even though the chances of dying from preventable disease and malnourishment are about 33 times greater than the chances of dying in a conflict' (Mahbub ul Haq 1995:9).

In international political economy structural conceptions of power have become increasingly significant and are often related to hegemony. Neo-realist work implies this, but Marxist analysts are more explicit. The Gramscian notion of hegemony as developed in the study of the global political economy, clearly involves a historically determined combination of relational and structural power (Gill and Law 1993). Even if many of the assumptions of such 'critical' political economy may be unacceptable, the emphasis on the structural bases of control and consent is difficult to contradict. The possession of (or perhaps the ability to benefit from) structural power implies much more than the ability to set agendas and to control international trading and monetary regimes:

> Structural power, in short, confers the power to decide how things shall be done, the power to shape frameworks within which states relate to each other, relate to people, or relate to corporate enterprises. The relative power of each party in a relationship is more, or less, if one party is also determining the surrounding structure of the relationship (Strange 1987:25).

Thus, concepts of structural and relational power, although they may be analytically distinct, are both likely to be employed in the analysis of particular problems.

# Conclusion

The student of global politics will have to be aware of the existence of a complex of structures, which are often disjointed and contradictory. In this chapter we have surveyed political and economic international structures composed of state units and the emerging structures of a globally integrated system.

The post-Cold War debate amongst realists about the new international power structure has reached no very certain conclusion. The collapse of bipolarity leaves American primacy but in a world that remains insecure and perhaps more conflict-prone. The causes of insecurity and conflict are not readily subject to control by the United States and in any case realist analysis predicts that unipolarity cannot endure. Structural change in the political and military order can be examined in relation to long-run alterations in the underlying international economic structure. It is, in fact, somewhat surprising that so few predicted the precipitate collapse of the USSR from its evident economic weakness. Perhaps this was because so much attention was being paid during the 1980s to the supposed loss of US hegemony.

The end of the Soviet Union was also hastened by other structural changes occurring in the global economy and its associated communications systems, which in retrospect, made Stalin's closed totalitarian system impossible to sustain. The development of a functionally differentiated global system was uneven, and its most marked feature was extreme inequality between centres and peripheries. It should not be forgotten that for the overwhelming majority of the earth's population it was this deep structural conflict between North and South and centre and periphery that mattered rather than forty years of East–West bipolarity.

An important question for the future is the disjunction between the international structure and the underlying structures of a globalizing system. Such structures have enormous significance because of the ways in which they channel and constrain human activity, rendering some powerful and others relatively powerless. However, they do not predetermine the future. To take a concrete example, we cannot make reliable predictions based upon American primacy or hegemony in the current power structure for at least two reasons. The first involves the tensions between the international and global structures. However dominant a state government may appear, recent experience suggests that economic globalization makes it extremely difficult to exert control over financial and production structures organized across national boundaries. The second reason refers again to the 'agent–structure' question. Structural power does mean that on many occasions events will favour the powerful without conscious action on their part, but we still require leadership from a government enjoying a position of primacy. Here structural position may, on occasion, count for little if its members are hamstrung by the demands of electoral politics and confounded by the uncertainties of human agency.

## Notes

1 The use of the term 'structuralist' may cause some confusion because it has become common to divide the study of international relations up into a trinity of paradigms; realist, pluralist and structuralist. Here, structuralist connotes a Marxist-inspired analysis of North–South inequality, theories of dependency and the writings of Johan Galtung and others (Smith, Little and Shackleton 1981).

2 The draft DPG and the reaction to it is discussed in Layne (1993:5–7). Offending parts of the original document were redrafted. During 1992–3 the Pentagon apparently prepared a 'new NSC–68' which emphasized the instability of a multipolar world.

3 Waltz's varying positions on the bipolar or multipolar state of the system are chronicled and criticized by Lebow (1994).

4 Buzan for example writes that the category of aggregated state power collapses:

> What in the late 1980s was one to make of an ostensibly bipolar system in which one of the two 'superpowers' had only the third largest economy in the system, and the other two had the biggest debt? How did one weigh the relative importance of the Soviet Union's large territory and endowment of resources against China's large population and ethnic coherence? How does one weigh China's weapons against Japan's wealth ? . . . How does common sense enable one to assess polarity in the fluid conditions of the 1990s when plausible arguments can be made for unipolarity, bipolarity and multipolarity all at the same time? (Buzan, Jones and Little 1993:58)

5 Comecon, the Council for Mutual Economic Assistance (established 1949 and dissolved in 1991) was a regional organization under Soviet direction.

6 The 'Westphalia Model' was coined by Morse (1976) to describe traditional statecraft. The reference is to the Treaty of Westphalia 1648, usually taken as the starting point of the modern system of sovereign states.

7 Satellite-based long distance communications are being increasingly challenged by new broadband fibre-optic cables which can be very efficient on heavily used routes. However, satellites will remain pre-eminent in transmitting messages to populations scattered across wide areas, because, unlike cable, costs are insensitive to distance travelled.

8 The main contenders are Motorola's Iridium system and the equivalent sponsored by Inmarsat, the International Maritime Satellite Organization.

# 3

# North–South Relations and Globalization after the Cold War

## Colin Parkins

The end of the Cold War has understandably been greeted as a major turning point in world affairs. The threat of a global nuclear conflict has receded after more than thirty years. The disappearance of the socialist bloc in eastern Europe and the general decline of central planning as a model have removed the main historical alternative to capitalism. Bipolarity has ended, and with it a period of superpower rivalry whose ramifications touched millions of lives throughout the world. Above all, the certainties of the post-Second World War international political system have collapsed. The fact that they have been replaced by a sense of doubt and uncertainty about the prospects for a stable new world order only reinforces the feeling that something significant has changed. But how significant? The global apartheid that separates the rich industrialized North from the underdeveloped South remains intact and for many, even at the height of the Cold War, this has always been a more significant division than the East–West conflict.[1]

In part this claim fails to compare like with like. The Cold War was a form of military and ideological competition between social systems. Economic competition was secondary, though it proved to be decisive in the end, and relations between the two blocs were marked by open conflict. The division between North and South, on the other hand, is the product of structural inequalities in the capitalist world economy. This translates into a profoundly unequal distribution of political power, and a relationship which combines localized episodes of aggression by one side against the other with elements of clientalism, dialogue and interdependence. Moreover, the East–West conflict and North–South relations have been closely interrelated from the start.

The fact that the Third World emerged on to the international stage at a time when this was dominated by the superpower rivalry has shaped its relations with the industrialized North in important ways.

The first object of this chapter, therefore, is to examine the impact of the Cold War on the Third World and to examine the extent to which its disappearance has altered the shape of North–South relations. In both cases the impact has been important but limited as the position of the Third World in the global system has been determined principally by long-term structural factors. The end of the Cold War has provoked a great deal of reflection and debate about the changing nature of the international system, during which the concept of globalization has gained widespread currency. The extent to which this concept helps us to understand the nature of North–South relations and the position of the Third World in the post-Cold War era will be considered in the later part of the chapter, where it will be argued that the idea of globalization is used in a number of different and partially contradictory ways.

Before we move on to these questions, however, we must deal with a prior one: whether in the mid-1990s it is still possible to talk about a Third World with common characteristics, interests and demands.

## The Idea of the Third World

The idea that the countries of the Caribbean, Latin America, Africa and Asia can be referred to collectively, whether as the Third World, the South, the developing world or in some other way, is a product of the post-war period. It reflects important changes in world politics during this time: the appearance of a group of new states conscious of their common weakness in the global system, and the emergence of development as an important global issue. In the aftermath of the Second World War, economic development became, for the first time, both a universal goal and a measure by which to classify states. Underdevelopment became the identifying characteristic of countries in the South and they, in turn, began to recognize a set of common interests and demands. Underlying this recognition was a shared history: the experience of colonialism and the way in which this had shaped the incorporation of these areas into the world economy.

Colonialism itself was a diverse phenomenon. There were significant differences among the imperial powers; the majority of Latin American countries had achieved independence decades before most of Africa and parts of Asia were colonized; some areas in Asia and Africa were never under formal colonial rule. However, this is less important than the fact that the European powers' expansion profoundly affected the local economic and social structures in these areas and tied them into global economic relationships that shaped their subsequent development. The impact of colonialism took several forms: the disruption of indigenous processes of development, the imposition of market relations, the consolidation of authoritarian political structures, and above all the formation of an international division of labour in which the colonized areas acted as primary commodity producers and labour reserves for the industrialized world. After an initial phase of conquest and plunder, the driving force behind this process was the expansionary needs of European capital, at first in search of trade and then increasingly in the form of investment. The result was an unprecedented accumulation of wealth and capital in the metropolitan countries.

The patterns of global apartheid referred to earlier are a product of this history. Its legacy can be clearly seen in the continued dependence of many Third World countries on the export of primary products, and in the dominant role played by foreign capital in their economies. Ismail-Sabri Abdella's definition of the Third World as, 'All those nations which, during the process of formation of the existing world order, did not become rich and industrialised' (quoted in Allen and Thomas 1992:4–5) is therefore a useful starting point. It makes clear that the formation of the industrialized North and the underdeveloped South must be seen as part of a single process. However, as indicated above, the Third World is not simply an analytical category. It also provides a collective identity which unites an otherwise disparate group of states and, in this sense, it is a product of the post-colonial era.

A number of internal and external factors – the exhaustion of the European colonial powers, the emergence of United States hegemony, the impact of the rhetoric about self-determination that underpinned the success of anti-colonial movements – combined to make a continuation of colonial rule untenable at the end of the Second World War. The most significant aspect of the decolonization process, however, was the role played by nationalism as a corrosive force in undermining colonial rule. This meant that nationalism became the dominant ideological force in the newly independent states. More significantly though, it was the vehicle through which the nation-state spread to Africa and Asia and this in turn determined the political form the Third World would take: a group of sovereign states within the international state system.

The new states that emerged as a result of decolonization did so in a context marked by two principal features. The first of these was the new-found conviction that economic forces could be controlled and, therefore, that economic and social development could be planned. At the international level this became a declared aim of the new United Nations system which, early in its life, organized a series of expert groups to study the problems of the underdeveloped areas (Meier and Seers 1984:12–13). At a national level, development became the central legitimizing project throughout the Third World. A further element can therefore be added to Ismail-Sabri Abdella's definition: the states which make up the Third World all define themselves and are defined by the principal institutions of the international system as developing countries.

The second important feature of the international environment into which the Third World emerged was the Cold War. The forum in which Third World states first came together as a force in the international system was the Non-Aligned Movement (NAM). As its name suggests, the NAM was conceived as a counter-weight to the two rival Cold War blocs. It was founded on five basic principles: peace and disarmament; self-determination, particularly for colonial peoples; economic equality; cultural equality, and multilateralism, in the shape of strong support for the United Nations (Singham and Hune 1986:13–32). However in practice, with the exception of its anti-colonialism about which there could be strong agreement, the aim of creating an independent force in world politics quickly succumbed to the pressure of Cold War alliances. Furthermore, as initial optimism about the prospects for development in the Third World faded, the economic concerns of its members came increasingly to the fore. By the 1970s, therefore, the NAM had largely become an advocate of Third World demands for a New International Economic Order (NIEO); a role it shared with the Group of 77, the caucusing group of Third World states within the United Nations. Given the relative economic weakness of the Soviet Union, these demands were directed essentially at the West.

In analytical terms, then, the idea of the Third World, the South or the developing world, identifies a group of states whose common history of colonialism has left them in a position of economic and political weakness in the global system. As a collective actor in that system, while it began life as an anti-imperial coalition with aspirations to an independent place in world politics, the Third World bloc has found cohesion mainly around a set of common economic demands directed at the developed capitalist world. In neither sense does the recent realignment in global politics appear to undermine the coherence of the idea or suggest that it should be abandoned. Before we accept it wholeheartedly, however, a number of complicating factors and objections must be taken into account.

For some theorists the idea of a fundamental division between North and South is misguided. On the one hand neo-liberals such as Peter Bauer (1984) reject the notion that Third World countries face particular problems because of their position in the international division of labour, or that they have internal characteristics which mark them out from the industrialized North. For these theorists the beneficial effects of market discipline and the superiority of liberal values have a universal law-like quality that admits no boundaries. To ignore this can only have negative consequences: attempts at planned development have been fruitless at best and, at worst, have needlessly held back development in the South. At the other end of the political spectrum, Marxists such as Bill Warren (1980) and Nigel Harris (1986) emphasize the continued dynamic and unifying, if uneven, thrust of global capitalism. Their primary concern is to challenge the pessimism that has dominated radical assessments of capitalist development since Lenin, which claims that capitalism has ceased to be a progressive transformative force. The consequence of their analysis, however, is to dissolve the idea of the Third World as a bloc of countries that are characterized by underdevelopment and subject to imperialist domination. From this perspective the spread of capitalist relations of production has already led to strong economic development in some parts of the South.

Both these strands of argument have successfully challenged orthodoxies in the analysis of development, although the neo-liberal version has been by far the most influential. Having been marginal for most of the post-war period, it gained considerable importance in the late 1970s and 1980s when it formed the basis of what John Toye (1993:17) has called the 'counter-revolution in development economics'. As we shall see below, quite apart from any merits it might have as analysis, it has been associated with a significant change in North–South relations in the 1980s and 1990s.

In the work of the above writers, neo-liberals and orthodox Marxists alike, the idea of the Third World, or 'Third Worldism', is understood as a legitimizing ideology that promotes the interests of southern elites. For neo-liberals the main point is that Third World governments exploit a misplaced sense of guilt in the North to extract aid, which is used to sustain a bloated and corrupt state machine. Similarly, for Harris and Warren 'Third Worldism' is the ideology of the bourgeois nationalist leaders who took power in the new post-colonial states. The general argument that ruling elites in the Third World are best understood as self-interested actors rather than the representatives of a common national interest is also made by writers such as Stephen Krasner (1985) and Chai-Anan Samundavanija (1991). This in turn points to a wider concern; the danger of obscuring the complexity of the societies concerned. It is important, therefore, to take into account the class, gender, ethnic and other divisions within Third World societies in any analysis of North–South relations.

The homogenizing effects of the idea of the Third World have also been criticized. The emphasis on economic and social development associated with Third Worldism inevitably underplays the importance of culture and therefore of cultural difference. Moreover, it is argued that the implicit or explicit use of the West as a standard against which to measure development denies legitimacy to other forms of social organization. Thus environmentalists who oppose the post-war growth based model of development such as Sachs (1992 and 1993) and feminists, such as Chandra Mohanty (1986), concerned with the politics of identity, have echoed this criticism.

In one way or another, the above strands of criticism are all sceptical of the idea of the Third World as such. A further criticism sees the term as having been overtaken by events. Here it is argued that the image of the Third World as a group of largely agrarian, low income, primary commodity producers may have been accurate in the immediate post-war period. However there has been too much differentiation among Third World states over the last thirty years for them to remain confined within a single category.

At one end of the scale are the least developed countries (LLDCs), a category created by the UN in 1968 to differentiate the poorest countries from those that had already had modest success in development. The original group of 25 has since grown to 50, with 37 concentrated in Africa, reflecting that continent's increasing marginalization (Adedeji 1993). At the other end are a group of small oil exporters, who have used their control of a strategic commodity to dramatically raise export earnings, and the Newly Industrializing Countries (NICs), a group of states that have managed to transform the structure of their economies over the last twenty-five years. The oil producing states were extremely important in the 1970s because they demonstrated that it was possible to successfully challenge northern control of the world economy. However, their cohesion broke down in the 1980s. Moreover, although attempts were made by the producers of other commodities to follow a similar path, none of these was successful. The example of the NICs has therefore been of more lasting importance for this argument.

There is disagreement as to which countries should be included in the category of NICs, but the undisputed core is made up of Hong Kong, Singapore, Taiwan and South Korea (the 'Four Tigers'), Mexico and Brazil. Each experienced rapid growth of manufacturing output during the 1970s and the Asian tigers became significant exporters of manufactured goods. In 1988 these four countries alone were responsible for 55 per cent of all manufacturing exports from the Third World in value terms. The South American NICs were unable to maintain their high growth rates in the 1980s but their Asian counterparts continued to forge ahead and, according to some estimates, by the early 1990s Hong Kong and Singapore had overtaken most developed countries in real GDP per capita (UNDP 1994).

For some, therefore, the idea of a Third World that includes both Ethiopia and Singapore has become unwieldy. However, the NICs are still highly unrepresentative. The combined population of the four Asian tigers in 1992 was just 73 million and, as figure 3.1 shows,

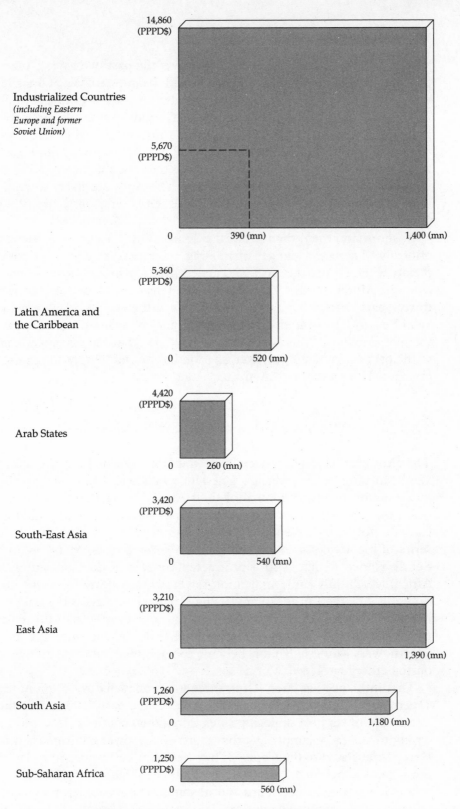

**Figure 3.1** Population and real GDP by areas
Adapted from United Nations *Human Development Report 1994*

however impressive their achievements over the past twenty-five years, the fundamental division in wealth between the industrialized countries and the Third World remains. In fact it has increased over this period.[2] This would not be so significant if the NIC model was easily replicable and therefore pointed the way forward for other states. But there must be considerable doubt about this. Gerald Tan (1993), for example, has found that of a group of countries suggested as possible future NICs in the early 1980s only two, Malaysia and Thailand, are likely to reach that status in the foreseeable future, though, significantly, he offers China as a possible addition to that list.

In summary, then, the idea of the Third World needs to be viewed critically. There is a danger of missing an important degree of complexity when we use the term, and generalizations should be made with caution. Moreover the Third world itself has changed over the last thirty years, becoming more diverse. Nevertheless the idea remains valid because it captures a fundamental and enduring division within the global system. This is not to say, however, that the disappearance of the other significant post-war division has not had important consequences. It is to that question that we now turn.

## The Third World and the Cold War

The European colonial powers have not been absent from the Third World in the post-war period. The late 1940s and 1950s saw a rearguard action to retain control of their Asian, African and Caribbean colonies, or at least to manage what had become the unavoidable clamour for independence (Adams 1993:46–53). The result was a series of bloody conflicts in Indochina, Algeria, Kenya, Malaysia, and South Yemen (Aden) and a protracted process of decolonization in Africa, which only came to fruition for many new states in the 1960s. Subsequently the European powers have had some success in retaining influence in their former African colonies. Nevertheless, the configuration of the post-war international order meant that the two superpowers would inevitably become the dominant external influence on the emerging Third World.

That influence has been felt in three interconnected ways: First, the superpowers intervened repeatedly between the early 1950s and the late 1980s to support opposing sides in regional conflicts. It would be wrong to see these simply as proxy wars: superpower confrontation in Europe translated to the tropics. They were conflicts whose roots lay in the regions concerned. Moreover, as John O'Loughlin (1986:264) has pointed out, 'Leaders in Third World states, anxious to defeat external enemies or score internal political victories, blithely invite[d] the superpowers to help achieve success and dr[ew] their states on to the front line of global competition'. However the scale of these conflicts and the suffering caused were magnified through being caught up in the logic of global ideological competition.

Secondly, the superpowers have intervened militarily and covertly to topple, undermine or shore up numerous regimes in the Third World. There is no doubt, however, that in this respect the US has had a much greater reach. While the Soviet Union was able to subjugate Eastern Europe for forty years through the threat and use of force, in the Third World it committed itself militarily only once, in Afghanistan. Otherwise its role was confined to providing support for autonomous revolutionary processes or opposition groups whose nationalist, anti-colonial ideologies gave little scope for determining the nature of the regimes or movements concerned. Moreover, interventions by the Soviet Union outside its European sphere of influence were always strenuously opposed by the United States and its allies. The USA, on the other hand, made largely uncontested use of force and a range of covert techniques to undermine left-wing and over-assertive nation-alist regimes, and to ensure the survival of repressive clients. The human cost of this policy was high, both through the destruction of popular development programmes and the routinization of state terror, particularly in the Latin America of the 1960s and 1970s.[3]

Thirdly, the superpowers maintained a series of worldwide alliances through the provision of trade concessions, aid and arms. It is in this area that the East–West and North–South dimensions of global politics merge most clearly. The appearance of development as a significant issue in the late 1940s, while not a product of the emerging Cold War rivalry, was certainly conditioned by it. In the Third World the ideological rivalry between East and West largely took the form of a competition between opposing development models. Equally, the competition for influence centred on the provision of aid. In this last respect, however, any appearance of parity between the superpowers is once again misleading. The Soviet Union – a military but never an economic superpower – could not seriously rival the United States in providing material assistance to its Third World allies or in influence within multinational institutions. It did, however, play a full part in one of the most destructive aspects of the Cold War, the militarization of the Third World through arms sales.

These forms of intervention were constant throughout the Cold War period, although their impact was never uniform. The focus of super-power attention shifted and widened over time. In the immediate post-war period the Soviet Union had little or no presence in Africa or Latin America; Cold War tensions were concentrated in Europe and Asia. The importance of Asia lay, first, in the unstable situation left by the Japanese occupation of former European colonies and, secondly, in the fact that in 1949 China fell to communist rule. Asia, therefore, was the first area where Cold War turned hot: in Indochina, Malaya and Korea. It was also the area where economic aid and the promotion of internal reforms were employed for the first time to build up an anti-communist alliance. Thus Taiwan and Korea both enjoyed significant United States aid and trade concessions from the late 1940 onwards, and both underwent important US assisted agrarian reform programmes.

This strategy of supporting economic development in front line areas of the Cold War evolved in the 1960s into 'containment liberalism' (Bello 1994); a mixture of anti-communism and attempts to promote stable economic growth with some redistribution of wealth. The main impetus for this new approach was the Cuban revolution of 1959. This not only gave the Soviet Union a foothold in Latin America but also demonstrated that, if left unaddressed, demands for social justice in the Third World could provide a breeding ground for opposition movements. The result was the Alliance for Progress, announced by President Kennedy in his inaugural address in 1960. This committed large amounts of aid to support land reform and social programmes in Latin America and was complemented by a programme of counter-insurgency training for the military and police.

From the 1960s onwards the Third World began to play an increasing role in the Cold War, for a number of reasons. On the one hand, the Soviet Union began to look beyond its traditional concern with Asia to reach out for influence in Africa, and to some extent in Latin America. On the other hand, a new wave of revolutionary victories in the 1970s, from the fall of Haile Selassie of Ethiopia in 1974 to the triumph of the Sandinistas in Nicaragua in 1979, provided several new points of conflict (Halliday 1986). By the time of the US Presidential elections in 1979 concerns about the Third World had come to figure as prominently in foreign policy discussions as fears about Soviet nuclear strength. Thus the 'Second Cold War' that followed Ronald Reagan's election was justified in part by the need to roll back supposed Soviet gains in the Third World. The right wing offensive in the United States, however, was not simply concerned with the Third World as an area of Soviet expansion. The 1970s had seen not only a period of revolutionary victories but also the Organization of Petroleum Exporting Countries' (OPEC) price shocks, demands by the South for a New International Economic Order (NIEO) and the appearance of the NICs as serious competitors in the world market. In consequence increased US belligerence in regional conflicts was paralleled by a more hostile attitude to Third World assertiveness in the economic arena.

The profound change in analysis and policy that followed Mikhail Gorbachev's appointment as general secretary of the Soviet Communist Party in 1985 led to a re-evaluation of the Soviet Union's alliances in the Third World. This 'new thinking' amounted to a general retreat from previous levels of involvement and the abandonment of erstwhile allies. Foreign policy was viewed instrumentally, in line with the belated recognition of the Soviet Union's serious internal problems. Hence the need for a rapprochement with the United States and western Europe took precedence over considerations of international solidarity. For the Soviet Union's Third World allies, the consequences were profound. Most were forced to abandon any attempt at a centrally planned development strategy and adopt a more accommodating attitude to the world market.

A number of conclusions can be drawn from the above analysis. First, the Third World played a central role in the Cold War which cannot be understood simply as an extension of superpower rivalry. Decolonization, development and political struggles within the Third World shaped the East–West conflict as much as they were shaped by it. Indeed Fred Halliday (1990) suggests that the resolution of the outstanding Third World conflicts was a precondition for, rather than a consequence of, the end of the Cold War. Secondly, there was an asymmetry between the superpowers in their relations with the Third World. The Soviet Union offered diplomatic support for the decolonization process and allied itself with Third World countries whose foreign and domestic policies led them into confrontation with the United States. It also offered an alternative model of development to that being presented by the West. However its ability to back this up with material support was severely limited. The USA was clearly the dominant economic and military power in the Cold War period and its impact on the Third World was consequently much greater than that of the Soviet Union.

This raises the question of how the disappearance of the Soviet Union will affect the Third World. Here one argument suggests that bipolarity gave Third World states political leverage by allowing them to play one superpower off against the other. The prospect of a unipolar world order therefore appears entirely negative, as it seems to give the remaining superpower free rein. However this view is based on the questionable assumption of undiminished US power. The new world order proclaimed by President Bush at the time of the Gulf War has shown a marked reluctance to appear and, although it undoubtedly remains the only military superpower, the US has, for some time, faced a serious challenge to its leading position in the world economy. This clearly opens up the possibility of a multipolar system emerging. The end of the suffocating ideological competition at the heart of the Cold War may also bring about significant changes in the United States itself. The absence of a supposed Soviet threat makes it increasingly difficult for the US government to justify to a sceptical electorate the sort of intervention that took place in 1980s. Thus, in relation to Latin America, it has been argued that 'With the end of the Cold War . . . the

US propensity to intervene should be considerably reduced and Latin America should enjoy a consequently greater room for manoeuvre for social experiments' (Hirschman 1990:176). For the moment the prospect of a new wave of left-wing governments appearing is somewhat remote. Nevertheless the conditions of the poor in the Third World remain desperate and, as recent experience in Mexico and Brazil demonstrates, the disorientation felt by the Left in the developed world is not necessarily shared by progressive movements in the South.

## North–South Issues in the 1990s

We have seen that the characteristics which distinguish the Third World, and the interests that have united it as a political force, are the product of long-term structural inequalities in the world capitalist economy. The Cold War also had a considerable impact on the Third World and its relations with the North. We now consider some of the main North–South issues of the 1990s in order to more clearly assess the relative importance of these two factors.

Current North–South issues fall into three broad groups. First, those such as debt and trade that are of long-standing importance but concern relations between the South and the developed capitalist world which were only marginally affected by the Cold War; secondly, issues such as aid, political conditionality and military intervention that either played an important role in the Cold War or have emerged as result of its disappearance; thirdly, issues such as the environment that have emerged relatively recently. Of these three types of issue, the first continue to play the most significant role.

### *Debt and structural adjustment*

The debt crisis was the most high profile North–South issue of the 1980s. Mexico's default on its external debt repayments in August 1982 ended a period of uncontrolled lending by northern commercial banks that had grown throughout the previous decade. In 1983 and 1984, twenty-five Third World countries were forced to reschedule $126.4 billion of outstanding commercial debts, $118.1 billion of which was owed by Latin American governments. It was argued at the time that 'Never have so many nations owed so much money with so little promise of repayment' (Corbridge 1993:49). Although centred on Latin America, the crisis appeared to threaten the stability of the international financial system as a whole. It was this concern which occupied the attention of northern governments in the mid-1980s and determined their strategy for managing the crisis. This consisted of defining the problem as a temporary shortage of liquidity to be dealt with on a case-by-case basis through International Monetary Fund (IMF) coordinated rescue packages that guaranteed new funding in exchange for economic reforms.

This strategy was successful in the limited sense of preventing a collapse of confidence in the international financial system and allowing the major northern banks gradually to reduce their exposure to Third World debts. However, underlying the banking crisis was a more deeply rooted crisis of development, attributable largely to changes in the international economic environment in the 1970s: recession in the industrialized countries, slow growth, falling commodity prices and rising real exchange rates. The debt rescheduling of 1982–4 followed several years when governments throughout the Third World had experienced repayment difficulties. Africa, where commercial lending had never played an important role, was particularly affected. Unsurprisingly then, the debt crisis proved to be far from temporary. Indeed it dominated the 1980s – a 'lost decade for development' – in both Latin America and Africa, and contributed to a profound change in the nature of relations between Third World states and the multinational financial institutions.

The collapse of commercial lending to the Third World meant that official aid was the only source of external finance for countries in need of new loans to cover repayments on existing debts. However, access to this additional finance was dependent on IMF and World Bank approval. In the first instance this meant the agreement of a stabilization package with the IMF. By 1985, however, it was obvious that stabilization was not enough and the Baker Plan was announced. This held out the promise of additional, longer-term, Structural Adjustment Loans (SALs) from the World Bank in exchange for a further set of economic reforms. The IMF's primary concern has been to deal with balance of payments deficits by reducing excess demand in the economy, particularly through cuts in state spending, and by achieving what it considers a realistic exchange rate. The World Bank's programmes, however, have traditionally been concerned with supply-side measures to reform the productive structure of the economy. Nevertheless in the 1980s the loan conditions imposed by the two institutions converged to the extent that they can now be treated as a single structural adjustment package.

The specifics of the agreements with individual countries varied, but typically they included the following elements: severe cuts in government spending, particularly in price subsidies and public sector employment; currency devaluation; export promotion and import liberalization; the removal of restrictions on foreign capital; privatization of state enterprises, and a general deregulation of economic activity. These measures ensured that an ever greater proportion of economic activity in the Third World was devoted to debt servicing, with the consequence that between 1982 and 1990 there was a net transfer of resources from the Third World to the OECD countries equivalent to six Marshall Plans (George 1992:xv). This in turn has deepened the crisis of development in many areas. In Africa and Latin America, the 1980s were characterized by falling living standards, high unemployment, negative growth and worsening social welfare indicators, with lasting consequences for the social and political structures of the countries concerned (Ghai and Hewitt de Alcántara 1990).

Needless to say, the burden has fallen disproportionately on poor households and, in particular upon poor women. For the advocates of structural adjustment these consequences are the unfortunate but necessary price of economic recovery. For many in the Third World, however, it appears that the multilateral institutions' primary concern has been to act as debt collectors for the northern banks. Resistance has consequently been widespread, giving rise to what have become known as 'IMF riots' (Walton and Seddon 1994).

Structural adjustment involves the imposition of a specific market-based development model on the Third World in the name of economic prudence. Susan George has described it as, 'the most enormous, ideologically driven, economic experiment ever devised' (George 1993:67). In consequence it is hardly surprising to find that it has had important political as well as economic and social consequences. The management of the debt crisis by the leading industrialized countries has helped to undermine the statist development model of economic nationalism favoured by many Third World governments until the 1980s and replace it with an export based model in which foreign direct investment is encouraged.[4] There is widespread agreement that economic nationalism as it developed in the 1960s and 1970s was unsustainable. However the debt crisis has effectively ruled out alternative responses to its failure such as delinking 'the suppression of external relationships to the needs of internal development' (Amin 1993:138). At the same time the gains made by Third World states in international forums during the 1970s have been reversed. In particular calls for a New International Economic Order have been silenced and institutions such as the United Nations Commission for Trade and Development (UNCTAD), the main forum through which the South pressed its economic demands on the North, have been marginalized.

This picture has not changed substantially in the 1990s. In 1989 the Baker Plan was replaced by the Brady Plan, which, for the first time, accepted the need for some reduction in debt service requirements. However, for the vast majority of debtor countries the crisis is far from over; indeed it may be spreading. By 1989 five countries in Asia had long-term debt stocks of over $10 billion (Corbridge 1994:83) and UNCTAD has identified 61 non-OECD countries with debt service difficulties at the end of 1992 – 31 in Africa, 12 in Latin America and 10 in Asia (UNCTAD 1993:165). Meanwhile, the disappearance of central planning as a viable model has further discredited economic nationalism, while the continued strong performance of the East Asian NICs in the 1980s is held up as an example that vindicates the export oriented approach to development. Despite widespread criticism of its effectiveness and social consequences, structural adjustment and liberalization remains the order of the day.

## *Trade*

Trade has always been central to North–South relations. UNCTAD was founded on the premise that the international division of labour established by colonialism, in which southern primary products were exchanged for northern manufactures, was a significant handicap to the Third World's prospects of development. Implicit in this view was the idea that development would only be achieved through diversification into manufacturing, and this in turn implied the need for the protection of infant industries. In the short to medium term, however, it also implied the need for a more effectively managed system of international trade that provided greater rewards to primary commodity producers. This was the one of the main objectives of the NIEO.

The crisis of the 1980s marginalized this argument and the liberal counter-revolution in development theory challenged its underlying assumptions. At the same time many countries were forced to orient an increasing proportion of their economic activity towards the production of primary products for export in order to service their debts. A number of factors combined to undermine this strategy, however. In the short term, the fact that a large number of countries moved into the same areas of export production, urged on by the IMF and the World Bank, led to over-production and falling prices. Meanwhile, slower growth and structural changes in the northern economies – technological changes in production; agricultural protection in the North, and the advent of biotechnology and new materials that could replace traditional Third World exports – combined to ensure that the long, post-war trend for commodity prices to fall continued through the 1980s and early 1990s (ODI 1988). A large number of Third World countries were, in consequence, obliged to export more to earn less.

The picture was different for those countries that had successfully or partially industrialized, particularly the Asian NICs whose spectacular growth was based on the export of manufactures to OECD countries. This success had its price, however, as it led to the rise of protectionism in the North in the form of non-tariff trade barriers (NTBs). These measures – principally anti-dumping clauses and 'voluntary export restraints' (VERs) – in reality export quotas imposed under the threat of trade sanctions – were introduced by the European Community, Canada and Australia in the 1980s, but the protectionist pioneer was the USA. Between 1980 and 1991, the United States imposed 125 export restraint agreements on Third World countries, including LLDCs such as Bangladesh and Haiti, compared with 31 imposed upon industrialized states (Bello 1994:135–6). The countries most frequently the subject of VERs were Korea (16), China (7) and Taiwan (6). Two of these were front line allies of the United States in the Cold War and long-time recipients of aid and trade concessions. It is therefore worth noting that the change in American attitudes towards them came well before the end of the Cold War rather than as a consequence of it.

This combination of rivalry between the developed industrialized countries and the reassertion of northern economic control over the South was not confined to bilateral trade relations. At a multilateral level it was also evident in the negotiations around the GATT. In the 1970s the NIEO debate provided an alternative, specifically Third World, view on world trade which centred on the need for international commodity agreements. However, the only significant forum in which the international trade regime has been discussed in the 1980s and 1990s is the GATT Uruguay Round, which lasted from 1986 to 1994 and was dominated by a northern agenda.

The object of the GATT is to achieve the maximum trade liberalization possible on the basis that free trade benefits all. Nevertheless, as Martin Khor Kok Peng (1992:41) has argued, 'When a strong party insists that a weaker party subject itself to the "free flow of goods and services, trade and investment", it does not take an expert to predict that the weak party may grow even weaker while the majority of the benefits accrue to the strong'. Thus a widely quoted OECD study in 1993 estimated that a successful Uruguay Round would produce an annual increase in world income of $213 billion by 2002. Two thirds of this, however, would go to the developed world, especially the European Union, while Africa as a whole and individual countries such as Indonesia would find themselves worse off as a result (*Financial Times* 4.10.93). Further discussion of the GATT can be found in chapter seven.

The measures pursued by the industrialized countries in the Uruguay Round concerned, for the most part, extending liberalization into new areas: agriculture, services, trade related investment measures (TRIMs) and trade related intellectual property rights (TRIPs). In each case the final agreement was significantly prejudicial to Third World interests. The proposals on agriculture led to a protracted dispute between the United States and the European Community, but it is Third World producers who have most to lose from opening up domestic markets to imports and a reduction of subsidies to farmers.

Indeed it is the proposals on agriculture that account for Africa's poor showing in the OECD study. The effect of the proposals on services and TRIMs is to deal a further blow to the idea of national economic development through effectively stripping Third World states of any powers to control the penetration of northern corporations into their economies. Finally, TRIPs are designed specifically to ensure that patents, held overwhelmingly by northern corporations, are enforced in the Third World. On the one hand this blocks the way for these countries to follow the path taken by late industrializers such as Japan, for whom imitation laid the foundations of their current level of technical advancement. On the other hand, it ensures that the benefits from developments in areas such as biotechnology will flow directly back to the laboratories and corporate headquarters of the North, even when the genetic resources being used have been developed over generations by peasant communities in the South (Watkins 1992; 1994).

### Aid and the role of non-governmental organizations

Development thus became an important international issue in the post-war period and development aid, or Overseas Development Assistance (ODA), was frequently used as a weapon in the East–West conflict. Since the end of the Cold War, as might be expected, there have been changes in the aid environment. A recent report on ten OECD donor countries (Hewitt 1994) notes a reduction in North–South aid flows in the early 1990s which it attributes, in part, to changes in eastern Europe. Not least among these is the transformation of the former Soviet Union from a modest donor to an aid recipient. The end of the Cold War, however, has also witnessed calls for a change in the form aid will take in the future.

The idea and practice of post-war ODA has been subject to a great deal of criticism.[5] First, the underlying economic justification of aid – that the Third World is in need of capital and technical know-how which the developed world has in abundance – suggests that development is essentially a technical problem rather than a process of social change in which conflicting interests are at stake. It also suggests that development means replicating the experience of the West, an assumption that has produced a number of unfortunate consequences, not least severe environmental damage. Secondly, bilateral aid is often tied: it is given on condition that the funds provided are spent on goods produced in the donor country, thus greatly reducing their value to the recipient. Thirdly, the Cold War practice of using aid to support strategic allies has skewed its distribution considerably, so that in 1991 China received aid worth $1.7 per head while Israel received $353.6 (World Bank 1993). Perhaps the most telling indictment, however, is that aid has helped to finance the militarization of the Third World. In

1992 half the ODA went to just twelve countries, whose combined expenditure on armaments in that year equalled the amount of aid received. It appears therefore that ODA can simply release funds to be spent on arms.

Several of these criticisms are accepted even by supporters of aid, and the case for its reform has been made widely. The United Nations Development Programme, for example, has proposed a 'new design for development cooperation' at the heart of which is the call for a 20:20 compact on human development (UNDP 1994:77). Under such an agreement 20 per cent of Northern ODA and 20 per cent of public spending in developing countries would be committed to achieving a specific set of social targets, including universal access to basic education, clean water and primary health care, the elimination of malnutrition, and stabilization of the world's population at 7.3 billion by 2015. This proposal is an example of what Michael Lipton and Simon Maxwell (1992) call the New Poverty Agenda, a return to the sort of emphasis on poverty reduction promoted by multilateral agencies in the 1970s and subsequently swept aside by structural adjustment in the 1980s. Whether the end of the Cold War will act as a catalyst for any significant move in this direction remains to be seen. As the Pergau Dam case shows, the non-humanitarian motives for granting aid have frequently been economic rather than strategic. Such motives are likely to be enhanced as global economic competition increases.

An alternative solution to the problems of official aid is to reinforce the role of Non-Governmental Organizations (NGOs) in both North and South. This approach has considerable support. For neo-liberals, NGOs represent a private solution to development problems, while for some northern governments they are a cost-effective way of distributing ODA for small community-based projects. For many, however, they are important not because of their efficiency but because they promote an alternative model of development based on local needs and community control. This is also true of community-based development initiatives (CDIs), a rapidly growing form of development cooperation that links municipalities in the North and South through twinning, the provision of technical and administrative support and grants to community groups (Shuman 1994). Both NGO links and CDIs have become important alternative channels for North–South contact in recent years. They have also had considerable practical impact in humanitarian and political terms. According to one estimate 'NGOs currently benefit some 100 million people out of the 2 billion rural poor' (Ekins 1992:200) while, as Michael Shuman (1994:4–5) points out, 'The 86 US–Nicaragua sister cities sent more humanitarian assistance to Nicaraguan towns than all the aid the US government provided to the contras.'

## Political conditionality

Democratization has been the most significant political development in the Third World in the 1980s and 1990s. It is dealt with extensively elsewhere (see chapter nine) but one aspect of democratization, the emergence of political conditionality, is particularly relevant to analysis of North–South relations in the 1990s. Political conditionality refers to 'the linking of development aid to demands concerning human rights and (liberal) democracy in recipient countries' (Sørensen 1993:1).

The debt crisis made economic conditionality central to the provision of some forms of multilateral aid in the 1980s, and at first political conditionality was simply an extension of this process. In response to difficulties experienced in implementing structural adjustment in Africa, the World Bank produced a report in 1989, entitled 'Sub-Saharan Africa: From Crisis to Sustainable Development', which stressed the importance of 'good governance' as a precondition for successful development (Moore 1993). The idea of governance signalled a concern with the issues of accountability, corruption and administrative efficiency, and this became a theme in negotiations between individual Third World countries and the multilateral institutions. However, in the aftermath of the fall of communism in eastern Europe the idea was taken up by a number of European aid donors and linked to calls for democratic reforms. The role of political conditionality in the tide of democratization that swept through Africa in the early 1990s is debatable. The struggle for democracy and human rights within Africa has its own history that predates the belated concern of the European powers (Allen et al. 1992). However it is important for what it represents: 'a potentially dramatic change of basic principles of the international system: putting the human rights first means that respect for individuals and individual rights acquires priority over respect for the sovereignty of states' (Sørensen 1993:1).

Given their colonial past and vulnerability to external pressure, Third World states of all types have always been staunch defenders of the principle of non-interference. Clearly, the reality of global politics bears little similarity to the legal fiction of an international system composed of self-determining, sovereign states, particularly if the states concerned are in the Third World. Nevertheless a weakening in the principle of non-interference does have important implications for the manner in which the international system operates. It has implications for human rights, as Sørensen argues, but it also has implications for military intervention; suggesting, perhaps, some potential for humanitarian intervention. These issues are discussed in some detail in chapters six and ten.

## *The environment*

The growing significance of environmental issues in global politics is also dealt with at length elsewhere (see chapter eight) but it is important to note two things here. First, the environment is of central importance to the future of North–South relations because it is one of the few areas where the South appears to have some leverage over the North after the setbacks of the 1980s. Whereas southern interests are either routinely ignored or subjugated to northern interests in bodies such as the GATT, the IMF and the World Bank, it will be difficult for the industrialized countries to deal coherently with problems such as global warming and ozone depletion without coming to some agreement with the developing world. This was recognized, at least formally, when the two issues were linked at the 1992 Rio Earth Summit – the United Nations Conference on Environment and Development. Indeed Marc Williams (1993:8) has suggested that northern concerns about the planetary dimensions of environmental degradation may give 'fresh impetus to the stalled North–South dialogue and revive the dormant Third World coalition'.

Secondly environmental issues graphically demonstrate how North–South relations have changed since the 1970s to incorporate a wider range of interests. The priority of northern governments is clearly to manage the environmental crisis without questioning existing power relations within the global system or the profligate lifestyles of their own societies. Their southern counterparts, on the other hand, are principally concerned with defending the right to develop through industrialization. However, the growth-based concept of development shared by both parties has been widely criticized by environmental groups over the last twenty years and, as Alain Lipietz (1992) has argued, neither of their positions pays much attention to the fundamental class, gender or community interests of the poor in the Third World. One response to this situation has been the appearance of a parallel agenda which unites NGOs in both North and South in a fundamental rejection of economic growth. The impact of this agenda on formal negotiations about environmental change has so far been slight.[6] However, the growing importance of NGOs leads Marc Williams to suggests that 'a re-vitalised Third World coalition will reflect a set of priorities which has not been set exclusively by political elites' (1993:28).

## *Summary*

The end of the Cold War has had important consequences for the Third World. It has had a significant impact on aid policies, in particular through the introduction of new forms of political conditionality which emphasize democratization and respect for human rights, and has increased the possibility of humanitarian intervention in Third World states under the aegis of the United Nations. However, the major economic issues that divide North and South, and recent developments such as the increasing importance of environmental issues and the growth of grassroots contacts, have been largely unaffected by the end of the Cold War. Thus long-term structural inequalities of power and wealth, and growing awareness of planetary interdependence, are more important determinants of North–South relations in the 1990s. We now consider one important way of understanding this situation theoretically.

## Globalization

The idea of globalization has come into widespread use in the 1990s. It plays an important part in many current policy debates and has become a key concept across a range of academic disciplines. Here we consider the extent to which the concept of globalization allows us to understand the place of the Third World in the global system and, more specifically, how it illuminates the issues in North–South relations examined above.

In general terms, globalization refers to a unifying process of social change, or a way of seeing social relations, that takes in the world as a whole. As such it goes beyond forms of analysis centred on social relations within and between national societies and tries to identify structures and processes that exist at a global level. This is clearly a rich theoretical seam. It promises to reveal aspects of social reality not illuminated by other perspectives and provides a way of understanding important social changes at a time when the role of the state is being questioned both analytically and practically. At the same time it also suggests the possibility of a less Eurocentric vision of the global system – one in which the concerns and interests of the four-fifths of humanity who inhabit the Third World become more central. However, beyond the general, intuitive idea that global relationships are becoming more important, the concept is open to a number of interpretations.

At present globalization is used in at least four different ways: to refer to a new consciousness of global interdependence, particularly in relation to issues such as the environment that extend beyond the compass of individual states; as a project, in the sense of global business strategies and attempts at global governance; as a process of change in economic and cultural relations which intensifies links at a global level; and as an explanatory framework, a way of understanding social relations by considering the world as a single social system. These various senses of globalization are not necessarily incompatible. However the term has slipped into political and social science discourse without much systematic effort to reconcile or integrate these different approaches. Conceptual imprecision has a number of consequences, the most important of which concerns periodization.

If we think about globalization primarily as the emergence of a new form of behaviour or consciousness, this suggests a relatively recent phenomenon, particularly as the underlying cause is usually said to be rapid technological change over the last thirty or forty years. The communications revolution has contributed directly to a growth in awareness of issues such as the environment, human rights and development cooperation, and this in turn has led to new forms of transnational activism. Meanwhile, rapid technological innovation in a number of areas has enabled, or forced, economic agents to operate at an increasingly global level. Twenty-four-hour, worldwide financial markets have emerged; transnational business corporations have moved increasingly towards global production and marketing strategies, and the growth of transnational media corporations has greatly increased the flow of cultural commodities. These developments are often said to have had two main consequences: first they have undermined the capacity of governments to intervene coherently in their respective national economies and, secondly, they have contributed to the emergence of an increasingly homogeneous global culture. A reading of globalization that concentrates on these developments, therefore, sees it as a recent growth in transnational links among non-state actors, whose significance lies chiefly in the fact that it undermines existing state-based forms of political, economic and cultural organization.

Alternatively however, if we think of globalization as a particular way of understanding social relations or as a process of structural change, then it appears as a much longer-term phenomenon. World-systems theory, for example, argues that social relations can only be properly understood if they are seen in the context of an evolving world capitalist system that dates from at least the sixteenth century (Taylor 1986), while social theorists such as Anthony Giddens (1990) and Roland Robertson (1992) take a similarly long-term view and see globalization as one of the central processes in the formation of the modern world.

To a large extent these differing emphases can be reconciled if we identify recent developments as the latest stage in a longer process. However this still leaves important discontinuities. In particular, a great deal of writing on globalization takes as its starting point the idea of an international system based on the nation-state. Global relationships are described as either superseding or transcending interstate relationships. However, the interstate system is itself the result of a globalizing process; and this is particularly clear from the perspective of the Third World. As we have seen, it was the spread of nationalism to Africa and Asia, and the subsequent process of decolonization, that finally established the nation-state as the universal form of political organization (Anderson 1991). At the same time, though, decolonization can also be seen as a *de*globalizing process, in the sense that the aim of all post-colonial states was to create national economies in which control could be exercised over economic activities formerly subject to external economic forces. In other words, the universal acceptance of planned development as a desirable goal led to an increased nationalization of economic activity. It is clear, therefore, that globalization cannot be seen as a unilinear process and especially not one which moves simply from an interstate to a global system.

The experience of the Third World also brings into question the idea of globalization as a recent growth of global consciousness. Governments in the South have always acted in the knowledge of their vulnerability to external economic forces, and the national cultures that were formed under colonialism and after were the product of both global and local influences. Equally, most analyses, particularly radical analyses, have traditionally understood development in global as well as national terms. This raises the question of what exactly is new in the idea of globalization. In the North – where it is has been easier to believe in the sovereignty of the nation-state, the relative solidity of national cultures and what Hugo Radice (1984) has called the 'Keynesian myth' of the self-directed national economy – the idea may appear novel. But it appears much less so from the point of view of the South. From this perspective, globalization seems in many ways to be a repackaging of some already well analysed themes.

There can be gains from such a repackaging, as is demonstrated by Leslie Sklair (1991) in his innovative analysis of transnational practices, possibly the most interesting overall account of globalization so far. But there can also be losses; and according to Peter Waterman (1993) and Jan Nederveen Pieterse (1994) one particularly important loss in the work of some theorists is the idea of imperialism. Specifically, they criticize Anthony Giddens (1990) for losing sight of international power relations in his account of globalization as one of the principal characteristics of modernity. More generally though, Pieterse suggests that the idea of globalization is redundant if it is simply equated with westernization, as is often the case. He proposes instead that it should be seen as a process of hybridization in which disparate cultural forms and social structures combine to produce a new, composite global system. If the concept of globalization is to bring anything new to analysis of the Third World it will be in this form. An idea of globalization that takes into account both hybridization and inequalities of power would be a useful new tool in understanding the place of the Third World in the global system.

The idea of globalization, then, has a variety of meanings and it is consequently difficult to accept or reject in its entirety. It focuses attention on some significant changes in North–South relations over recent years, and it provides a useful framework for analysing the rise of global activism. It also potentially provides an innovative way of thinking about the growth of the global system that does not focus exclusively on the expansion of the West. However, many of the themes that are considered important to analysis of globalization from a northern perspective – such as the growing influence of transnational cultural flows and the impact on the state of global economic forces – are not new to the South. More specifically, it is difficult to see how the idea of globalization can contribute much to analysis of issues such as debt, aid and North–South trade flows.

## Notes

1   On the resemblance between the present global system and the structure of apartheid see Falk (1993:629). He quotes the American strategist Thomas Schelling:

> We live in a world that is one-fifth rich and four-fifths poor; the rich are segregated into rich countries and the poor into poor countries; the rich are predominantly light skinned; most of the poor live in 'homelands' that are physically remote, often separated by oceans and great distances from the rich. Migration on any great scale is impermissible. There is no systematic redistribution of income. While there is ethnic strife among the well-to-do, the strife is more vicious among the poor.

However he notes that the comparison should also be extended to military force: 'the rich, light-skinned countries enjoy a decisive military superiority and engage in frequent interventionary operations against the poor, dark-skinned countries' (ibid.).

2   The use of Gross National Product (GNP)/Gross Domestic Product (GDP) figures as a measure of development has been widely criticized. Figure 3.1 uses Purchasing Power Parity Dollars rather than the United States Dollar as a measure of GDP to avoid distortions caused by exchange rate variations. However this only deals with one of the problems posed. For a comprehensive list of these see Anderson (1991).

3   See Edward Herman's judgement that 'the United States, as dominant and perhaps only *real* superpower, has been the supreme terrorist in recent decades' (Herman 1992:18).

4   Philip Daniel (1991:1) has described economic nationalism as having 'rejected foreign direct investment as an agent of socially acceptable growth. It espoused instead nationalisation of foreign-owned enterprises, capital formation in state-owned enterprises, deficit financing, trade and exchange restrictions and protectionism.'

5   It is important to distinguish here between development aid – itself a catch-all category – and emergency aid sent in response to droughts, famines, refugee crises, etc. The criticisms here apply to development aid.

6 Nicholas Hildyard (1993:22–3) has pointed out that the Rio Conference Secretariat 'provided delegates with materials for a convention on biodiversity but not on free trade; on forests but not on agribusiness; on climate but not on automobiles. Agenda 21 – the Summit's "action plan" – featured clauses on "enabling the poor to achieve sustainable liveli- hoods" but none on enabling the rich to do so; a section on women but not on men.'

# 4

# The End of the Soviet Era: Implications for Global Politics

Geoffrey Ponton

After a period of relative stagnation the impact of Mikhail Gorbachev's assumption of the general secretaryship of the Communist Party of the Soviet Union (CPSU) in 1985 not only led to the collapse and disintegration of the Soviet Union itself in December 1991, but dissolved the arrangements for global stability and security which had developed since the Second World War. Three main questions arise as a result of this dramatic collapse: Why did the Soviet empire fall apart? What has been the effect on other communist states? And what are the implications for Russia's future role in the world, in particular its relations with the successor republics and the states of central and eastern Europe? Understanding and answering these questions requires the identification of relationships between long-standing historical, cultural and ethnic issues and the intrusion of global political and economic forces from which the communist world had previously been isolated.

The end of the communist world as it had been known since the Second World War was largely unanticipated by commentators on Soviet affairs. One school of thought had seen the communist states as essentially stable, with slowly developing characteristics of a quasi-pluralist system (Hough and Fainsod 1979). Others, such as Jeanne Kirkpatrick, United States Ambassador to the United Nations, considered the communist world to be too atomized to generate significant change from within. Long-standing anti-communists claimed credit for being justified, as they saw it, in arguing that communism had to be destroyed by economic and military pressure from the West. Nevertheless they could not easily explain the advent of Gorbachev and policies of *glasnost* and *perestroika* – except as a clever KGB plot to sustain the regime in power (Remnick 1994:20–6). Yet others felt that the fundamental changes in political and economic circumstances experienced in the Soviet Union and Eastern Europe resulted from interaction of ideas and events generated both internally and externally. The process, from attempts at reform, through collapse, to the rebuilding of economies and the adoption of new political systems, is best seen as a series of major adjustments, involving both confusion and continuity, as citizens and politicians attempted to adapt to a new and uncertain future.

## The Historical Antecedents

The Bolshevik revolutionaries restored and developed the multi-national and multifaith empire of the tsars. Although they tried to use Marxist-Leninist ideology to unify these peoples – to create 'socialist human beings' – there remained many underlying attitudes, beliefs and practices inherited from the past. Between the two World Wars Joseph Stalin established a dictatorship and terror; his death in 1953 seemed to herald the end of a stultifying, oppressive period of communist rule, both in the Soviet Union and the east European countries it dominated. Stalin's successor, Nikita Khrushchev, and his allies saw that the country had to be given a new lease of life, politically, economically and in foreign affairs. In practice, however, most of Khrushchev's initiatives did not survive the resistance of bureaucratic and military interests. The Communist Party held the empire together and kept other political, economic, cultural and nationalistic pressures under control.

The following two decades saw decline in all major areas. Politically an ageing leadership presided over increasing bureaucratic stagnation and a failure to deal with growing problems such as environmental pollution, nationalism and corruption. Corruption also entered the economic sphere at a time when the Soviet Union and the other communist countries were increasingly unable to keep up with the technological information revolution of the 1970s. The emphasis on heavy industry and manual labour, together with failure to integrate into the worldwide economic and financial system, created increasing difficulties. Although there were variations among the constituent republics of the Soviet Union, the country was essentially run as one vast integrated economy based on monolithic, monopolistic producers. In foreign affairs and defence there was an apparent thaw in the Cold War after an attempt by the Soviet Union to develop a policy of detente. However the Reagan Presidency in the United States saw the development of a further arms race from 1979. The Soviet Union was unable to compete and further economic difficulties ensued.

The situation in other communist countries was complex. Before their post-Second World War development the communist countries were mainly agrarian economies (except for the German Democratic Republic (GDR) and Czechoslovakia). They all adopted or had Soviet-type systems imposed upon them to varying degrees. The particular economic, social and political circumstances of these countries is significant as an explanation of their differing responses to the collapse of communism. Albania and Cuba have histories of foreign domination, while the GDR and North Korea, as poorer halves of divided nations were, not surprisingly, reluctant reformers – radical change was an admission of defeat. Success in the call for more individual initiative, responsibility and enhanced performance required material incentives – better supplies of consumer goods and services. In China and Hungary it was believed that the answer lay in reforming agriculture first and in encouraging a healthy private sector. The relatively independent situation of Yugoslavia facilitated a unique type of market socialism based on self-management by workers' councils of 'socially owned' enterprises. However tinkering with the command economy was usually ineffective, although China and Vietnam showed that partial reform could be made to work. China especially raised the question of whether political liberalization was a prerequisite for reform, at least in the short term.

The economic explanation of the collapse of the communist regimes in these countries has been challenged by the view that their weakness was primarily ideological. The real problem, it has been argued, was the failing legitimacy of a system to which the post-war generation was no longer committed. Sociological studies, available for the first time, showed that there was no real commitment to the socialist system, especially among the young. It is revealing to compare the idealism of youth in the inter-war period, remarked on in memoirs of later dissidents such as Andrei Sakharov and Alexander Solzhenitsyn (Sakharov 1990:20,32; Scammell 1986:63–4) with the general air of cynicism and disillusionment reflected in the sociological surveys made available in the 1970s (White 1977:328–42; 1979). This trend was even more emphatically evident by 1990 (Merridale 1991:28).

These problems were exacerbated by a growing expectation of change when a new, younger leadership was in place. That new leadership came when Gorbachev became general secretary of the CPSU in 1985. Gorbachev set about a thorough-going reform of the existing system based on the principles of *glasnost* (openness) and *perestroika* (reconstruction). He believed that a more open society was an essential basis for economic and social revival. Instead he released pent up political forces, especially those of nationalism, which placed intolerable strains on the political and social system and rapidly undermined the integrity of the Soviet Union itself. Yet during the Gorbachev period the Soviet economy was not radically reformed. Increasing economic crisis encouraged the view in the constituent republics that they would be better either independent or at least with a much greater degree of autonomy than hitherto.

In foreign affairs and defence Gorbachev and his foreign minister, Eduard Shevardnadze, abandoned the principles which had previously governed Soviet policies. Pressured partly by economic considerations, they rejected the policy of sustaining regimes through economic and military aid on the basis of their support for the Soviet Union (or at least their anti-Americanism), but regardless of the wishes of their populations or the quality of their regimes. Instead they proclaimed the right of states to self-determination and the virtue of agreements freely entered into between states having mutual interests and common principles. Countries such as Cuba faced crisis as economic support from the Soviet Union was drastically reduced.

The most dramatic impact of this change was the withdrawal of Soviet troops from the countries of central and eastern Europe (CEE). Above all, Gorbachev and Shevardnadze accepted the reunion of East and West Germany, hitherto seen as unthinkable. What was not faced was the question of how the Soviet Union (and later Russia) would redefine its relationship with states within what it considered to be its sphere of influence.

The Soviet Union now began a period of cooperation with the West which, given the confusion that prevailed in the economy and elsewhere, particularly among the armed forces, meant that western priorities were largely accepted. Both Comecon and the Warsaw Pact soon ceased to operate and the CEE countries found themselves without security guarantees.[1] What all this amounted to was the collapse of the post-Second World War settlement, which had provided a significant degree of stability and security in Europe for over forty years. The thinking of politicians and defence chiefs, however, continued to be governed by the parameters of the Cold War. They had extreme difficulty in contemplating a united Europe within the common security system envisaged by Gorbachev when he used expressions such as 'Europe – our common home' (Smith 1992:325).

## The Communist World Disintegrates

Political, economic and nationalist crises came to a head after the attempted coup by anti-Gorbachev forces in August 1991. This finally discredited the CPSU and the existing Soviet institutional system, causing the constituent republics of the Soviet Union, with varying degrees of enthusiasm, to decide that independence was preferable to any form of central government from Moscow, however modified.

Most joined a loose association – the Commonwealth of Independent States (CIS) – originated by the Slavic republics, Russia, Ukraine and Belarus.

Outside the Soviet Union the communist world reacted in different ways. Like the Soviet Union, Yugoslavia disintegrated. Czechoslovakia split into Slovakia and the Czech Republic while other east European countries moved towards western-type political and economic systems, at different speeds and with varying levels of confusion. At first Hungary and Slovenia were the most successful, Albania the least. Some (such as Hungary) adopted the gradualist approach. Others (such as Poland) looked to economic shock therapy. Cuba and North Korea retained traditional command economies with communist party control. China and Vietnam retained communist control but with market oriented reform. Indeed China had experimented with market reforms since 1978, particularly successfully in agriculture in the shape of the 'household responsibility system'.

President Bush of the United States spoke of a new world order, but in many of the newly independent states there was little prospect of the smooth transition to democracy implied by liberal triumphalists – an issue taken up more fully in chapter nine. Increasing economic difficulties, the inexperience of politicians and the lack of any democratic traditions in many states meant that some (such as those in Central Asia) maintained authoritarian systems, others degenerated into armed conflict (Azerbaijan and Georgia) or faced serious divisions (Ukraine and Moldova). The CEE countries faced severe difficulties in achieving economic adjustment and problems involving ethnic minorities including, in the case of Czechoslovakia, pressure for the country to divide into its constituent parts.

The result in many states was a turning back, if not to communism, then to former communist leaders. Indeed, in Central Asia and Belarus, the communist leaders remained in office throughout, albeit under different party political names. In Russia many of the new leaders, including Boris Yeltsin, the President, were former communists, while in other countries such as Poland, Hungary, Lithuania and Azerbaijan former communists were elected or called back, as nationalist radicals' movements showed themselves incapable of adjusting to the new situation or of remaining united with a coherent political programme. This was not a return to the *status quo ante*, however. Rather it was a reversion to leaders who had some experience of government and had shown a willingness to adjust to the changed situation by accepting some elements of democracy, economic reform and nationalist aspirations.

An essential element of the western conception of democracy is the healthy activity of 'civil society' – the area of life where citizens can freely promote their interests. Fukuyama points out that the development of civil society in the former communist states has not been uniform. Hungary, Poland, the Baltic states and the Czech Republic all had non-communist elites waiting to take over when communism collapsed, while in countries such as Romania, Ukraine, Belarus and even Russia there was a heavy reliance on former communists to run ministries and newly privatized enterprises. In Central Asia and the Transcaucasus clan, ethnic and sub-regional loyalties were revived (Fukuyama 1994:3).

## Post-Soviet Russia: The Experience of Independence

Russia, newly independent from the Soviet Union from 1991, faced formidable economic and social difficulties. The problems of privatiz- ation, modernization and efficiency, and of converting military enter- prises to domestic production without causing socially disruptive unemployment were great enough. To these must be added pressure from the constituent republics and regions of the federation for more autonomy or even independence (Chechenia did unilaterally declare independence) and a growing extreme Russian nationalist movement which potentially threatened President Yeltsin's position.

The economic policies of the new government were controversial. Prices were freed immediately but some thought this was a serious error. Many manufacturers were in a virtual monopoly position and simply put up their prices while failing to improve productivity, thus fuelling inflation. Overall the government favoured the fashionable 'shock therapy' approach to economic reform, aiming at low inflation and drastic cuts in government spending, which was also the policy advocated by potential lenders such as the IMF. Nevertheless this policy failed to address the problem of the political and social conse- quences – in a country which had come to take full employment for granted – of the high levels of unemployment likely to ensue.

In the event, the principal source of instability in the first twenty months or so of an independent Russia came from an all-consuming political struggle between President Yeltsin, on the one hand, and the speaker of the parliament, Ruslan Khasbulatov, supported by Yeltsin's vice-president, Alexander Rutskoi, on the other. Disagreement over economic policy was one significant aspect of this dispute, with Rutskoi and Khasbulatov emerging as supporters of the 'social market' – a more cautious and, they believed, less socially damaging road to a market economy, involving more government management than envisaged by the liberal economists of the Yeltsin government. The dispute extended to a political struggle between the presidency and parliament as well as a personal power struggle between Yeltsin, Rutskoi and Khasbulatov.

The parliament had been elected in 1990 under the reformed Soviet system and, although relatively democratic by previous Soviet standards, contained a large number of communist sympathizers and those who saw in their position of deputy an opportunity for personal advantage rather than for playing a constructive role in the government of the country. On the other hand, many feared the accretion of power which Yeltsin seemed to be aiming for; demanding (and getting, for a time) emergency powers. As the struggle between presidency and parliament continued, consideration of urgent economic reforms languished. Nevertheless parliament gained one victory when Yegor Gaidar was replaced as prime minister by Viktor Chernomyrdin, who had an industrial management background and espoused more moderate policies.

Various ploys were attempted by Yeltsin in order to resolve the situation, including calling a referendum and commencing a debate on institutional reform. These efforts failed, however, because of parliamentary intransigence, regional divisions and the limited nature of the proposals themselves. Eventually, at the end of September 1993, Yeltsin took a step he had long threatened and suspended the legally elected parliament – a move that was, strictly speaking, unconstitutional. A dramatic confrontation ensued, culminating in troops storming, and overwhelming, the White House, where parliament sat. There was considerable loss of life and much psychological shock at this violence in the capital. Yeltsin's reputation was not enhanced by this episode, even among those who were exasperated at parliament's behaviour. Rutskoi and Khasbulatov were also discredited by their reliance on extreme right-wing nationalist forces during the seige. Yeltsin announced elections for a new parliament to take place on 11 December 1993. At first he also announced an early presidential election but later decided to see out his term until 1996.

## The effect of the December 1993 elections

As it turned out, the December 1993 election marked a major turning point in the short life of post-communist Russia. It was fought between four principal political groups: the radical reformers, supported by Yeltsin and Gaidar; the moderate reformers whose main protagonist was Gregorii Yavlinsky; former communists and nationalists represented by the Russian Communist Party and led by Gennardii Zyuganov; and the right-wing Russian nationalist Liberal Democratic Party led by Vladimir Zhirinovsky. Zhirinovsky acquired notoriety by expressing extreme views concerning the restoration of the Russian empire. In the event the radical reformers were at a disadvantage because they were held responsible for the country's difficulties. They also fought an election campaign which suggested that the extreme right was the only alternative to themselves, with the result that the moderate centre was squeezed out of the campaign. Consequently the nationalist right made considerable gains and Zhirinovsky's Liberal Democrats emerged as one of the largest groups in the new parliament.

Russia illustrated a situation of transition in which ideas, attitudes and conventions from the past vie with externally induced pressures. The Soviet economic and financial system lumbered on, with productivity falling as its channels of supply broke down. Thus populists such as Zhirinovsky were able to play on, and gain advantage from, government mismanagement and widespread discontent. His success highlighted the exasperation of the Russian electorate, but the implications of the election result spread far beyond Russia. In the West confidence in the economic future of Russia was undermined, affecting, in particular, the terms of economic and financial assistance.

## International aid

Stability and progress in Russia, and indeed the other former communist states, was highly dependent on aid from the West. This, in turn, meant negotiating terms which would be acceptable both to the countries concerned and to the international economic institutions such as the World Bank and the IMF. However the IMF had always laid down strict conditions for lending and saw no reason to make an exception for Russia or other former communist countries (Pringle and Torday 1992).

The whole question of aid was given new impetus by a memorandum from former United States president Nixon in which he argued that the United States was missing a historic opportunity to secure long-term peace in the successor states. United States' aid to Russia was, he stated, a

> pathetically inadequate response in light of the opportunities and dangers we face in the crisis in the former Soviet republics. We have to realize that if Yeltsin fails, if freedom fails, the new despotism that will take its place will mean that the peace dividend is finished and we will have to re-arm, and that is going to cost infinitely more than would the aid that we provide (Usborne 1992:14)

Despite divisions over the degree of support that could be offered, IMF membership for Russia was approved in April 1992. While Yeltsin had to state (for the benefit of his right-wing critics) that he would never allow western financiers to dictate to his country, in accepting western aid he was implying acceptance of western conditions as well. Indeed at the July meeting of the Group of Seven major industrial countries (G7), Yeltsin agreed to tough IMF conditions in an attempt to expedite aid payments. By this time there was, in Russia, growing scepticism about the West's honesty and reliability. Little western government or private money had been invested in Russia and Russian exports were being met by restrictions everywhere.

Western concerns were greatly exacerbated, however, by the success of the nationalist and populist right in the December elections. Harvard economist Jeffrey Sachs, who resigned in January 1994 as economic adviser to President Yeltsin, stated: 'The communist old guard has reasserted its political dominance in Russia . . . the reformers could not win without our help, but help never arrived' (Sachs 1994:16). Thus the setback for the radical reformers was attributed by some critics to the failure of the West to provide support, while western leaders felt they had more than adequate reasons for caution, notwithstanding calls for bold initiative from such as ex-President Nixon. Late in March 1994, however, the IMF agreed to grant Russia a long-delayed loan. IMF policy makers were aware that the political and economic situation in Russia would continue to deteriorate unless (increasingly unconditional) aid was provided. Without aid to give non-inflationary support to state industries, Yeltsin had to choose between accelerating inflation or the risk of mass unemployment. As the economic situation deteriorated further, the authority of the federal government was collapsing in the face of refusal by provincial governors to forward tax revenues collected.

## The Wider Impact of the Collapse of the Soviet Union

The prospect of instability in Russia following the collapse of the Soviet Union caused widespread concern, which was exacerbated by ultra-nationalist statements from such as Zhirinovsky. In particular, the CEE countries feared falling once again under *de facto* domination by Russia, while the three Baltic states were not entirely assuaged by the withdrawal of Russian troops from their territories at the end of August 1994. There were, in addition, profound political, economic and social consequences throughout all fifteen successor republics of the Soviet Union. Their histories and development varied widely as did their relationship to the Russians and to the Soviet government in Moscow. However, over the years of Soviet power they had acquired some common characteristics of organization and development, not the least being the integration of their economies, which meant that none could embark on independence without being aware that they remained economically dependent on Russia and, to a lesser extent, on other successor republics.

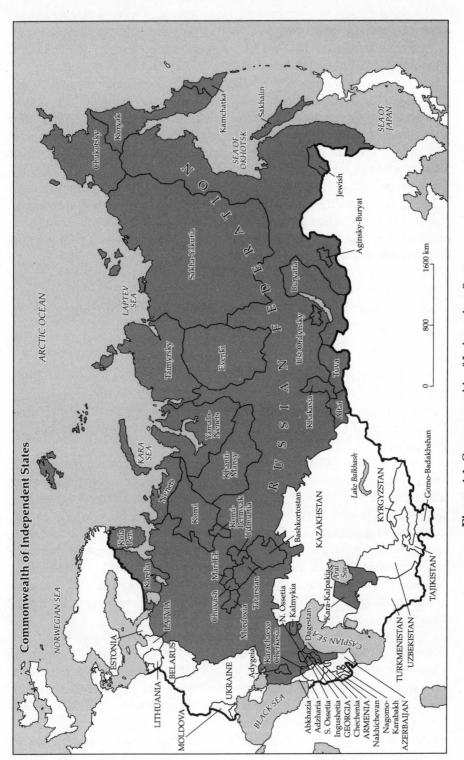

**Figure 4.1** Commonwealth of Independent States

Adapted from Russia and the Successor States Briefing Service, vol. 3, no. 1, February 1995: 2

In Russia itself the collapse of the empire was hard for most people to come to terms with, and the idea that Russia could and should retain significant influence throughout the area of the former Soviet Union was prevalent among politicians of every sort, from radical reformers to the extreme nationalist right. Thus President Yeltsin argued, in his speech to the opening session of the Federation Council (the upper house of the new Russian parliament elected in December 1993), that 'Each state is increasingly realizing that it cannot cope with those most difficult problems single-handed, that it cannot survive on its own. Rapprochement between our countries is under way. It is Russia's mission to be first among equals' (Higgins 1994:13). In effect, the story of the successor republics since the collapse of the Soviet Union is one in which Russia has steadily sought to regain influence, and even control in many areas, mainly by exploiting the economic, military and political weaknesses of the republics.

## The Situation in the Successor Republics

### Central Asia

Central Asia has strategic importance because of its proximity to China and Afghanistan. It contains a large number of ethnic minorities, while significant proportions of the major ethnic groups live outside their own republics. The northern part of Kazakhstan has a majority Russian population.

Although the CPSU maintained a firm hold over the area through the associated republic communist parties, there remained a strong undercurrent of regional and clan loyalties which affected the choice and influence of leadership personnel. There was no tradition or experience of democratic government as understood in the West so that, when the Soviet Union collapsed, political leaders changed the name of the Party and their rhetoric, but retained power by building on the local loyalties which had always underpinned their position. This caused some social conflict, with hostility being directed primarily against rival clans.

A major concern of politicians, both in Russia and the West, has been the possibility of so-called Islamic fundamentalism gaining in influence throughout the region. Religion certainly experienced a strong revival after the fall of communism, but most commentators have felt that the traditions of the area and decades of secularization will prevent fundamentalism from developing popular appeal. Most people in Central Asia belong to the more moderate Sunni branch of Islam and, even with the religious revival, a majority of the area's population is not significantly practising their religion. The exception here has been Tajikistan with its Iranian connections and a border with Afghanistan; ethnic groups such as the Tajiks and the Uzbeks having a significant presence on both sides of that border. A struggle ensued soon after independence when the Tajik government (still the communist government under another name) was overthrown by a combination of democrats and the Islamic Revival Party. This was short-lived and the ex-communists were restored by Russian intervention, tacitly supported by the United States, both fearful of inroads by Islamic fundamentalists from Afghanistan. The Russian army took over the security of the country, guarding the border with Afghanistan. The governments of other Central Asian republics were very much in favour of these firm measures.

With their historical links in Central Asia, both Iran and Turkey looked to extend their influence following independence. Turkey in particular has made great efforts to forge political ties and commercial links. It is clear, however, that official Turkish policy does not extend to envisaging the creation of a Turkestan – a unified Turkic nation across the area which had, for many years, been the dream of some activists. The Iranian government lacks the contacts and resources to mount an effort comparable to the Turks but has supplied some material and religious support. None of these activities has been on a scale which could seriously challenge the predominant influence of Russia in the region, and the governments of the central Asian countries clearly preferred this state of affairs. They had wanted more autonomy and accepted full independence only reluctantly, and are therefore quite content to maintain their ties with Russia.

Nuclear weapons were based in Kazakhstan but the republic's leadership raised no objection to abandoning nuclear status and transferring the weapons to Russia. The announcement of the unifying of the Russian and Kazakh armies reflected the strength of Russian influence and Kazakhstan's desire for very close ties with Russia. The security significance of the region will depend on Russia's relations with China and developments in Iran and Afghanistan. Despite the potential for foreign investment, especially in oil and gas resources in Turkmenistan, difficult times lie ahead economically. In consequence, authoritarian regimes are likely to remain, with the potential for increasing repression should ethnic or clan conflicts erupt.

## The Caucasus

The Caucasus is a region containing many nationalities, divided between Christians and Moslems. It includes southern Russia as well as Georgia, Azerbaijan and Armenia (the Transcaucasus). Historically it has been an area of instability: there were long-standing animosities and fears between ethnic groups in the region, most of which were suppressed, but not forgotten, under communism. Nevertheless many of the smaller ethnic communities felt more secure under Soviet rule than in the newly independent republics where the local majority nationality is in control. Following the collapse of the Soviet Union, ethnic groups living in the mountains of southern Russia were stimulated to seek greater autonomy from Moscow and also to provide support for other minority groups, especially those in Georgia.

The conflict which erupted in Chechenia in December 1994 was pre-dated by a long-standing territorial dispute between the Chechens and Ingush in southern Russia. After the attempted coup of August 1991 the Chechen leader, Dzhokhar Dudayev, declared independence from Russia. No country recognized the independence of Chechenia and relatively little action was taken by President Yeltsin until late in 1994, when a full-scale military attack was launched on the autonomous republic. Through this action Yeltsin hoped to ally himself with the Russian nationalists, who were growing in strength, and also to end any aspirations for greater autonomy or independence in other regions of Russia. But he took great risks by alienating public opinion opposed to war within the Russian territories, by revealing division and demoralization within the armed forces, and by creating the possibility of a prolonged conflict with Chechen guerrilla forces.

In Georgia, the South Ossetian people have sought union with North Ossetia (which is situated within Russia) or at least to have guaranteed Russian protection. They were unwilling to live in an independent Georgia where they believed they would suffer discrimination. The Georgian government strongly opposed these moves, but only after severe fighting between North Ossetian and Georgian troops was a cease-fire agreed with the help of Russia.

Georgia had other problems of an even more serious nature. After the overthrow of the increasingly authoritarian president Zviad Gamsakhurdia, in the first days of 1992, the country was in the hands of military leaders. Later, Eduard Shevardnadze, a Georgian who was Soviet foreign minister under Gorbachev and who, under Brezhnev, had been a ruthless Party secretary in Georgia, was called in to try to reunite the country. Nevertheless resistance to rule from the Georgian capital, Tbilisi, grew among the Mingrelians in the west and the Abkhazians in the north-west, the latter being by far the most serious conflict. Although the Abkhazians made up only 18 per cent of the population of the area, they put up resistance so fierce that the Georgian forces came close to defeat, raising suspicions of involvement by Russian troops. It is argued that, having thoroughly destabilized the region, the Russians were in a position to dictate terms to the Georgians, mainly regarding rights to a military presence in Georgia and economic agreements. With Russian assistance peace was restored but Abkhazia, although devastated, still regards itself as independent so that the issue cannot be said to have been resolved. Again Russia remains the key to the future and it is significant that Shevardnadze also supported Yeltsin's attempt to crush the Chechens by force.

The remainder of the Transcaucasus consists of Christian Armenia and Moslem Azerbaijan. The most serious conflict resulting from the collapse of the Soviet Union, coming close in severity to the situation in the former Yugoslavia, occurred over a long-standing dispute concerning an Armenian enclave in Azerbaijan, Nagorno-Karabakh. The weakening of Soviet control encouraged Armenians to campaign for the removal of Karabakh from Azeri control. However, this was resisted for political and geographical reasons. Prolonged fighting ensued and, although both sides had successes and losses in the early stages, the Armenians slowly gained the upper hand. Their army was well trained and disciplined while Azerbaijan relied on a mercenary army raised and financed by local leaders. A severe refugee problem developed involving Iran, where many fled. Iran was also concerned for the stability of Azerbaijan because a large Azeri minority lives in northern Iran. In a desperate attempt to remedy the situation, the Azeris recalled their former communist leader, Geydar Aliyev.

Suspicions have been aroused as to how the Armenians were able to achieve their success and who was aiding them. In the early days of the dispute Russia favoured Azerbaijan, much to the chagrin of the Armenians who tended to see themselves as defenders of Christian society against the encroachment of Islam, and expected Christian Russia to support them. However, the Russians changed their policy apparently because Aliyev, the Azeri president, was not prepared to agree to Russian military bases in his country. Azerbaijan suffered severe defeat, with 20 per cent of its territory, going far beyond Nagorno-Karabakh, in Armenian hands. An uneasy cease-fire prevailed but peace efforts by Russia and by the Conference on Security and Cooperation in Europe (CSCE)[2] failed to move either side. The Azeris were demoralized and humiliated but the Armenians, too, seemed to have had enough of the war and had increasing difficulty in recruiting troops. Meanwhile Turkey and Iran continue to be interested although their involvement has been very limited so far. Neither has given entirely wholehearted practical support to their fellow Moslems in Azerbaijan; indeed the Azeris have accused Turkey of actively supporting Armenia. Historically relations between Turkey and Armenia have been very bad, following massacres of Armenians by the Turks in 1915, but in recent days the Armenians have shown themselves willing to develop better relations with Turkey, thus prioritizing practical considerations over historical enmity.

## Ukraine and Moldova

Ukraine had no real tradition or experience of independence and the vote for independence on 1 December 1991 was perhaps the greatest of many shocks for Russians as the Soviet Union collapsed. For most Russians, Russians and Ukrainians were inseparable. Historically Kievan Rus was the region from which Russia developed, and for the Ukrainians to go their own way was hard to accept. A large Russian speaking population lives in the east and south of Ukraine but the west of the country has a very different history, having once been part of the Austro-Hungarian empire, and dominated by Poles in the twentieth century. It was strongly nationalist, many belonging to the uniate Ukrainian ('Greek') Catholic Church and looking westward rather than towards Russia. West Ukraine also contains Polish and Hungarian minorities. Indeed Ukrainians had never been fully united until incorporation into the Soviet Union and maintaining that unity is likely to be a very difficult task.

The communist leadership was never really replaced, although the party name was changed. Leonid Kravchuk, who became president, was a communist leader who opportunistically embraced nationalism to preserve his position. Although Ukraine, with a population of over 50 million, has great industrial and agricultural potential, its progress since independence has been very poor. A new currency was introduced which was rapidly devalued, but the government failed to embark on an effective programme of economic reform. This meant that western aid was not forthcoming on any significant scale. Three issues have dominated Ukrainian politics since independence – nuclear weapons, the future of Crimea and the fate of the Black Sea Fleet. All three have implications for global stability and security going well beyond the immediate area.

Immediately after independence, along with the other nuclear republics – Belarus and Kazakhstan – Ukraine agreed to give up its nuclear weapons leaving Russia as the only nuclear power in the area. But fear of Russia and pressure from nationalists caused a reversal of this policy. Only prolonged pressure from the West at last persuaded Ukraine to agree to the transfer of its nuclear weapons to Russia. It was realized that Ukraine did not have the expertise or resources to maintain, use or even dismantle the weapons. Promises of aid, including that towards the cost of dismantling, evidently helped in this decision.

Difficulties with Ukraine over the disposition of the Black Sea Fleet were heightened in July 1993 when the Russian Supreme Soviet voted to reclaim the port of Sevastopol in Ukraine, and bring the entire Black Sea Fleet under Russian control. In doing this they had the support of the military. Yeltsin moved rapidly to repudiate the Supreme Soviet's decision, but an alarmed Ukrainian parliament urged the United Nations Security Council to help resolve the dispute. The Security Council duly denounced the Supreme Soviet's claim as incompatible with the Charter of the United Nations. The controversy was as much over status and prestige as military necessity; the fleet itself was out-dated and too large for contemporary needs. A whole series of agreements was reached over the division of the fleet, all of which collapsed. Several incidents increased tension and fears were raised of serious conflict, while the fleet's personnel were divided and confused. Increasingly it was realized that Ukraine did not need a significant share of the fleet and, in any case, was not capable of maintaining it. Nevertheless, until the situation is resolved it remains a source of potentially serious conflict and destabilization of the region.

The Black Sea Fleet's headquarters is at Sevastopol in the Crimea. The political position of Crimea itself is another serious problem affecting relations between Russia and Ukraine. Although separate from Russia proper, Crimea was part of Russia until ceded to Ukraine by Khrushchev in 1954. Now, with the opportunity for self-determination, the large Russian population is demanding at least a much greater degree of autonomy and closer ties with Russia, while some want complete reunion of Crimea with Russia. The Ukrainian government is strongly resisting these pressures but Crimea has elected its own president (Yuri Meshkov) who has a policy of much closer links with Russia. Such policies are fuelled by the economic crisis in Ukraine (even more serious than that of Russia) which encourages disgruntled Russians to turn to Russia as a better option. Thus conflict over the future of Crimea must also be regarded as a serious potential source of instability in the region.

Moldova consists of Romanian territory annexed to the Soviet Union in 1940. It has no boundary with Russia proper, while changes in its boundary with Ukraine mean that it has a Ukrainian minority living alongside Russians in the industrial area known as Trans-Dneistr. On independence these minorities feared that Moldova would seek reunion with Romania and so formed their own unofficial 'Trans-Dneistr Republic' which was *de facto* supported by the former Soviet 14th Army stationed in the area. While it became clear that Moldova had no intention of reuniting with Romania in the foreseeable future Russian interests were, nevertheless, threatened by this serious revolt in such an economically important area. In addition, Moldova had difficulty with the Gagauz, a community of Turkish Christians in the south, who had tried to gain more autonomy as a result of the Soviet Union's crisis. Most of the difficulties with this community occurred before independence but they remain a potential source of friction. Still further, before independence, Moldova was confronted with a threat of destabilization from irregular armed bands. Only firm action supported by Moscow enabled this threat to be diminished. Moldova's difficulties are as much with Ukraine as with Russia. Ukraine believes that trouble-making elements (for example, Cossack mercenaries) may enter the country from the Trans-Dneistr area, and so they closely supervise the border.

## The Baltic Republics and Belarus

The three Baltic republics regarded themselves as states which had been illegally annexed to the Soviet Union by Stalin in 1940, an annexation which was not recognized by most western governments, although the *de facto* situation was accepted in subsequent agreements. They had become independent countries following the 1917 Russian revolution, and strong nationalist sentiments continued to exist. Gorbachev's *glasnost* and *perestroika* policies gave the opportunity for nationalist movements to be set up openly and so the first popular fronts came into being. Ostensibly formed to support the CPSU's policy of *perestroika* they soon developed into political movements for independence and were copied in many other republics. Lithuania took the lead among the three republics and it was the Lithuanian Communist Party which made one of the most significant decisions of the Gorbachev period when it became the first of the republic communist parties to break from the CPSU and embrace a nationalist programme.

Many members of the Soviet government viewed events in the Baltic states with great concern, and in Lithuania and Latvia this was associated with violent attempts by old-style communists to wrest power from the governments of those countries. Hence both historic and contemporary events gave rise to nervousness in the three republics concerning the intentions of their powerful and unfriendly neighbour. In consequence there was determination in the Baltic states to regain independence and help was sought, particularly from the West, to achieve this. The situation was considerably exacerbated by the presence of Russian minorities in all three republics, amounting to 29.4 per cent of the population in Estonia and 33.5 per cent in Latvia. In Lithuania, Russians constituted 8.5 per cent (Klatt 1994:35). Other minorities further reduced the proportion of the indigenous population (especially in Latvia).

These issues, and the presence of Russian military forces in the three republics, dominated relations between the Baltic states and Russia in the early years of independence. In addition, they had in common with all other republics severe economic and financial problems with a dependence on Russia for many needs, and energy in particular. In all three countries the popular fronts, which had been at the forefront of the independence movements, were unable to stay sufficiently united or coherent to retain power for long. They were replaced, after democratic elections, by right of centre governments in Latvia and Estonia, while the former Communist Party, now renamed the Democratic

Labour Party, won power in Lithuania under its popular leader, Algirdas Brazauskas.

The question of citizenship was particularly serious in Latvia and Estonia because of their proportionately large Russian populations. Both tried to develop citizenship laws that would put heavy pressure on the Russians formally to commit themselves to the countries in which they resided, even though significant proportions of the Russian minority in each country had voted for independence. Basically, citizenship revolved around the condition of having been a citizen before annexation in 1940, or a descendent of such a person. Others were subject to residence requirements, quotas and – the condition most objected to – some knowledge of the local language. This not only annoyed the Russian government and encouraged Russian nationalist feeling, but caused difficulties with the United Nations and the CSCE, who saw these conditions as being incompatible with international principles concerning human rights. Under pressure from Russia and the United Nations, therefore, both countries had to look at their citizenship laws again.

Citizenship was not unconnected with the presence of the Russian military in the three countries. They had traditionally been popular retirement places for Soviet military personnel and after independence many military personnel in their thirties and forties had 'retired' in the Baltic states. This seems to have been a move by the Russian government to avoid the responsibility of resettling these people in Russia, but in the Baltic states they were seen as a potential security risk. Further problems arose during negotiations for the withdrawal of the Russian military from the three republics, which were fraught with tension especially in Estonia and Latvia. In the case of Lithuania, the negotiations were complicated by the need of the Russian military to have access, through Lithuania, to the Russian enclave of Kaliningrad. Ultimately, however, the agreed date of withdrawal, 31 August 1994, was honoured by the Russian government.

Belarus, formerly Belorussia, had never been independent but had been ruled by Poles and Russians. In more recent times part of Lithuania, including Vilnius the present capital, had been included in Belorussia. Therefore the sense of a separate national identity was not strong. Belarusians are Slavs and identify with Russians, their fellow Slavs. Independence came unsought by most, although there was a popular front and there had been some industrial unrest. Communists largely retained control after independence and, after a short period of rule by a relatively moderate acting president, Stanislav Shushkevitch, ousted him and looked to have an 'establishment' president elected. They also negotiated an agreement with Russia aimed at reintegrating the country's economy and financial system with that of Russia – the two had in reality remained closely intertwined anyway. But, in one of the great surprises of the post-independence period, a populist, Alexander Lukashenko, who had been chair of the parliament's anti-corruption committee, won the presidential election. He promised to sweep away the old guard and to renegotiate the economic and financial agreement with Russia, thus creating yet another area of uncertainty in Russia's relationship with the newly independent states.

Thus the overall situation among the successor states is that they are struggling with political, economic and security problems, and seeking with varying degrees of intensity to maintain their independence in the face of the reality of economic dependence on Russia and military insecurity alongside a major nuclear power.

## Russian Foreign and Security Policy: Issues of Regional Stability

### *Policy towards the successor states*

The Russian government has argued that it is realistic and practical for countries in a region with such close ties to work together in economic development and the creation of effective security arrangements. All this would be achieved under the natural and inevitable leadership of Russia. While this may be acceptable in Central Asia and Belarus, and to Russian minorities in the successor republics, it causes tension and anxiety elsewhere. This means that cooperation with and reliance on Russia, economically and militarily, is accepted only reluctantly by many. However the Russian government, in turn, seems reluctant to acknowledge the considerable degree of suspicion and distrust that exists towards it throughout the region.

Observers are divided over the intentions of Russian policy towards the 'near abroad' of newly independent states. Does it simply represent a realistic appraisal of the situation – that the region is a natural sphere of interest for Russia and that responsibility for policing the region will inevitably fall to Russia? Or does Russia's policy suggest covert imperialism, an attempt to restore the Soviet empire under another guise?

The evidence in the early years after independence was inconclusive. Russia did indeed show a great interest in acting as peacemaker in the region, in claiming rights to military bases in the successor republics and reaching economic agreements with them. On the other hand, Russia has worked cooperatively with the United States as well as with the United Nations and other international organizations such as the OSCE, and it has withdrawn its troops in accordance with agreements reached with the governments of the Baltic states. How Russia's policies will develop in the future depends on internal political developments, in particular the presidential election due in 1996, the degree to which suspicions in many in the successor states can be assuaged, and a range of external factors – in particular the policies of western governments towards the region.

Clearly Russia's security policies have considerable bearing on these issues. Early in November, 1993, President Yeltsin approved new principles of military doctrine to meet the needs of Russia in the post-Soviet world. From its emergence in the 1920s until the break-up of the Soviet Union, military doctrine had been overwhelmingly concerned with large-scale warfare – the Third World War. There was little consideration of low intensity conflict. From 1988 the doctrine had been redefined as a system of views on the prevention of war and this definition was maintained in the new military doctrine. It emphasized smaller conflicts, within Russia and on its borders, as well as support for United Nations peacekeeping operations. The main purpose of the Russian armed forces is said to be 'localization of the foci of tensions and curbing military action at the earliest possible stage . . . the most rapid normalization of the situation, the restoration of law and order, guaranteeing security for society, giving necessary help to the population and the creation of conditions for regulating the conflict by political means' (Bellamy 1994:9).

Significantly, the new doctrine sanctioned the use of Russia's troops beyond Russia's immediate borders. Operations outside Russia would 'conform with all international norms' and respect the sovereignty of other countries. It also defined the military's internal role by stating that the army had the duty to intervene in crises where the established power structure was threatened by violent revolt.

The new doctrine was recognized in the West as an important statement of aims. It was seen as based on practical rather than ideological considerations and not as constituting a threat. However, some felt that the West was condoning a Russian sphere of influence in the area of the old Soviet Union. Russia's foreign minister, Andrei Kozyrev, wrote at that time: 'Either we learn to conduct military actions to support an established peace in the zones of our traditional geopolitical interests, or we lose influence there, and the vacuum will be filled by others' (Black 1993:13).

The arguments against the benign view of Russia's intentions towards the 'near abroad' have been put by Jonathan Eyal (1993:19). He contends that Russia's tactics to force states into the CIS and to increase Russian influence have been of three kinds:

1   Through exploiting ethnic rivalries in order to destabilize neighbouring
    states such as Georgia. Separatist movements arose and were well

equipped; then Russia intervened to separate warring parties and impose a peace which involved the stationing of Russian troops.

2    In Moldova and Tajikistan local Russian residents were encouraged to demand the permanent presence of Russian troops.

3    There was a creation of enclaves which were controlled by or supportive of Russian interests, like the Dneistr region in Moldova, and Kaliningrad.

One should also note Yeltsin's rhetorical declaration that the Tajik–Afghan border was Russia's border.

The Russian government also continued to press the West to allow the Conventional Forces in Europe (CFE) Treaty provisions to be modified to allow a greater Russian military presence in the Caucasus. Kozyrev, the foreign minister, had asked the West to allow Russia to take responsibility for peacekeeping in the area but, Eyal argued, there was no cease-fire in these countries, Russian troops were not impartial and, to accord with the traditional principles of peacekeeping, the contending parties needed to accept such a role for Russia. In any case, the Russian military were already active in these areas.

A considerable argument thus ensued over whether the Russian government's interest was one of peacekeeping in areas close to Russia's borders or whether it was manifesting imperial ambitions under another guise. The necessity for the deployment of peacekeeping forces in volatile areas was acknowledged. But the Russian government's demand for military bases in many of the successor republics, together with the deployment of the Russian military on the Tajik–Afghan border and on the Iran–Turkish border with Azerbaijan seemed to many to go far beyond the requirements of peacekeeping, at least as traditionally understood (see chapter six pp. 137–8). In addition, the Russian government utilized the economic dependence of the successor republics on Russia to bind them closer to itself. Many republics were in too weak an economic state to resist Russian pressure. The instrument of this reintegration by stealth was the CIS, as Russia steadily asserted its influence over the organization. By April 1994 all the successor republics except the three Baltic states had joined the CIS.

The counter to these arguments was that the Russia does have a legitimate responsibility in the region covered by the successor states, and that the West had neither the interest nor the resources to undertake major peacekeeping operations in the region, especially when United Nations resources were already deployed in other parts of the world. The point was to ensure that Russia acted under the auspices of the United Nations and in accordance with the principles laid down by that organization for peacekeeping operations. Once again, opinion on this matter was affected by the degree of distrust which Russia had to overcome. The evidence as to whether it was acting in ways acceptable to the international community was not conclusive.

## The Yugoslav Conflict

The escalation of conflict in Yugoslavia and the Federal Republic's subsequent dissolution followed closely upon the disintegration of the Soviet Union. The Russian government was looking for an opportunity to assert a significant role in world affairs and, in many ways, the conflict in the former Yugoslavia provided an excellent issue in which Russian intervention could be effective. The Serbs are Slavs and, historically, the Serbs have been allies of Russia, although the Soviet Union and Yugoslavia had unfriendly relations after the Second World War. Indeed Norman Stone has argued that pan-Slavism is an artificial creation without deep roots (Stone 1994:18).

Russia retains the potential to play a significant role in the conflict through its position as unchallenged inheritor of the Soviet Union's permanent member status of the United Nations Security Council. This gives the Russian government power of veto over all Security Council decisions, and the Serbian government has repeatedly sought Russian support in reducing or delaying United Nations interventions in the crisis.

Since the spread of the conflict to Bosnia in 1992 there has been increased Russian involvement. Efforts by the West to get tougher United Nations sanctions imposed on Bosnian Serbs were delayed by Russian opposition, faced as they were by traditional ties with the Serbs and vociferous right-wing support for them. On the other hand, Yeltsin's special envoy, Vitalii Churkin, worked hard to keep dialogue going with the Serbs. He made it clear to them that Russia would continue to support the international community's position over Bosnia. But he also reiterated Russia's opposition to the use of military action against the Serbs. The position of the Russian government has been that all parties to the conflict have committed atrocities and it would be wrong to single out one of them.

In January 1994 members of the North Atlantic Treaty Organization (NATO) took the decision, under United Nations resolutions, to use air strikes against the Bosnian Serbs if they continued to beseige Sarajevo, the Bosnian capital. All Russian factions were united in opposing the decision and nationalists tried to portray Russia and Serbia as Slavic allies against the western world. Consequently, President Yeltsin badly needed foreign policy success in the Balkans and, indeed, the situation changed dramatically when he intervened directly in February 1994. He pledged to provide peacekeeping forces for

Sarajevo and persuaded the Bosnian Serbs to withdraw their heavy weapons. The Russians regarded this as a diplomatic triumph.

Throughout the years of conflict in the former Yugoslavia there has been continued, albeit uneasy, cooperation between the Russian government and European Union and NATO member governments. Nevertheless the notion of a Russian–western strategic partnership is a myth, Eyal has argued, because their interests often do not coincide. In particular, if Russia is to accept NATO intervention in eastern Europe, the West must make concessions to Russia (Eyal 1994:8). In Russia NATO intervention is interpreted as expansionism and a desire to appease the Moslem world. European security should be based, it is argued, not on the Cold War system of blocs but on an overall arrangement centred on the OSCE.

## The European Security Architecture

The collapse of the Warsaw Pact and the subsequent disintegration of the Soviet Union left European security in disarray. NATO had lost its principal *raison d'être*. At the same time many former communist countries or newly formed states found that they were without effective security arrangements. For the governments of the CEE countries, in particular, Russia was perceived as the principal security threat, and it was from the western Alliance that these governments sought security guarantees. Thus the problem for western governments has been, and remains, the need to set up a European security system which would reassure the successor states and the CEE countries without generating fears among Russian political and military leaders that Russia will be isolated or marginalized.

In an early attempt to address these problems, NATO established a new consultative organization, the North Atlantic Cooperation Council (NACC). The Council, set up on 20 December 1991, is a political forum which originally consisted of representatives from the sixteen NATO states, nine CEE states and the three Baltic republics, but soon came to embrace other Caucasus and Central Asian republics. Its main purpose is to provide a forum for discussion of security issues and to help CEE countries and the former Soviet republics with the restructuring of their defence industries. Subsequently, in early 1994, the Partnership for Peace scheme was devised with the purpose of giving eastern countries (including Russia) some form of association with NATO military structures which falls short of full membership. Apart from the considerable political difficulties, it was clear that some eastern countries did not yet have a military sufficiently trained and experienced fully to participate in NATO. The success of this scheme has been somewhat mixed, in that it has failed to provide the full security guarantees desired, particularly by CEE governments, while at the same time contributing to feelings, increasingly evident across the political spectrum in Moscow, that Russian interests are being marginalized.

For some years the CSCE has been seen by the Russian government as the most appropriate forum for discussion of European security issues, with the potential to play a significant role. The successor republics were able to join the CSCE, and in June 1991 its role was enhanced when it was agreed that it could meet at short notice, at the request of twelve of its members, in response to emergencies defined as major human rights violations or 'major disruptions endangering peace, security or stability'. A speech by James Baker, United States Secretary of State at this time, apparently envisaged the CSCE as a major institution in a future 'Euro-Atlantic community' which would embrace the former Soviet republics and eastern and western Europe, as well as the United States and Canada. But this idea did not evoke a positive response in the West and was not followed through. Only Russia continued to press for a central security role for the CSCE.

Speaking in Warsaw at a Polish–Russian conference 'Towards a New Europe' early in 1994, Kozyrev, the Russian foreign minister, argued that the future security of the region should be guaranteed both by Russia and the West. He called for a pan-European partnership in which Russia would be fully included and the establishment of a security system in which 'there cannot be a division into countries which are threatened and those which are not'. He reiterated Russia's strong objections to CEE countries joining NATO. While not ruling out the possibility, he said that such an act would create new political barriers and could provoke counter-measures. He developed the Russian view that pan-European relations should develop within the framework of the CSCE and, in the political/military sphere, within the North Atlantic Cooperation Council. All this did not change the view of CEE country representatives that Russia does not yet see them as truly independent. They reiterated the opinion that they would only feel safe by joining NATO (Bridge 1994:11).

Subsequently, at the CSCE summit in December 1994, these divisions became increasingly evident. Thus NATO representatives expressed clearer commitment than hitherto to extension of full membership to CEE countries, whereas the Russian delegation found itself increasingly isolated in urging a central role for the CSCE, now renamed the Organization for Security and Cooperation in Europe (OSCE). The hardening of attitudes evident at the summit led President Yeltsin to accuse western governments of creating a climate of 'cold peace' involving the creation of new lines of division across Europe. This raises the possibility that Russia's largely pro-western foreign policy might be abandoned, and that policy-makers may seek, through tighter control of the CIS, to strengthen Russia's position as a Eurasian power.

## Conclusion

There are two main interpretations of the significance of the collapse of communism. One is that the post-Second World War Yalta settlement, guaranteed and stabilized by the two great powers within the parameters of the Cold War, had disintegrated, leaving only disorder, uncontrolled nationalism leading to the fragmentation of large states into smaller entities, ethnic conflicts, the breaking of treaties and the revival of fascism and racism, together with various forms of religious and political fundamentalism (Ascherson 1994b:20). An alternative and more positive analysis emphasizes, not chaos and disintegration, but the inevitable confusion in a period of change. As time passes order returns, political systems settle down to more or less working order and economies begin to show signs of stability and then growth. Positive change is seen as requiring time and inevitably creating some confusion and failure. But essentially movement is in a constructive direction.

In relation to the domestic political systems of the successor states and the CEE countries, the paradox of the contemporary situation is perhaps illustrated most dramatically by the return of communists into positions of political and economic authority. The names of the former communist parties may have changed into social democrats or something similar, but essentially these parties are comprised of 'reformed' communists, and they have acquired significant roles in Hungary, Poland, Romania, Lithuania, Belarus and Ukraine, while they are also strong in Slovakia, Bulgaria and Germany (in the form of the SPD) as well as in Azerbaijan and the Central Asian republics.

Among explanations for the return of the communists is that it reflects a reaction against the free market, following inevitable economic and social disruption. The ex-communists are seen as protectors and defenders of order. But against this it is argued by Schopflin (1993:16–34) and others that those who have suffered most severely from the changes have turned, not to the former communists, but to populists and nationalists of the extreme right who offer either instant solutions or blame all the troubles on some identifiable group, typically an ethnic minority. The supporters of former communists are those still in work at medium and junior levels who want reform but at a cautious and manageable pace. Thus they exist not just in countries where reform has been too hectic but also in those like Ukraine where it has been too slow. This also explains the development of the Czech republic where governmental reforms, although drastic, have been undertaken without alienating the working public, hence lessening the tendency to turn to former communists. Thus the success of these former communists reflects the fact that communism was never so monolithic as some in the West assumed. Since the 1960s there had been reformers within the communist parties, working cautiously at first, but with increasing confidence throughout the 1970s and with a growing volume of hard evidence to support their case.

The prognosis for the future of the former communist states is variable. The major republics like Russia and Ukraine have the greatest problems because they have to face the bulk of political and economic restructuring. The less developed states may be able to improve their situation by means of foreign aid and links with neighbouring states, but they also face the danger of political confusion and economic collapse which could relegate them to a position among the world's poorest states.

In terms of the broader issues of global politics, the end of the Soviet era has considerable implications. Central, here, is the future role of Russia in the global political system. Despite the difficulties experienced in economic and political restructuring, Russia remains a significant power militarily and the foreign and security policies of the Russian government are of great importance. The pro-western policies which have largely been followed since Russian independence in 1991 have increasingly been challenged – primarily but by no means exclusively by Russian nationalists – and there is some evidence to suggest that Russian policy is increasingly oriented towards strengthening ties with other successor states with the intention of emphasizing Russia's position as a Eurasian power. Certainly the considerable potential for conflict and instability in the region suggests, at minimum, a role for Russia as regional mediator or peacekeeper.

## Notes

1  Comecon – the Council for Mutual Economic Assistance (CEMA) was the communist economic development organization. The Warsaw Pact refers to the unified military command of the European communist states, dominated by the Soviet Union.

2  The Conference on Security and Cooperation in Europe (CSCE) was formed in 1975 during the Cold War period. It was renamed the Organization for Security and Cooperation in Europe (OSCE) in December 1994. The CSCE produced the Helsinki Accords which the Soviet Union hoped would reinforce the security status quo and the West attempted to use to draw the Warsaw Pact countries into a reform process. Now that the Cold War is over, the future role of the OSCE is the subject of much debate, but it does provide a forum for discussing problems and carries out monitoring functions.

# 5

# Contemporary Sources of Armed Conflict

## Charlotte Bretherton

The ending of the Cold War did not bring peace; the period since 1989 has witnessed a major interstate war in the Gulf and a number of bitter, lengthy – and seemingly intractable – conflicts elsewhere. Of particular significance has been the emergence or escalation of intercommunal tensions which have generated pressures for, or processes of, disintegration of existing states. In consequence United Nations Secretary-General, Boutros-Ghali, has raised the spectre of a fragmented and unmanageable international system comprising 400 states by the end of the century – thus suggesting that conflict and fragmentation rather than globalization might be the dominant characteristics of global politics in the 1990s.

This chapter examines the sources of and potential for armed conflict in the contemporary world, and attempts to relate these issues to the principal themes of the book – the impacts of globalization and of the end of the Cold War. The issues of avoidance and management of conflict are addressed in chapter six.

A diminution in the incidence of armed conflict in general, and of war between states in particular, might be suggested by the globalization thesis. The intensification of global connectedness associated with economic globalization and ecological interdependence, for example, would indicate that cooperation between states is more than ever necessary. Moreover the end of the Cold War, in ending the ideological conflict between capitalism and communism, has raised the possibility of the globalization of liberal democracy – a phenomenon traditionally associated with peaceful interstate relations.[1]

Conversely, however, the end of the Cold War and the dissolution of the Soviet empire have generated considerable uncertainty and instability, which may be temporary, or may presage an increase in armed conflict. Aspects of the globalization thesis, too, might suggest similar conclusions. Thus economic globalization may be associated with rapid social change and increased economic inequality, while the globalization of ideas presents significant challenges to cultural identity. Both have the potential to generate or exacerbate social instability and, ultimately, armed conflict.

These prognoses are apparently incompatible. Closer examination, however, suggests parallel tendencies – a diminution in war between states and an increase in intrastate or transboundary communally based conflicts. Clearly this hypothesis raises important issues for understanding and analysis of the sources of armed conflict and, in particular, challenges the realist focus upon interstate relations. Consequently, in examining potential sources of armed conflict, we have attempted to distinguish between interstate and intercommunal conflict. In each of these two broad categories a range of issues is examined, with particular emphasis upon resource conflicts between states and conflicts associated with aspects of cultural identity which are intrastate or transboundary in nature.

Two important problems arise from the approach adopted. First, armed conflicts are, in practice, highly complex phenomena which arise from a number of interrelated sources. Thus interstate conflicts are likely to be associated with issues of cultural identity as well as disputed borders and access to resources, as in the case of the 1979–88 Iran–Iraq war for example. They are frequently, also, characterized by both interstate and intercommunal elements, as has been the case in the conflict in Bosnia–Herzogovina from 1992. Nevertheless the distinction between interstate and intercommunal conflicts is useful in examining changing patterns of conflict in the contemporary period. Second, concentration on overt conflict inevitably neglects and obscures the fundamental conflicts of interest associated with structural inequalities, which may be deep underlying sources of armed conflict. Alternatively structural conflict – in particular between North and South – may cause death through starvation or disease rather than war. Nevertheless, while structural and overt conflict are frequently interlinked, and both must be addressed in the interest of a just and peaceful global order, it is the immediacy of overt, armed conflict which concerns us here.

According to a recent study, 'Armed conflicts are contested incompatibilities . . . where the use of armed force by two parties, of which at least one is the government of a state, results in at least 25 battle related deaths in a single year' (Wallensteen and Axell 1993:332). This definition suits our purpose, in that it encompasses conflict both within and between states. Nevertheless the criterion that one of the parties should be the government of a state requires some relaxation in circumstances such as occurred in Somalia in 1992–3, and Rwanda in 1994, where authority had deteriorated to the extent that no formal government existed. The inclusion of a stated number of battle related deaths is a traditional, if distasteful, method of differentiating between conflicts according to their severity. Setting the number of fatalities at 25 denotes an inclusive approach, which allows us to consider relatively minor incidences of armed conflict.

Wallensteen and Axell's study explicitly tests competing hypotheses concerning the implications of the end of the Cold War for the incidence of interstate conflict – that is the realist proposition that interstate armed conflict would increase following the end of bipolarity's stabilizing influence; and the liberal internationalist view that the emergence of a more cooperative world order would enable conflict to be better managed in the future. This latter view echoes the assumption implicit in theses about globalization, that interstate conflict is increasingly obsolete.

A number of Wallensteen and Axell's conclusions are of interest. During the period studied (1989–92) 82 armed conflicts were recorded, of which only four could be described as interstate – that is the 1991 Gulf War, which was a major conflict, and the relatively minor conflicts between Mauritania–Senegal in 1989–90 and the USA–Panama in 1989, together with intermittent conflict between India and Pakistan throughout much of the period. Effectively the study reveals a continuation of the Cold War pattern; in that armed conflict has remained overwhelmingly intrastate rather than interstate. Nevertheless there have been changes to the pattern of conflict since the end of the Cold War. Overall there was an increased incidence of armed conflict (from 46 in 1989 to 54 in 1992) with a marked decline in Latin America being more than compensated by a marked increase in Europe (see figure 5.1). It is undoubtedly the return of armed conflict to Europe that has generated the impression of an upsurge in conflict since the end of the Cold War; as Colin Parkins argues in chapter three, the end of the Cold War has had rather less impact in the South.

The evidence cited above can be interpreted in a variety of ways. The period studied may follow too closely after the end of the Cold War to reflect the consequences of the end of bipolarity. Moreover the increase in intrastate/intercommunal conflict may be a short-term consequence of the ending of the Cold War rather than necessarily invalidating liberal internationalist predictions of a more peaceful world order.

Further examination of the sources of contemporary armed conflict may help us to address these questions. As indicated, discussion centres upon two broad areas – interstate conflict and intercommunal

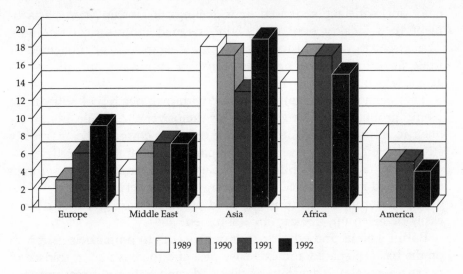

**Figure 5.1** Incidences of interstate and intrastate armed conflict 1989–1992
Adapted from Wallensteen and Axell (1993)

conflict. It is the latter, apparently growing phenomenon, with which we begin.

## Intercommunal Conflict and the Politics of Identity

Issues of identity will inevitably impinge upon the incidence of armed conflict, whether this is between or within states. Thus national identity, ethnicity or religious affiliation is likely to contribute to the outbreak of conflict or to be used as a source of legitimation for recourse to arms. Our present concern, however, is with the relationship between identity politics and the apparent increase, in recent years, of intercommunal conflict. Hence we discuss two forms of conflict, or potential conflict, associated with identity – civilizational conflict, which would transcend state boundaries; and conflicts arising from demands for ethnic–national self-determination, which would involve the creation of new states. Initially, however, let us consider the meaning of identity politics and the reasons for its contemporary upsurge.

Identity politics refers, here, to the growth of movements organized around aspects of cultural identity and seeking to assert this identity through a reordering of existing political arrangements in accordance with the proclaimed preferences of the cultural community.[2] This involves the establishment of group membership, delineated in terms of cultural criteria such as religious affiliation or ethnicity. Movements founded upon these criteria provide for their followers powerful

emotional satisfactions based upon feelings of kinship and/or attachment to a locality or a way of life steeped in historical tradition.
The extent to which histories and traditions are real or 'imagined' is
irrelevant provided the necessary sense of continuity and security is
generated (B. Anderson 1991).[3]

The feeling of belonging associated with membership of religious or
ethnic groups is reinforced by their exclusiveness. While nominally
open to all, the self-identification of religious communities is greatly
strengthened by the presence of the unconverted and the irreligious –
the 'infidel' at the gate. Similarly, exclusiveness is important to ethnic-
ally defined groups; indeed it is central to their very existence. Whatever its criteria, ethnicity is regarded as natural, or given. It cannot
easily be given up, nor can it be assumed.

Both religious and ethnic communities seek to unite their members
on the basis of shared and exclusive ties, and to subsume or transcend
the socio-economic divisions of class and gender. For this reason social
scientists have regarded as modernizing, or progressive, the processes
of *state* building (often referred to, erroneously but tellingly, as *nation*
building) but have tended to regard movements which seek to assert
cultural identity as regressive; as more appropriate to traditional, pre-
modern societies. Consequently such movements have, until recently,
been treated as an anachronism; they have rarely been analysed in
terms of their capacity to promote change, nor have they been widely
discussed in the international relations literature. However the increasing significance, globally, of identity politics demands that we seek
explanations for this upsurge at this time. This we attempt through
application of our central themes – the impacts of the end of the Cold
War and the process of globalization.

## The impact of globalization

Globalization, we have argued, involves (among other things) the thesis
that technological innovation, particularly in the field of communications, has enabled a range of ideas, issues and processes to become
increasingly global in scope; and that, as a consequence, the capacity of
states to meet the needs of their citizens is diminishing.

These two aspects of globalization are complementary in effect.
Governments are perceived to be ineffective in managing the impacts
of increasing economic and financial globalization or in dealing with
environmental issues. In the 1990s lack of confidence in government is
by no means confined to those parts of the developing world or the
former Soviet bloc where change has been particularly destabilizing
and governments are poorly legitimated; it is increasingly a global
phenomenon, as we shall see from discussion of the problems of
democracy in chapter nine.

This aspect of globalization, while socially disruptive and potentially threatening to existing political arrangements, can provide both stimulus and opportunity to movements seeking to assert cultural identity. Firstly, it can be argued, the existing, failed order must be replaced by a new order which expresses more clearly the identity needs of the cultural group. Secondly, in a situation of economic globalization characterized by relatively flexible production processes, the size of political units has become less relevant. The economic success of small states such as Singapore and Taiwan appears to provide evidence for this, and in Europe such arguments have been strongly put by academic economists as well as nationalist leaders from Slovenia to Scotland.[4]

While political fragmentation may not be inconsistent with economic globalization, the rise of cultural particularism clearly sits ill with the broader globalization thesis, which includes the contention that a range of ideas is becoming increasingly universal. Here the upsurge of identity politics can be seen as a reaction against modern ideas and values and against cultural globalism, which directly challenges cultural identity.

Modern thought involves the dualistic separation of the human from the natural world; belief in progress through the application of human knowledge; individualism; secularism. While it is not contended that these ideas are universally accepted, nor that their impacts are necessarily homogenizing in effect, we would agree that 'modern environments and experiences cut across all boundaries of geography and ethnicity, of class and nationality, of religion and ideology . . . weakening and subverting them, eroding the lines of continuity which hitherto stabilised our cultural identities' (Hall 1989, citing Berman:119).

Modern values, then, undermine cultural identities. In time, the notion of cultural globalization implies, particularistic cultural values will be replaced by a universal, media-led cultural globalism which juxtaposes the values and commodities of mass consumerism with an eclectic mixture of ethnic and folk themes and electronic music. Evidence of the challenge deemed to be associated with this 'cosmopolitan culture' is provided by the (largely unavailing) efforts of governments from Tehran to Beijing to suppress these images.

Despite the evident appeal of this media-produced cultural globalism, it is, as Anthony Smith has argued, essentially synthetic and devoid of the very characteristics which are fundamental to cultural identity. Thus:

Cultures are not patchwork parodies of selected motifs . . . thrown together for some visual effect. Cultures are expressive wholes, spatially particularised and historically embedded. The images that have greatest impact . . . are just those which have this expressive, particular and historical character – the ceremonies, the monuments and works of art that bear witness to an heroic and emotion-laden collective past (Smith 1992:12).

Ultimately, of course, both cosmopolitan and particularistic values have appeal, albeit to different constituencies at different times. Both, too, can be linked – as product or reaction – to the processes of globalization. Nevertheless, in situations of change, instability and social dislocation individuals need, more than ever, the reassurance provided by membership of a defined group and the security of its myths of historical continuity. Globalization may well generate change and contribute to social destabilization; it is, however, essentially a process involving an extended time scale. Consequently, it is in the impact of the end of the Cold War that we may locate more immediate reasons for the resurgence of identity politics.

## The impact of the end of the Cold War

It is evident that the events and processes associated with the end of the Cold War have contributed both directly and indirectly to new expressions of identity politics. The most obvious direct impact relates to the decline in Soviet power over the past decade, the collapse of Soviet authority in Central and Eastern Europe and the subsequent disintegration of the Soviet Union itself. Two effects of these changes are of particular significance – the social dislocation associated with rapid, and extensive, change; and the power vacuum left by the ending of Soviet domination. This latter has essentially involved a decolonization process during which previously subject peoples have been able to rediscover their cultural heritages and identities; a process which, as the previous chapter has demonstrated, is far from complete.

A further, direct impact of the ending of the Cold War relates to the global reach of the superpowers during this period. As an aspect of Cold War competition, both the United States and the Soviet Union actively sought to extend their influence through attempts to guide the policies of newly independent states. The support extended by the superpowers ensured the persistence of client regimes even in situations where their domestic legitimacy was dubious. The ending of the Cold War ended Soviet support for such regimes, while the willingness of the United States to intervene has also eroded. The impacts of this withdrawal of support can be seen, for example, in the separation of Eritrea from Ethiopia and the armed conflicts in the Horn of Africa, Liberia and Angola.

The indirect impacts of the ending of the Cold War are also far reaching and concern, once again, the issue of political legitimacy. Firstly, the apparent supremacy of liberal ideologies has considerably reduced the relevance of socialist ideology as a mobilizing or legitimating formula. The implications of this are evident as regimes throughout the erstwhile socialist world adjust to the apparent inevitability of marketization. They nevertheless reverberate more widely: the ideological vacuum left by the devaluation of socialism appears likely to be filled by some form of identity politics. In relation to Africa, Julius Ihonvbere provides a chilling scenario. While previously it was thought that, 'in the context of the deepening crisis in Africa, the choice is not between capitalism and socialism but between socialism and barbarism, it would seem that the situation has so deteriorated since 1978 that the choice today is either a radical and popular restructuring in favour of the majority or extinction' (Ihonvbere 1994:57). The logic of Ihonvbere's statement has already been witnessed in Rwanda.

A further aspect of delegitimation associated with the ending of the Cold War involves the sudden loss of a powerful external enemy. Some commentators have emphasized the difficulties this poses for western governments, which can anticipate divisive struggles over basic principles rather than 'a return to some mythical halcyon normalcy' (Deudney and Ikenberry 1994:23). A common reaction, among international relations scholars and western politicians alike, has been the attempt to find a replacement for the old enemy, or at least to identify new risks to western security. Prominent among such risks has been the challenge deemed to arise from movements associated with identity politics, whether these are based upon religious or ethnic criteria.[5] The evident dangers, here, of self-fulfilling prophecy are associated in particular with the notion of civilizational conflict.

## Civilizational conflict

Conflict between civilizations, it has been argued, will follow the conflicts between nations of the nineteenth Century and between ideologies of the twentieth to become 'the latest phase in the evolution of conflict in the modern world' (Huntington 1993:22). According to Huntington, a civilization is 'the highest cultural grouping and the broadest level of cultural identity people have short of that which distinguishes humans from other species. It is defined by common objective elements, such as language, history, religion, customs, institutions, and by the subjective self-identification of people' (Huntington 1993:24). Huntington identifies seven, or possibly eight, major civilizations in the contemporary world – Western, Confucian, Japanese, Islamic, Hindu, Slavic-Orthodox, Latin-American and 'possibly' African (ibid.:25).

A number of arguments is advanced to support Huntington's thesis, several of which are associated with notions of globalization. Thus processes of modernization and the communications revolution, involving – for Huntington – dissemination of predominantly western cultural values, are seen as factors which have generated strong rejectionist responses, articulated through an assertion of non-western cultural values. Of particular significance for Huntington is the timing of this resurgence of non-western civilizations: that is when, following 'victory' in the Cold War, western power has reached its apogee and Western civilization can only decline, as other civilizations before it.

Economic globalization is also considered to be of significance, particularly through the promotion of defensive regional responses which, as in the case of the European Union, tend to be *within* civilizations. Thus problems experienced in creating the North American Free Trade Area, and in particular the strong reaction by Mexico's indigenous peoples, demonstrate the difficulties of cooperation between Latin American and western civilizations, providing an example of a 'civilizational fault-line'.

While a 'West versus the rest' scenario is implicit in Huntington's arguments, the potential for armed conflict arising along civilizational fault-lines varies considerably. Thus, while the fault-line between western and Slavic-Orthodox cultures in Europe is fraught with danger, it is that between western and Islamic civilizations which is considered most problematic. Here the West, in its relations with the Islamic world is:

> facing a mood and a movement far transcending the level of issues and policies and the governments that pursue them. This is no less than a clash of civilizations – the perhaps irrational but surely historic reaction of an ancient rival against our Judeo-Christian heritage, our secular present, and the worldwide expansion of both. (Bernard Lewis in Huntington ibid.:32)

A number of criticisms of Huntington's arguments can be advanced. The most fundamental of these relates to his contention that the broad cultural groupings he refers to as civilizations will to some extent replace states or nations as significant, coherent actors in global politics. The extent to which it is meaningful to speak in this way of western civilization is an interesting question which Huntington leaves unaddressed. Indeed the assumption that the West has common interests which it will unite to defend is poorly supported by evidence: the Vatican has made common cause with the Iranian Islamic regime on the subject of population control; the twelve member states of the European Union followed twelve distinct policies during the Gulf War and have shown similar disunity in relation to the conflict in the former Yugoslavia.

The conflict in Bosnia–Herzogovina is of particular relevance, in that it suggests to Huntington evidence of civilizational conflict. This is based on the support provided to the Bosnian Muslims by fighters from 'over two dozen Islamic countries', together with indications of substantial funding from Saudi Arabia (Huntington 1993:36–7). However the confused and disunited response of the West tells us more about the ability of western civilization to respond to challenges than the potential of Islamic civilization to mount them – a point which is central to Huntington's warning to western policy makers.

The rise of Islamism has, of course, been identified by commentators other than Huntington as a significant risk to western security, and Islamists themselves proclaim commitment to the establishment of the Khalafah, a global Islamic state. Consequently we need to consider whether Islamism can be considered a coherent, transnational movement with potential to challenge civilizations having conflicting values, whether these be western, Slavic-Orthodox or Hindu.

Islamic revivalism, encouraged by the 1979 Iranian revolution, was greatly strengthened by success in driving the Soviet Union from Afghanistan. According to Ghassan Salame, 'Afghanistan is viewed as a spectacular example of Islamists' ability to win a war against an alien expansionist power. Many returnees from the Afghan war play leading roles in the most extremist groups in Algeria, Egypt, Tunisia and the Gulf countries' (Salame 1993:27). Nevertheless the subsequent bitter power struggles between rival Islamist groups in Afghanistan and elsewhere, the sectarian nature of Islam itself and the historic enmity between Arabs and Persians all suggest that doctrinal and ethnic differences may be difficult to overcome, and that Islamic civilization is no less disunited than western civilization.

Despite this evidence of disunity, it is possible to identify significant common elements of an Islamist programme, of which a central theme is rejection of western values and influence, coupled with the desire to restore the former prestige of the Muslim world. However, while the seeds of civilizational conflict may be found here, for the moment the principal targets of Islamist action are the existing governments of Muslim countries, which have failed to honour their early, anti-imperialist commitment to eradicate western influence. They have failed, also, to fulfil promises of improved material well-being for the masses, and of democratization. Thus Islamists are able to claim inheritance of the anti-imperialist mantle while, in the absence of alternative opposition movements in countries where opposition has been much discouraged, they are also well placed to benefit from any belated democratization.

The Islamists' success in the 1992 Algerian elections, and the subsequent military overthrow of the democratically elected Islamist government, provided a salutary lesson for governments of other Muslim countries. For the most part they have preferred to make concessions to Islamist demands rather than risk competing with Islamic movements in election processes (ibid.:26).

Salame's conclusion concerning the potential of Islamist movements reflects, to some extent, Huntington's concerns about civilizational conflict. However Salame's assessment is itself contested. Thus Fouad Ajami maintains that such arguments greatly underestimate commitment in the Muslim world to modernity and secularism, particularly among the middle classes, who would choose to 'scramble for their market shares, learn how to compete in a merciless world economy, provide jobs, move out of poverty . . . tell us men want Sony, not soil' (Ajami 1993:5).

Ajami's words may well highlight the principal impediment to the long-term success of Islamism as a formula for mobilization and hence a source of conflict. In advocating rejection of modernity, and the secular, individualistic values which have underlain the modernization process, Islamists have provided an important focus for marginalized or excluded social groups. While appealing directly to the masses, however, Islamist leaders have excoriated the degeneracy of the group most closely associated with modernity, that is the urban middle class. Hence, for example, 'bourgeois dolls' (westernized, middle-class women) have been a particular target, and the imposition of the Islamic dress code and of Shari'a family law has been deeply resented by such women (Moghadam 1993:89). This suggests that Islamist movements, unlike nationalist movements, will fail to unite communities across the social divisions of class and gender.

Clearly the appeal, and potential, of Islamism cannot be dismissed. It provides a focus for popular identification and a highly developed moral and social code, legitimated by divine authority, which explicitly rejects western cultural and ideological domination. However, while Islamism provides a substantial and immediate threat to governments in the Maghreb, and to a lesser extent elsewhere, its potential to develop as a broad-based transnational movement is less evident. The apparent strengths of Islamism conceal a weakness common to fundamentalist movements: the level of commitment and self-sacrifice required by the faithful, not merely in times of crisis but in their daily lives, proves difficult to sustain. Ultimately the fundamentalist message may be less effective in mobilizing and sustaining support than appeals based upon ethnic or national identity. It is to these categories that we now turn.

## Nationalism and ethnic conflict

Kamal Shehadi has argued that: 'The drive towards ethnic-national self-determination is one of the greatest challenges facing the international community in the 1990s. From the Balkans to Burma, from the Caucasus to the Horn of Africa, communal groups are asserting claims to self-determination by force' (Shehadi 1993:3). These words echo the concern, expressed at the beginning of this chapter, that fragmentation rather than globalization, particularism rather than universalism, will be the defining characteristics of the post-Cold War period.

Factors contributing generally to the revival of identity politics have already been discussed. We now examine the meaning and implications of ethnicity as a source of identity and investigate the mechanisms through which ethnicity becomes politicized, or associated with a programme for action. Hence our central concern is with the links between ethnicity, nationalism and demands for self-determination.

Ethnicity is a cultural rather than a political concept. It refers to the diverse characteristics which make up cultural identity – origins, physical appearance, language, customs and beliefs – and which are recognized as the basis of differentiation between peoples. It is both more, and less, than a checklist of criteria; indeed the characteristics suggested above are common but by no means necessary aspects of ethnicity. For example, the experience of mountain dwelling has been a particularly salient aspect of Kurdish identity (Entessar 1989:87). Moreover, despite the significance frequently attributed to language, ethnic groups may share a common language as is the case with the Hutu and Tutsi peoples. Ethnicity, then, is a highly fluid concept associated with a range of objective and subjective criteria and, in the present context, it is the latter which are of particular significance. Clearly the intensity of emotional attachment involved in ethnic identification largely determines the extent to which group membership inspires loyalty and, ultimately, action in defence of group interests.

The sources of attachment to ethnic identity are disputed. For some commentators the ties of ethnicity are aspects of a fundamental human need to belong and are, therefore, among 'the persistent primordial attachments of kinship, the ties to one's own: one's own children, one's own "people", and one's own land' (Grosby 1994:166). This view, which regards emotional attachment to the ethnic group as essentially an extension of family feeling, is reflected in the abundance of allusions to be found, in the rhetoric of ethno-nationalist politics, to ties of blood, to ancestry, to mother tongue and fatherland (Connor 1993).

The dominant view among academic commentators, however, has been that ethnicity, in common with other aspects of identity such as gender, is socially constructed; so that the values and beliefs constitutive of a culture reflect historically specific socio-economic and political determinants (Gellner 1983; Hobsbawm 1990). Subsequently, however, these commentators have expressed concern at the renewed vibrancy of ethnic politics, albeit continuing strongly to reject the 'primordialist' approach (Gellner 1991; Hobsbawm 1992).

Debate concerning the relative significance of psychological and sociological determinants of ethnic attachment will doubtless continue; indeed it is essential that our understanding of ethnic identification be enhanced. The willingness of large numbers of people to die, and to kill, on behalf of their ethnic group has contributed significantly to the incidence of armed conflict in the world and has led to the coining, initially in the context of the conflicts in the former Yugoslavia, of an ugly new concept – ethnic cleansing. Such phenomena suggest that greater attention than hitherto must be given to the psychological determinants of ethnic identification if we are to understand how ethnicity is politicized, for, 'In sharpest contrast with most academic analysts . . . those who have successfully mobilized nations have understood that at the core of ethnopsychology is the sense of shared blood, and they have not hesitated to appeal to it' (Connor 1993:377).

Ethnicity, then, is associated with sentiments of kinship and loyalty which can be appealed to for purposes of political mobilization; hence it is significant not so much for what it is, but for what can be achieved in its name.

Ethnicity attains political significance, and is linked to action, by nationalism: that is, in Gellner's succinct formulation, 'the principle which holds that the political and national unit should be congruent' (Gellner 1983:1). As is well known, however, the correspondence between states – legally defined territorial units – and ethnic groups is poor. No more than fifteen states can accurately be referred to as nation-states, while 40 per cent of all states contain five or more politically or statistically significant ethnic groups and some, such as Nigeria, contain more than a hundred ethnic groups. Interestingly, in almost a third of states (31 per cent), the largest ethnic group does not even constitute a majority (Connor 1993:374–5).

In very many cases, of course, ethnic groups are simply culturally distinct groups within a state. Such groups, while retaining their cultural identity, largely accept the existing legal and political framework of the state and do not seek self-determination. In these circumstances a distinction can be made between nations and ethnic groups by reference to the political aspirations expressed on their behalf, thus: 'A nation is a group of people with a strong cultural and political identity that is both self-defined and acknowledged by others. Nations are defined as those groups who have exercised political control over their destinies at some point in the past and still see such control as a possible future strategy' (Clay 1989:225).

According to this formulation ethnic groups *become* nations through a process of increasing self-awareness leading to demands for greater independence or for self-determination. Such demands – which may involve secession, as in the case of Slovenia, or may seek to unite a people across state boundaries as envisaged by the notion of Greater Serbia – have increased both in intensity and in number since the end of the Cold War. Self-determination is a principle having internal and external implications, in that it refers both to internal self-government and to freedom from external domination. Consequently the reasons for this increase must be sought in the domestic situation in which ethnic groups are situated as well as in the changing international environment.

The domestic sources of self-determination claims lie in the relationship between the ethnic group and the regime. In circumstances where there is successful accommodation, self-determination is not an issue. In a number of cases, however, such accommodation has been limited or, indeed, non-existent, and self-determination has been a long-term demand – examples here include the Timorese, the Kurds and the Palestinians. In other cases demands for self-determination arise only when the benefits of accommodation are perceived as diminishing. Thus the destabilizing effects of rapid social and economic change may disproportionately threaten the well-being of particular ethnic groups, while the delegitimation of political authority may, at the same time, provide the opportunity to challenge the existing political order. As we have observed, both the globalization process and the ending of the Cold War have generated considerable change and instability; both have contributed, also, to the widespread delegitimation of authority.

While a range of internal factors, from human rights abuses to economic exploitation, may be associated with self-determination claims, until recently their success has related almost exclusively to the external aspect of self-determination. Thus, given the legal convention of state sovereignty, demands for self-determination have tended to succeed only where there has been external domination as a result of colonization or conquest. When ethnic groups have sought to secede, even if there has been a strong case for self-determination coupled with evidence of severe repression, as in the case of the Tibetans and the Timorese, the principle of sovereignty has taken precedence over that of self-determination. Former United Nations Secretary-General U Thant stated this very clearly in 1970:

> You will recall that the United Nations spent over $500 million in the Congo primarily to prevent the secession of Katanga from the Congo. As an international organization, the United Nations has never accepted and does not accept and I do not believe will ever accept the principle of secession of a part of its Member state. (Quoted in Shehadi 1993:19)

Throughout the Cold War, with the single exception of the secession of Bangladesh from Pakistan in 1971, which was achieved following substantial intervention by India, U Thant's assertion remained valid. In 1991, however, recognition of the Baltic Republics' secession from the Soviet Union was followed by recognition of all the former Soviet Republics and of Slovenia and Croatia. Subsequently the separation of the Czech Republic and Slovakia and the secession of Eritrea from Ethiopia have also been formally recognized by the United Nations. It is hardly surprising that this apparent reversal of the United Nations position on these matters has been a source of encouragement to groups advancing new, or indeed old, claims to self-determination.

In this post-Cold War climate of selective tolerance of secessionist movements, Boutros Boutros-Ghali has set out the issues, if not their solution:

> The United Nations has not closed its door. Yet if every ethnic, religious or linguistic group claimed statehood, there would be no limit to fragmentation, and peace and security and economic well being for all would become ever more difficult to achieve. The sovereignty, territorial integrity and independence of States within the established international system, and the principle of self-determination for peoples, both of great value and importance, must not be permitted to work against each other in the period ahead. (Boutros-Ghali 1992:9–10)

In these circumstances, demands for self-determination are encouraged but no mechanisms exist for arbitration when such demands are resisted. Unless the sources of the current upsurge of ethnic particularism are better understood, and the issues raised by identity politics addressed within existing multi-nation states, resort to armed conflict seems almost inevitable. Its escalation will be encouraged as a consequence of continued failure to resolve the tensions between the principles of state sovereignty and self-determination of peoples – a failure which has implications for interstate as well as intercommunal conflict.

## Interstate Conflict

The incidence of interstate conflict, we have argued, is diminishing and will continue to do so. Nevertheless wars between states will doubtless occur and their potentially lethal nature, given the sophisticated weaponry at the disposal of governments, necessitates consideration of changing patterns of interstate conflict and examination of possible sources of such conflict in the future.

Kalevi Holsti (1991) has studied interstate armed conflict from the formal origin of the system of states in 1648 to the end of the Cold War in 1989. His study reveals two important trends in the period following the Second World War. First, there has been a significant decline in the proportion of armed conflicts primarily concerned with territory; from approximately half of all conflicts before 1945 to little more than a quarter after 1945 (ibid.:308). Two principal reasons are suggested for this – the reduced importance of territory to state power in an increasingly technological age, and the unravelling of the European colonial empires. Thus the 1982 Falklands War was a traditional territorial conflict over one of the untidier remnants of colonialism, although issues of cultural identity and of domestic legitimacy also played a major role. This reduction in territorial disputes in the post-Second World War period was more than compensated by conflicts associated with the creation and consolidation of states. Thus it was the legacy of colonialism rather than colonialism itself which provided the most common immediate source of armed conflict in the period between 1945 and 1989. Such issues continue to have significance, not only in relation to the West European empires, but also the dissolution of the Soviet empire.

The second important trend in the post-1945 period concerns changing attitudes towards the use of war as an instrument of policy. Indeed these changes date back to the period following the First World War, when the creation of the League of Nations initiated a significant departure from traditions of realpolitik or, indeed, of 'just war'. Following the Second World War the United Nations Charter expressly forbade the threat or use of force, reflecting, again, the aspiration to eradicate war between states. Indeed acts of aggression are increasingly regarded as aberrant or irrational, and state policies typically emphasize defence rather than the prosecution of war – exemplified, in the United Kingdom, by replacement of the War Office with the Ministry of Defence after 1945. This reflects a normative change associated not only with the deterrent effect of nuclear and other weapons, but also with changing attitudes towards the value of human life and the glories of war. While Holsti maintains that this is primarily a western perspective (ibid.:303) it is significant that both Argentina's invasion of the Falkland Islands in 1982 and Iraq's invasion of Kuwait in 1990 were strongly condemned by most Third World governments.

These broad trends between 1945 and 1989 suggest that the incidence of interstate war will continue to decline, a contention which is supported by the findings of Wallensteen and Axell for the period 1989 to 1992 (see figure 5.1). Nevertheless armed conflict between states will doubtless occur in circumstances where territorial disputes are exacerbated by other factors such as the presence of valuable resources or an unstable and unpopular regime seeking to unite its people against an external enemy. Moreover, despite its relatively low incidence compared with intrastate conflict, war between states continues to be the principal focus of realist and neo-realist analysis.

Below we examine, in addition to neo-realist arguments concerning the implications of post-Cold War systemic change, three further potential sources of interstate conflict – resource scarcity resulting from over-exploitation or degradation, the externalization of intrastate conflicts, and the impacts of population movements. These latter categories emphasize, once again, the essential interrelationship between intercommunal and interstate conflicts, and the pervasiveness of identity issues.

### Post-Cold War systemic change

According to the realist paradigm, states operate in circumstances of semi-organized anarchy and are 'engaged in a never-ending struggle to improve or preserve their relative power positions' (Gilpin 1975:35). Security, for the realist, is attained through military strength and, in a situation where several competing powers jostle for position, through a balance of power.

As we saw in chapter two, in an attempt to more clearly *explain* the unsociable behaviour of states predicted by their paradigm, neo-realists have introduced two major refinements to traditional realism. First, a structural perspective has been developed which, in common with all structural analyses, attributes to the structure itself the principal determining role. Basing their analysis on the work of the sociologist Emile Durkheim, neo-realists argue that conflict is inherent in a situation where the structure is characterized by anarchy and the actors (states) are functionally undifferentiated, and hence uninvolved in the division of labour which necessitates cooperation in domestic society. Secondly, neo-realists employ models derived from micro-economics to explain actor behaviour; thus states are conceived as behaving in a manner analogous to firms in a highly competitive and poorly regulated market. In this model, conflict is assumed to be an inevitable consequence of the structure of the international system and analysts have concerned themselves not so much with its probability as with its prediction or avoidance.

Since the end of the Cold War debate among neo-realists has been intense. The Cold War itself is considered to have been a period of uncharacteristic peace and stability, at least among the major powers. This stability was founded not so much upon the mutual nuclear deterrence strategies of the superpowers as upon the bipolar nature of the international system. Consequently, since the ending of the Cold War, neo-realists have speculated, with varying amounts of alarm, upon the system which may emerge to replace bipolarity. Their dilemma, which was dealt with more fully by John Vogler in chapter two, centres upon the view that considerable disadvantages attach to all but bipolar systems (Waltz 1993). Tripolar or multipolar systems, which may appear to be emerging in the wake of the Cold War, are considered to be particularly subject to conflict as a consequence of attempts to establish or prevent the attainment of primacy (Gilpin 1981; Mearsheimer 1990).

Neo-realist analysis of post-Cold War structural change can be criti-cized on a number of grounds. Despite its foundation in historical pessimism, it is essentially ahistorical and static, so that structural change is difficult to conceptualize; the implications of such change, in consequence, cannot be specified. More particularly the emphasis on structural determinants of state behaviour prevents consideration of normative changes in interstate relations, while ensuring that neo-realism fails entirely to engage with social and cultural variables, still less with human motivation. These are all factors which must surely be considered salient to the incidence of armed conflict.

Since the end of the Cold War the inadequacy of structural neo-realism as an approach to analysis has been increasingly apparent. Certainly it is not helpful in identifying potential sources of armed conflict and traditional realist approaches may prove more fruitful in this respect. We examine below issues which may be considered as potential sources of interstate conflict.

## Resource conflicts

The 1991 Gulf War provides a recent reminder that access to scarce resources can be a significant factor in the outbreak and escalation of armed conflict between states. In that case the global significance of oil as a strategic resource generated a major response to Iraq's invasion of Kuwait – from the United States, supported by twenty-seven other states, under the umbrella of the United Nations. More recently, in the early months of 1995, there have been incidences of armed conflict between Ecuador and Peru over a disputed stretch of their common border believed to be rich in gold, uranium and oil deposits.

In addition to the potential for conflict over strategic resources of this sort, there are a number of regions, predominantly in the South, where issues associated with depletion or degradation of natural re-sources are or may become sources of interstate conflict. For example, in the Sahel region environmental migration associated with loss of cultivatable land is already causing severe social dislocation.[6] Access to water is a further area where shortage of natural resources could be associated with armed conflict in the future. Indeed the issue of access to water, which is fundamental not only to economic development but to life itself, has already generated armed conflict between states in the basins of the Mekong and Parana rivers (Myers 1989:29–30).

It has been estimated by United States government intelligence services that there are at least ten areas, predominantly in the Middle East but also in North Africa and South Asia, where the diminution of shared water supplies could generate armed conflict. The extent to which attention has focused on water scarcity in the Middle East reflects, in part, the Cold War strategic interests of the United States, and alarmist predictions should, as Natasha Beschorner (1992–3) argues, be viewed with scepticism. Nevertheless, in a region where so many contentious issues remain unresolved, the potential for conflict over shared, diminishing and increasingly contaminated water resources merits consideration.

In 1989, while Foreign Minister of Egypt, Boutros Boutros-Ghali proclaimed the national security of Egypt to be 'a question of water' (cited in Starr 1991:21). This statement reflects concerns throughout the Middle East, where only Turkey and Iran enjoy secure water supplies. The region is predominantly arid or semi-arid and water supplies are both meagre and unreliable. More than two-thirds of all available water is devoted to irrigated agriculture. As a consequence of intensification of agriculture, coupled with growth and increasing concentration of populations in cities, water contamination is common.

Throughout much of the Middle East, concerns over water security are exacerbated in part by poverty but more particularly by dependence upon shared water sources. Thus the river basins of the Nile, Tigris–Euphrates and Jordan are crucial to the needs of riparian states which do not, in many cases, enjoy friendly relations. Here we will briefly examine the highly complex and volatile situations surrounding the Tigris–Euphrates and Jordan river systems.

The rivers of the Tigris–Euphrates basin supply Turkey, Syria, Iraq and Iran. Turkey controls the headwaters of both rivers and the Turkish government has an ambitious programme, begun in 1983, of extensive irrigation and hydro-electric power projects on both rivers (see figure 5.2). Syrian development schemes on the Euphrates are an additional source of concern in Iraq.

These tensions over control of and access to water supplies are a further destabilizing factor in a region where endemic border disputes are exacerbated by identity politics associated with Kurdish nationalism. In these circumstances cooperation in water management has proved elusive, and threats of military force to ensure access to water supplies are common.

It is in the Jordan basin region, however, that water shortages are most acute, and underlying tensions particularly intractable. The region includes Lebanon, Syria, Jordan and Israel, including the occupied territories and the recently liberated areas of Palestine. Lebanese supplies are relatively abundant, if poorly managed, and Syria controls the headwaters of the important Yarmouk tributary, which subsequently supplies the northern area of Jordan (see figure 5.3). Over the past twenty years Syrian water consumption has increased considerably while a number of additional irrigation projects are planned by the Syrian government. These plans have generated intense anxiety in

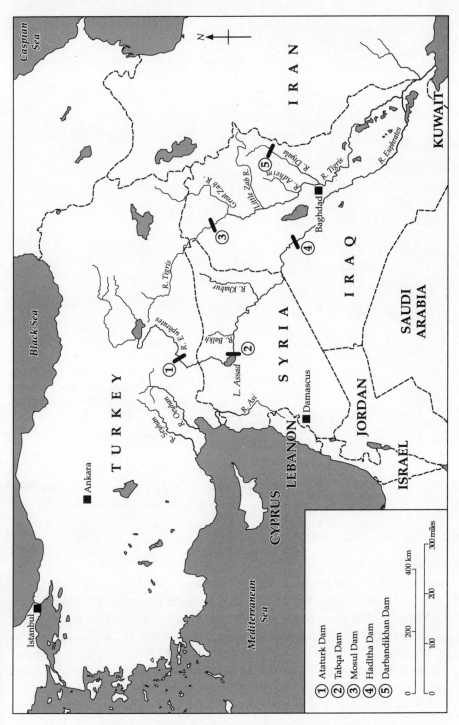

**Figure 5.2** The Tigris and Euphrates river systems
(Liverpool John Moores University, Cartographic Unit, 1995)

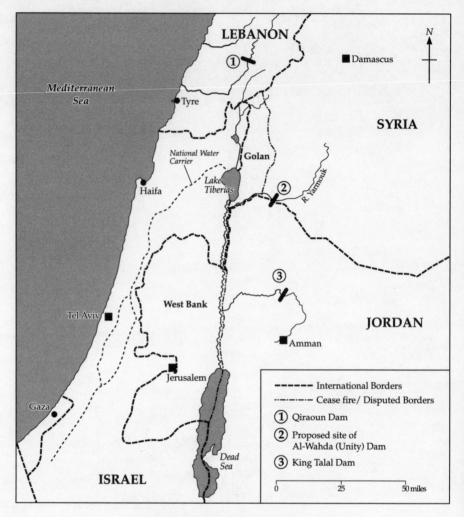

**Figure 5.3** The Jordan river system
(Liverpool John Moores University, Cartographic Unit, 1995)

Jordan, where the problem of water scarcity is particularly acute, and hostility between the two countries has been greatly exacerbated.

Disputes between Syria and Jordan notwithstanding, it is undoubtedly Israeli over-exploitation of the shared waters of the Jordan which is the most controversial issue. In this case tensions between riparian states are exacerbated by the fact that Israeli access to the Jordan, and several of its tributaries, is enhanced by control of the occupied territories on the West Bank and Golan Heights. Indeed the West Bank is crucial to Israel's water supply. Following occupation in 1967 the Israeli government introduced a number of restrictions upon water consumption by Palestinians; with the result that the area of irrigated land on the West Bank has decreased sharply (Beschorner 1992–3:14).

Restrictions on Israeli consumption were not introduced until the 1990s.

Undoubtedly access to water in this region is a highly sensitive political issue which fuels Palestinian and Jordanian grievances against Israel and greatly reduces the prospects for a successful outcome to the Israeli–Palestinian peace process. The rhetoric of 'water wars' has recently been replaced by joint proclamations of commitment to 'working together towards a common water future'. Nevertheless the Palestinian position remains that cooperation over water management must await resolution of the issue of Israeli settlements in Gaza and the West Bank (Kessel 25.7.94).

In the Middle East and elsewhere, pressure on diminishing water supplies is increasing steadily and it has been argued that 'Water security will soon rank with military security in the war rooms of defense ministries' (Starr 1991:19).

### Externalisation of intrastate conflict

Intrastate or intercommunal conflicts can, in certain circumstances, produce spill-over effects which have the potential to promote conflict between states. This, of course, links specifically with our discussion of identity politics and is particularly the case where national or ethnic groups straddle state boundaries or where large-scale population movements occur. This latter issue is dealt with separately below.

In the post-Cold War period the potential for interstate conflict associated with movements for national self-determination has increased significantly. Throughout Central and Eastern Europe and in the Soviet successor republics there exist resentments concerning the treatment of co-nationals residing in neighbouring states. The disputes between Hungary and Romania over Transylvania, between Armenia and Azerbaijan over the enclave of Nagorno-Karabakh and between Russia and Ukraine over the Crimea are but prominent examples of this broader phenomenon, which is discussed more fully, region by region, in the previous chapter. The potential for conflict between Soviet successor republics has inevitably been a matter of concern for western commentators, due to the perceived danger of spill-over effects from escalating conflict and instability in the region, and uncertainties concerning the future role of Russia.

Extension of domestic conflicts across state boundaries is not, of course, a specifically post Cold-War phenomenon; rather it is a typical consequence of the collapse of empire – in this case the Soviet empire – which allows the contestation of established but highly inappropriate, and deeply resented, state boundaries. In consequence there are regions throughout the developing world where old and new conflicts have important transboundary implications. A recent example is provided by the catastrophic civil war in Rwanda in 1994 between the Hutu and Tutsi peoples. Here the transboundary nature of Hutu and Tutsi settlement raised the potential of spill-over effects in neighbouring Burundi and, hence, for interstate war in the region. We return to this issue below, in our discussion of the impacts of population movements.

## Impacts of population movements

Mass movements of people within and across state boundaries are not a new phenomenon, they have historically accompanied famine, persecution and armed conflict, whether interstate or domestic. While population movements are frequently a consequence of conflict, they can also exacerbate or generate instability in both sending and receiving states and, ultimately, contribute to or cause conflict between states.

In periods of rapid change or instability, such as that following the end of the Cold War, it might be expected that there would be an increase in population movements, and this has indeed been the case. The Office of the United Nations High Commissioner for Refugees (UNHCR) recorded in 1956, the year of its creation, some 1.5 million refugees. By 1980 8.2 million refugees were recorded and by 1992 more than 18 million (Loescher 1992:9). Moreover these figures considerably underestimate the extent of population movement since they reflect the definition of refugees adopted in the 1951 United Nations Convention Relating to the Status of Refugees, that is: 'Persons who are outside their country because of a well-founded fear of persecution for reasons of race, religion, nationality, membership of a particular social group or public opinion.'

Application of this definition excludes persons whose migration has been caused by economic or environmental factors. Arguments urging extension of the definition of refugees reflect a broad, needs-based rather than legalistic approach to the issue. This suits our present purpose, since our concern is not with the causes but with the potential consequences of population movement. Accordingly, we have adopted a broad approach to population movement although the term 'refugee' is used when referring to persons covered by the United Nations Convention.

During the Cold War period large-scale population movements were confined to the developing world, and it remains the case that a high proportion of such movements occurs between countries of the South. Nevertheless, since the end of the Cold War substantial movements of persons have also occurred in Europe. There has been an exodus of ethnic minority group members from the former Soviet republics and Romania and of economic migrants from Albania. In addition conflicts between and within the former Soviet republics and, in particular, the former Yugoslav republics have generated large numbers of refugees.

Large-scale population movements are potentially destabilizing for a number of reasons. They are a source of embarrassment to the sending country, providing a highly visible demonstration of the inadequacy of its government; and they put pressure on the resources of the receiving country, potentially generating resentment among the host population. Here it is interesting to note that such resentment has been more evident in Europe, where population movements are smaller and resources more plentiful, than in countries such as Pakistan (hosting almost four million Afghanis at the height of the Afghan civil war) and Jordan where, as a consequence of the Gulf War, refugees comprised 25 per cent of the population in 1991.

The domestic impacts of population movement are likely to generate or exacerbate tension between receiving and sending regimes. In addition, migrant or refugee settlements provide both a refuge and a fertile recruiting ground for insurgent groups, whose activities may be supported by the host government or by third parties. The United States government, for example, has actively encouraged political and military organization among Cuban and Nicaraguan exile groups, while the complex political struggles among Cambodian and Afghan exiles were greatly exacerbated by external intervention.

The bitter conflict between the Hutu and Tutsi of Rwanda in the spring of 1994 demonstrated several of the characteristics discussed above. The unprecedented exodus from Rwanda of the majority of its population placed intolerable pressure on the resources of neighbouring states, particularly Zaire, while the confused and overcrowded circumstances of makeshift refugee settlements allowed the rival militias to regroup. This inevitably increased resistance to an early return to Rwanda on the part of many refugees and heightened an atmosphere of fear and suspicion which hindered attempts at external mediation. The activities of Rwandan 'refugee warriors' demonstrate that this phenomenon will continue whether or not it is encouraged by the intervention of Cold War protagonists.

Mass population movements, then are a humanitarian issue which must be dealt with urgently by the international community, not only because of their scale but also 'because of the serious consequences that mass displacements have for national stability, international security and the emerging new world order' (Loescher 1992:3). Thus the contemporary scale of mass population movements has implications beyond the interlinking of intercommunal and interstate conflict or the challenges posed to refugee and human rights organizations. It is a global phenomenon which has, itself, been identified as an important aspect of the globalization thesis with the potential, ultimately, for blurring national and ethnic differences (Castles and Miller 1993).

# Conclusion

This chapter has surveyed a number of actual or potential sources of armed conflict. The distinction made between interstate and intercommunal conflict is somewhat arbitrary, since conflicts tend to arise from a multitude of complex and overlapping sources. This distinction nevertheless reflects an important division between issues which have traditionally formed the subject matter of international relations and issues which have tended to be considered aspects of the domestic political process.

In the 1990s focus on interstate conflict is clearly inadequate. Nevertheless there exist a number of issues, for example the increasing scarcity of important resources such as water, which have the potential to exacerbate tensions between states and which might generate armed conflict if not properly managed. In addition failure to understand, and address, the sources of intercommunal conflict will contribute significantly to regional instability and, again, may ultimately lead to war between states through spill-over effects or as a result of destabilizing population movements.

The resurgence of identity politics based on ethnic or religious criteria is likely to remain a major source of intercommunal conflict. Ethno-nationalism and religious fundamentalism are at present filling the ideological void left by the decline of socialism, and the political void left by the delegitimation of regimes worldwide. The crisis of the state in Africa is but an extreme example of a more general malaise affecting western as well as developing states. At present the discipline of international relations is bereft of conceptual tools to assist our understanding of these phenomena. Cultural particularism is accessible neither to the state-centric perspective of realism nor the pluralist–universalist perspective of liberal internationalism. Its influence is too important to be dismissed as a passing, and pathological, reaction to change and instability, and we must seek insights from the disciplines of sociology, psychology and anthropology. Moreover, the contemporary upsurge of ethnic particularism is a global phenomenon which must be addressed in a determined and consistent manner as part of the agenda of global politics. These issues are the subject of the following chapter.

# Notes

1   This has been a central tenet of idealist thought from Kant to Woodrow Wilson. More recently it has been echoed by politicians such as Margaret Thatcher, who have asserted that democracies do not go to war with each other.

2   This restricted approach to the notion of identity politics reflects our specific concern with armed conflict. Identity politics generally refers, in addition, to movements associated with gender or sexuality. Such movements tend to be inimical to processes of mobilization based upon ethnicity or religion, which explicitly seek to unite groups across social divisions. In addition those based on ethnicity or religion frequently present a highly masculinized view of a heroic past and, in seeking to inspire military endeavours, promote symbols of masculinity in the present. For a discussion of this process see Enloe (1988). It is of interest to note that the promotion of Serb nationalism in the 1990s has been associated with harassment of feminist organizations, which are considered un*patriotic*.

3   Benedict Anderson (1991) has provided in 'Memory and Forgetting' – the final chapter of the second edition of *Imagined Communities* – a fascinating account of the processes by which nations imagine themselves to be old.

4   For the Slovenian case, see Senjur (1992) and Svetlicic (1993). These are two of a number of publications on the theme of 'the viability of a small state separating from a larger one' emanating from the Faculty of Social Sciences of the University of Ljubljana.

   In the case of Scotland, 'Independence in Europe' is the central policy position of the Scottish National Party.

5   See, for example, NATO's *Rome Declaration on Peace and Cooperation* which identifies 'violent nationalism' as a risk to European security (NATO 8.11.91).

6   Male migration in the Sahel, as a result of environmental degradation, is considered to have seriously disrupted the social fabric of that region and to have raised implications for its future political stability (Monimart 1991).

# 6

# Security after the Cold War: Towards a Global Paradigm?

## Charlotte Bretherton

*The concept of peace is easy to grasp; that of international security is more complex.*

*(Boutros Boutros-Ghali, 1992)*

This deceptively simple statement by the United Nations Secretary-General reflects important debates, which have intensified since the end of the Cold War, about our understanding of the concepts of peace and security. These debates, which have involved both practitioners and academic commentators, reflect the contrasting perceptions and analyses of liberal internationalists and neo-realists. They centre around two interlinked sets of issues, which are examined below. First, the extent to which the concept of security requires reappraisal and reformulation following the end of the Cold War and, second, the possibility of achieving global solutions, through the United Nations, to contemporary problems of security and insecurity.

In view of the increased incidence of intercommunal conflict in the contemporary period, we examine arguments concerning United Nations intervention, discussing both its justification and its potential for contributing to conflict avoidance or resolution. However, issues of peace and security require a broader focus than the immediate sources of armed conflict discussed in the previous chapter.

## The Meaning of Peace and Security during the Cold War

The concept of peace is not uncontroversial. During the Cold War it was frequently used to denote the absence of direct military conflict between the superpowers; hence NATO's claim to have 'kept the peace' for forty years. This treatment, unsurprisingly, is rejected by peace researchers in favour of an approach which emphasizes the priority of human needs over the interests of states. Nevertheless peace researchers themselves disagree about the meaning of their key concept. In particular there have been divisions between reformers – who see peace primarily in terms of the absence of overt violence – and radicals, who argue that the attainment of peace is contingent upon the achievement of social justice. According to this latter view peace is a distant goal, attainable only when structural conflict between North and South has ended.[1]

Security is also, as the UN Secretary-General suggests, a difficult and contested concept. As an idea, divorced from social and historical context, security implies freedom from harm and from threat, or fear, of harm. Hence, for the individual, insecurity derives not only from fear of a potential military aggressor but from a range of sources, including vulnerability to hunger or to violence in the home. These latter, and considerably more common sources of insecurity are not randomly distributed; they reflect patterns of social and economic inequality and the distribution of power. This might suggest that security analysts and radical peace researchers have much in common, but this has not been the case: indeed the concept of security has developed meanings inimical to peace and to peace research.

In discussion and analysis of international relations, the concept of security has traditionally been conflated with that of national security. This applies in general to the realist approach, with its emphasis on the military capabilities of states, and in particular to the Cold War notion of the national security state. Thus the Cold War produced the need for, or justification of, a vast state security apparatus which enjoyed privileged status and levels of secrecy incompatible with the needs of peacetime or the principles of democratic accountability, however minimally defined. In both East and West the internal manifestation of Cold War security was the repression of dissidence, while its external aspect involved espionage and massive arms proliferation, in particular the development of ever more sophisticated nuclear weapons technology.

During this period a much-used definition of national security was provided by Walter Lippmann: 'a nation is secure to the extent to which it is not in danger of having to sacrifice core values if it wishes to avoid war, and is able, if challenged, to maintain them by victory in such a war' (cited in Wolfers 1962:150). It is not surprising that, in the context of the Cold War, the identification of 'core values' should be seen as unproblematic. However, the notion that security is ultimately a function of the ability to achieve victory in war seems less than reassuring in the circumstances of Cold War nuclear confrontation.

During the Cold War period, then, security was unattainable, even when narrowly conceived. The nuclear age starkly illuminated the central paradox of the realist approach to national security: that attempts to enhance the security of one state inevitably increase the insecurity of its neighbours, thus prompting compensatory measures and ultimately creating a spiral of insecurity. Indeed, in western Europe many people considered the security policies of their *own* governments to be a major source of insecurity.[2] This paradox has been referred to as the 'security dilemma' (Herz 1950). In the climate of the Cold War little attempt was made to address this dilemma; indeed, insofar as realism remains the dominant approach to practice and analysis in this area, its resolution is impossible. The paradox remains – the pursuit of security by the governments of individual states continues to generate insecurities elsewhere, as is evidenced by the contemporary, competitive armaments build-up in South-East Asia and in Greece and Turkey.

Clearly preoccupation with the traditional issues of national security continues; nevertheless we have seen from the previous chapter that interstate conflict is not a common phenomenon. Nor is national security the concept to which Boutros-Ghali refers at the start of this chapter; he speaks of 'international security'. This concept is, as he states, complex, indeed ambiguous: it also reflects contemporary debates about the meaning of security in the post-Cold War period.

## The Concept of Security Reformulated?

An important contribution to contemporary debate has been provided by Barry Buzan, who explicitly aims to bridge the gulf between security analysts and peace researchers and has developed, from the perspective of neo-realism, an expanded approach to the concept of security (1991a:12). Buzan contends that a range of factors, including deepening economic interdependence and mutual vulnerability to environmental threats, has created 'common fates and security interdependencies' (ibid.:68–9). For Buzan, awareness of the diminishing utility of national security strategies in the face of such interdependencies is conducive to the development of an international system characterized by 'mature' anarchy.

In such a system, use of military force as an instrument of foreign policy would be constrained. This, then, forms the basis of Buzan's approach to international security, a concept which is 'best used to refer to the systemic conditions that influence the ways in which states make each other feel more or less secure. Individual national securities can only be fully understood when considered in relation both to each

other and to larger patterns of relations in the system as a whole'
(ibid.:22).

For Buzan the notion of international security reflects systemic
change which influences and constrains the decisions of statespersons
in an increasingly complex policy environment. However, state security
has not necessarily been enhanced by the decline in salience of external
military threats. Indeed the very conditions which have occasioned this
decline themselves threaten the autonomy of states, reduce their ability
to meet the needs of citizens and have the potential to 'trigger serious
conflicts of interest' between states (Buzan 1991b:451). Hence, it is
argued, consideration of security issues must include, alongside military threats, a range of threats not traditionally addressed within the
realist paradigm – that is political, societal, economic and ecological
sources of insecurity.

There is considerable overlap between Buzan's approach and our
discussion of sources of armed conflict. Political challenges threaten
the integrity and stability of the state, and are associated with
transnational movements such as Islamism, or transborder nationalism
of the type all too evident in the former Yugoslavia; societal challenges
threaten the cultural traditions of peoples within states and may generate secessionist movements, as in the Caucasus, or civil war, as in
Rwanda. Ecological threats were also considered in the previous
chapter, in terms of their potential to generate substantial and
destabilizing population movements or conflict over diminishing
natural resources.

The broader implications of climate change – the threats to well-
being, health and ultimately life associated with ozone depletion and
global warming – are not dealt with in our discussion of armed conflict,
nor are they seen by Buzan as capable of easy accommodation within
the meaning of security.

Similarly, economic issues were dealt with only indirectly in the
previous chapter, as an underlying rather than immediate source of
armed conflict. Buzan's position here is that, since participation in
market relations *inevitably* generates risk and uncertainty, economic
threats are particularly difficult to fit within the framework of security
analysis. Ultimately he concludes, in traditional realist manner, that
economic insecurity assumes relevance for the security analyst only in
circumstances where poor economic performance negatively affects the
military capabilities or international prestige of the state (Buzan
1991a:123–7).

This discussion reveals the limitations of Buzan's analysis. Those
factors with the most immediate implications for state security, as
traditionally formulated – and which we have identified as immediate
rather than fundamental sources of armed conflict – are most easily

accommodated within his expanded approach to security. Other issues fit less well, despite their significant implications for the well-being of all, or many, of the earth's people. Extreme poverty and/or vulnerability to environmental degradation or climate change are problems whose solution is beyond the capacity of states, and hence, ultimately, beyond the scope of the realist paradigm. We have identified these issues as global problems requiring global solutions but, for Buzan 'it is easy to see that global consensus is not the obvious response' (ibid.:133).

Buzan's recasting of the security dilemma, to emphasize security interdependence as a constraining factor in interstate relations, represents an important advance in neo-realist thought. Nevertheless his analysis remains state-centric and his approach to international security reflects the realist view that state egoism precludes cooperative solutions to global problems. In consequence Buzan has provided an extension rather than a reformulation of the concept of security, in which fundamental sources of insecurity are not addressed and global solutions are precluded.

The meaning of, and approach to, international security envisaged by the United Nations Secretary-General is, inevitably, somewhat different from Buzan's. Nevertheless a number of parallels are evident. For Boutros-Ghali, risks to international security include traditional military threats; racial tensions; social injustice; increasing economic inequality and ecological damage. In contrast to Buzan's neo-realist formulation, however, Boutros-Ghali particularly emphasizes the less traditional aspects of security, arguing that:

> A porous ozone shield could pose a greater threat to an exposed population than a hostile army. Drought and disease can decimate no less mercilessly than the weapons of war . . . the efforts of the Organization to build peace, stability and security must encompass matters beyond military threats in order to break the fetters of strife and warfare that have characterized the past. (Boutros-Ghali 1992:4)

International security, then, is both broadly conceived and indivisible; its meaning 'most clearly revealed through three objectives: peace, development and democracy. They are interlocking and mutually reinforcing' (Boutros-Ghali 1993a:3). This theme is echoed in the 1994 United Nations Development Report, which introduces the concept of human security.[3] Clearly, this interpretation of the meaning of security does suggest a fundamental reformulation of the concept. In addition, as would be anticipated, it embraces the optimism of liberal internationalists, expressed in its Charter, that the United Nations should assume a central role in facilitating international cooperation and in promoting 'peace, development and democracy'.

The ending of the Cold War and the new climate of cooperation between the superpowers appeared to provide opportunities for the United Nations to begin, at last, to carry out its tasks. In the contemporary period its role is more than ever necessary since: 'The world is being changed by powerful forces that no State, or even group of States, has the capacity to manage by itself' (Boutros-Ghali 1993a:7). In this view attempts to achieve global consensus – 'not an obvious response' to contemporary security issues for Buzan – are the only response available.

Contemporary reappraisals of the concept of security agree that a range of issues, extending beyond the traditional area of military threat, should be included among potential sources of threat to international security. Significant differences are apparent, however, concerning the appropriateness of including threats to human well-being associated with the operation of economic processes, or with global environmental issues such as ozone depletion and climate change. These controversies about the meaning of security are exemplified by debates concerning the appropriateness, and/or political expediency, of including environmental issues within an extended – rather than fundamentally reformulated – approach to security. Some environmentalists have explicitly sought incorporation of their concerns in the traditional understanding of security in the hope that the salience, urgency and resources accorded to national security issues might be extended, or indeed redirected, to environmental protection (Myers 1989; Starr 1991). Others have urged caution in this respect (Vogler 1993) or have opposed the creation of security–environment linkages on the grounds that the sources of traditional security and environmental threats are too divergent to permit a common approach (Deudney 1990). Indeed Deudney concludes that traditional approaches to security are inimical to environmental protection, so that: 'For environmentalists to dress their programmes in the blood-soaked garments of the war system betrays their core values and creates confusion about the real tasks at hand' (Deudney 1990:475).

Deudney's words express very clearly the dangers inherent in seeking to expand the content of the security concept without reformulating its essential meaning. This, however, may prove impossible as the meaning of security has been contaminated by its long association with national security. In consequence, we consider, alongside the concept of security, the concept of insecurity – which we see as including the numerous factors which may threaten the well-being of individuals or of groups. This involves identifying the fundamental sources of insecurity, and developing the capacity, and the will, to address them in ways which differ from traditional approaches to national security.

Divisions about the meaning of security are inevitably reflected in debates concerning the means of addressing security challenges. Buzan envisages the development of a mature anarchy, characterized by security interdependence, in which internally stable, well-established states mutually refrain from the use of force. Issues which are global in scope can be addressed neither by individual states nor through global consensus and are, it seems, insoluble. In contrast Boutros-Ghali envisages an important role for a strengthened United Nations Organization in promoting and coordinating international cooperation across a broad security agenda, including management of a range of global issues associated with economic and ecological factors.

These contrasting approaches to the meaning of security and to its realization are reflected in discussion of proposals for enhancing the role of the United Nations.

## Collective Action and the Role of the United Nations

Debates concerning the future role of the United Nations centre around three sets of arguments; those which emphasize moral issues, that is the role which the UN *ought* to play; those which emphasize legal issues, that is the role it is *entitled* to play; and those which emphasize political issues, that is the role it will be *permitted* by its members. Initially it is helpful to outline the legal position through consideration of the provisions of the United Nations Charter and their interpretation, in practice, during the Cold War period.

### The UN Charter: purposes and principles

The purposes of the United Nations as set out in its Charter, are far from modest. They range from maintenance of international peace and security (Article 1,1) to promotion of social justice and individual rights and freedoms (Article 1,3).[4] Despite the breadth of its compass, the Charter is a brief document. Nevertheless it provides considerably more guidance on traditional security issues than on sources of insecurity such as social injustice and violation of human rights: indeed in these latter areas the Charter fails to move beyond exhortation. Hence it is evident that the Charter privileges peace over justice, a priority which is unsurprising given its drafting during the closing stages of the Second World War – it was originally signed on the 26 June 1945.

In pursuit of its purposes, both the organization and its members are required to act in accordance with a set of principles, the first of which states 'The Organization is based on the principle of the sovereign equality of all its Members' (Article 2,1). The final principle reaffirms and expands upon the implications of the first:

Nothing contained in the present Charter shall authorize the United
Nations to intervene in matters which are essentially within the domestic
jurisdiction of any state or shall require the Members to submit such
matters to settlement under the present Charter . . . (Article 2,7).[5]

This strong emphasis on state sovereignty would appear to preclude
action by or on behalf of the organization in circumstances where states
fail to respect the social justice and human rights provisions of Article
1,3. Moreover the single area where state sovereignty may legally be
ignored – enforcement measures in the event of 'any threat to the
peace, breach of the peace or act of aggression' (Chapter VII, Article
39) – is dependent upon the unanimous support of the permanent
members of the Security Council.[6] Here, again, action by the organization is impeded by its Charter; the requirement for consensus could not
be met in the hostile climate of the Cold War period – as is evident
from the casting of 279 vetoes during the period up to August 1990.
During these years the United Nations was prevented from taking
action to achieve its primary purpose, and more than 20 million people
died in over a hundred major conflicts (Boutros-Ghali 1992:6).
Moreover, the very concept of permanent membership of the Security
Council, with right of veto, contravenes the first principle of the Charter – respect for the sovereign *equality* of states – by establishing a group
of five states in a position of privilege which effectively provides im-
munity from the Charter's provisions.

Thus the United Nations Charter places severe constraints upon the
organization's role. Its intergovernmental character, emphasis on state
sovereignty and non-intervention, and accommodation of the interests
of the 'great powers' of the period (the Second World War victors)
indicate strong realist influence. This juxtaposition of realism and
idealism has produced contradictions – between peace and justice as
priorities for the organization; and between commitment to the principles of social justice and human rights, and absence of the means to
take action in situations where those principles are violated.

For realists, these contradictions are simply indicative of the limited
role available to international organizations in a decentralized system
where power lies with the units. For liberal internationalists, however,
they provide room for manoeuvre and the opportunity to urge that the
Charter be reinterpreted in the interest of achieving a fresh balance
among its provisions. Aspirations for reform of the United Nations
received new impetus from the ending of the Cold War and are reflected *inter alia* in the proposals of the Secretary-General discussed
below. First, however, we briefly examine the historical record of
United Nations' involvement in traditional security issues – the anom-
alies of the Charter and the changes which have occurred in the

international system since its signature have already necessitated a degree of creativity in its interpretation.

## Evolution of the United Nations' Security Role

The development of the Cold War so soon after the organization's establishment created a climate of hostility between permanent members of the Security Council which precluded collective action as conceived in the Charter. This applies in particular to the provisions for enforcement action under Chapter VII, which provide a framework for global collective security.

### *Collective security*

Collective security, as a principle, was first institutionalized after the First World War, in the covenant of the League of Nations. The League's failure to prevent the outbreak of the Second World War resulted, in part, from lack of commitment – to the League in general and collective security in particular – by the major powers of the period. This problem was addressed in the United Nations Charter by creating a privileged group of Security Council permanent members intended to reflect the 'realities' of power politics. Thus the principle of collective security was retained, but diluted, while its realization in practice was again impeded.

Collective security as a concept is both simple and appealing. It is based upon deterrence, involving the threat that aggressive action by one state against another will be met by an overwhelming collective response 'by all the Members of the United Nations or by some of them, as the Security Council may determine' (Article 48). This involves recognition, by all participants, that a breach of the peace or an act of aggression by one member constitutes a threat to the system as a whole; and hence that security is indivisible. In principle, therefore, collective security affords protection to small or weak states and dissipates the insecurity inherent in the realist security paradox. Again in principle, collective security provides a strong deterrent to the adoption of self-help strategies by states.

In practice, the impediments to the establishment of a collective security system are numerous. The credibility of such a system demands a high level of commitment from its members in circumstances where there are considerable incentives to free riding. Indeed the Charter provisions for making forces available to the Secretary-General (Articles 43–47) were never put into practice and members have, in general, shown reluctance to pay their budget contributions in full or on time.[7] Members must, in addition, be prepared to participate in collective action in circumstances where they would prefer to remain neutral, or even to support the aggressor. Finally, and perhaps most importantly, the system must be universal and its sanctions apply to all transgressors equally. In the case of the United Nations the special status of the permanent members of the Security Council ensures that neither these states, nor their close allies, can be the object of collective action. In consequence, the Charter's framers must be seen as having

> repudiated the doctrine of collective security as the foundation for a general, universally applicable, system for the management of power in international relations . . . the new organization reflected the conviction that the concept of collective security has no realistic relevance to the problems posed by conflict among the major powers in the mid-twentieth century (Claude 1962:164–5).

In the context of the Cold War this repudiation had considerable impact. As a result of persistent use of the veto by permanent members, the Security Council agreed to identify threats to, or breaches of, the peace on only six occasions during the forty-five-year period up to June 1990.[8] In two cases economic sanctions were imposed (against Rhodesia and South Africa) but in only one case, the Korean War in 1950, was military action authorized. This authorization was possible only because of the absence from the Security Council of the Soviet Union's representative, in protest against the allocation of permanent membership status to the Republic of China (Taiwan) following the 1949 Chinese revolution. In addition the Korean operation did not conform to the Chapter VII provisions for collective action; it was authorized under United States command and other member states were merely *recommended* to participate. Had South Korea been the initial aggressor the situation would undoubtedly have been very different.

The end of the Cold War has brought considerable changes. The prospect of armed conflict between 'the major powers' now seems remote and, although the veto remains available to the permanent members, none has been cast for more than four years. However collective security as a concept applies most readily to situations of interstate conflict, in circumstances where it is possible to name an aggressor. This was the case on the second occasion when the Security Council authorized use of force, following Iraq's invasion and subsequent annexation of Kuwait in August 1990. On this occasion the Council reacted with unprecedented alacrity and determination, identifying a breach of the peace the day after it occurred and passing no less than twelve resolutions before the start of military action in January 1991.[9]

During the Gulf War, as in the Korean War, the conduct of operations showed scant obeisance to the provisions of the Charter. Again the action was commanded and dominated by the United States military; indeed on this occasion, unlike the Korean example, no attempt was made even to utilize the United Nations flag. Reports on the progress of the operation were made only retrospectively to the Secretary-General, who complained publicly, on more than one occasion, about the paucity of information supplied to him. Nevertheless the operation appeared to demonstrate the development of collective will on the part of the international community. Despite the preponderance of United States forces, a further twenty-seven states contributed to the overall military effort; of these seventeen contributed ground forces which, due to the likelihood of casualties, must be considered a strong indication of commitment. This impressive display of military force was evidently in excess of need, and was used punitively: Iraqi casualties are estimated at between 60,000 and 100,000; allied casualties totalled 857 (Matthews 1993). Indeed punitive measures against Iraq did not end with the hostilities; the cease-fire conditions imposed by the Security Council were stringent and were supported by the authority to take 'all necessary means' in securing their implementation (Resolutions 686, 687). As a consequence of Iraq's failure to meet the conditions imposed, mandatory economic sanctions were maintained, together with United Nations observer units on the Iraq–Kuwait border and intrusive surveillance of Iraqi military movements and capabilities.

The Gulf War could be seen as a demonstration of collective security in response to an act of aggression, and hence as a deterrent to such acts in the future. However, the exemplary effect of the measures against Iraq is mitigated by a number of factors peculiar to this case. These include the salience to policy-makers, in the United States and elsewhere, of the Middle East region in general, and the desirability of maintaining access to its oil resources in particular. These factors were augmented by the fears that the achievement of nuclear weapons capability by Iraq was imminent, and that urgent measures were required for its prevention. In situations where such circumstances are absent, potential aggressors may not be deterred.

Collective security, then, remains a problematic concept even in circumstances of interstate conflict where an aggressor can be clearly identified. In practice, such circumstances are rare; conflict situations – whether interstate or intrastate – tend to be complex. Ambiguity between acts of aggression and permissible acts of self-defence may be such that it is impossible for the Security Council to identify the aggressor, even in circumstances where its members could reach agreement on such matters. During the Cold War, when such agreement was not forthcoming, the United Nations security role developed in other directions.

*Peacekeeping*

Peacekeeping is a technique, developed during the Cold War, which enabled the United Nations to assist in controlling and resolving armed conflicts without recourse to the enforcement provisions of Chapter VII. Peacekeeping represents a creative interpretation of Chapter VI of the Charter 'Pacific Settlement of Disputes'. Thirteen peacekeeping operations were mounted in the period up to June 1990, of varying duration and character.[10] Despite the singularity of each operation a number of shared features can be identified.

First, peacekeeping operations were genuine United Nations operations under the command and control of the Secretary-General, paid for collectively by the member states who contributed forces voluntarily. Second, they were established with the explicit consent of all parties to the conflict, a factor which greatly reduced the risk of casualties among United Nations forces. Thus peacekeepers have traditionally been deployed after the cessation of hostilities to supervise cease-fire arrangements and provide mediation and conciliation facilities. Third, peacekeepers were committed to the principle of impartiality between the parties; a principle whose observance in circumstances of mutual distrust between former adversaries has been essential to the legitimacy of peacekeeping operations. Finally, peacekeepers have traditionally been unarmed or lightly armed, employing minimum force only in self-defence.[11] This factor, too, is regarded as having played an important role both in legitimizing peacekeeping operations and minimizing casualties (Connaughton 1992:172).

It is evident that there are a number of differences between collective security and the 'traditional' peacekeeping operations of the Cold War period. The principles of consent, impartiality and minimum use of force which characterize peacekeeping are entirely distinct from the mandatory enforcement measures envisaged by Chapter VII. These distinctive characteristics of peacekeeping have been regarded as essential to its success (Connaughton 1992; Rubinstein 1993). Indeed Rubinstein believes that it is precisely the ritualistic and symbolic nature of United Nations peacekeeping operations that enabled them to become an accepted feature of international diplomacy; the Blue Beret came to symbolize both the intention of the parties to resolve their differences, and the involvement and concern of the international community. Thus peacekeeping as an activity gained a legitimacy which was independent of the success or failure of individual peacekeeping operations (Rubinstein 1993:559).

This analysis suggests that any major departure from the traditional peacekeeping formula is likely to delegitimize peacekeeping as a technique, hence jeopardizing future operations. This is an important issue since, in the changed climate of the post-Cold War period, the practice of peacekeeping has been subject to modification as a consequence of increased willingness to authorize United Nations action in response to intense, intrastate conflicts deemed to threaten international security. As a result of the new demands made upon the organization, the Secretary-General has advanced proposals to extend and develop United Nations operations beyond the confines of traditional peacekeeping. It is to these proposals that we now turn.

## Agenda for Peace: Proposals for an enhanced United Nations Security Role

In January 1992 the Security Council requested that the Secretary-General produce recommendations for reforming and strengthening the security role of the organization to enable it to respond more effectively to the changing security needs of the post-Cold War period. His *Agenda for Peace* proposals centre upon four broad categories of operation: preventive measures, peacemaking and peace enforcement, peacekeeping and peace building. In addition to the more traditional tasks of assisting with management and resolution of conflicts and with post-conflict reconciliation, these proposals include a role for the United Nations in addressing fundamental sources of insecurity as well as immediate sources of armed conflict.

### *Preventive measures*

Preventive measures fall into two distinct categories. *Preventive diplomacy* builds upon traditional United Nations 'good offices' work, involving mediation at an early stage in potential conflict situations. In addition, a new category of United Nations military operation was proposed; *preventive deployment*. Preventive operations would be mounted either at the request of all parties, as has been the tradition for United Nations peacekeeping deployments, or of any party which feels threatened by aggression or by spill-over from nearby conflicts. This new form of deployment has been in operation since 1992 inside the Macedonian border. In this case, despite its departure from the principle of impartiality, the symbolic role of United Nations operations is maintained given the evident inability of a small, lightly armed force to prevent spill-over of the Bosnian war into Macedonia. Of significance, however, is the new meaning which must attach to the symbols. Preventive deployment does not symbolize consent and the concerned involvement of the international community; it is a deterrence strategy and, as such, symbolizes the will of the international community to act decisively should preventive measures fail. Thus the credibility of preventive deployment is contingent upon perceptions, and ultimately demonstrations, of the willingness of United Nations members to back up deterrence strategies.

### Peacemaking and peace enforcement

Peacemaking has traditionally involved conflict resolution measures, short of the use of force, as outlined in Chapter VI of the Charter. Peacemaking essentially involves mediation and arbitration procedures. However, *Agenda for Peace* recommends the development of two additional peacemaking mechanisms – *amelioration through assistance* and *peace enforcement*. The first of these involves adoption of a broad approach to security and insecurity which might more properly have been considered among preventive measures; the latter involves introduction of more forceful measures to deal with conflict should preventive measures fail.

'Amelioration through assistance' is intended to address factors underlying the outbreak of conflict and accords with a broad approach to international security which would involve input from various United Nations agencies and programmes. Thus, for example, assistance might involve coordinated efforts by Development and Environment Programme staff in addition to the High Commission for Refugees, which is more typically involved in conflict situations. In his subsequent discussion document *Agenda for Development*, the Secretary-General deals more fully with 'the deeper foundations of international peace and security. These are rooted in the great issue of development in all its aspects: economic, social, political and environmental.' (cited in Roberts 1993a:4). The implementation of amelioration measures is, of course, dependent upon acceptance of their principles by the member states and, more crucially, upon their willingness to provide funding.

*Agenda for Peace* also proposed that peacemaking should move beyond the traditional areas of arbitration and conciliation, based on consent of the parties, to include a new concept: peace enforcement. This would involve recourse to mandatory economic sanctions and/or military action under Chapter VII and, in consequence, represents a major departure from traditional peacekeeping operations. It is perhaps unfortunate that this type of operation is located within the broader category of peacemaking, which emphasizes the need to address the fundamental sources of insecurity. Clearly the Secretary-General recognizes the ambiguity of the notion that peace can be enforced, and he has subsequently suggested that 'cease-fire enforcement' might be a more appropriate title for the type of operation envisaged. He has also acknowledged that, in blurring the distinction between peacekeeping and coercive collective security, peace enforcement raises 'obvious difficulties' (Boutros-Ghali 1993b:93–4). These difficulties became all too obvious when attempts were made to enforce peace.

In Somalia in 1992–3 enforcement measures were instituted following the failure the United Nations operation (Unosom) to fulfil its role of providing humanitarian assistance to the Somali people. In an unprecedented Resolution (number 794) the Security Council authorized the use of 'all necessary means' to ensure the success of humanitarian relief operations and 'welcomed' the United States' offer to play a leading role. Operation Restore Hope's primary task of alleviating starvation involved attempts to enforce a cease-fire between rival armed clans engaged in a bitter civil war. In these circumstances casualties among United Nations forces were inevitable, although subsequent reprisals against particular 'warlords' represented a departure from the principle of impartiality which was both avoidable and unfortunate. By July 1993, it has been argued, 'the somewhat haphazard and *ad hoc* employment of weaponry had already succeeded in converting the US troops into a hostile force for some Somali factions' (Thakur 1994a:399). Operation Restore Hope demonstrated all too clearly the ease with which peace enforcement could be transformed into war fighting.

Differing explanations have been offered for the decision to mount this ill-fated enforcement operation, which exceeded the need to 'do something' in response to a situation of anarchy and mass starvation. For some commentators, the civil war in Somalia offered an opportunity to establish the credibility of the United Nations' collective security role.[12] An alternative explanation is that private reservations of United Nations officials concerning use of enforcement measures were mitigated by the prospect that, for the first time ever, United States forces would wear the blue helmet and operate under United Nations command. Their experience in Somalia suggests that they may never do so again.[13]

The problematic nature of enforcement measures was also demonstrated by their use during the protracted civil war in Bosnia–Herzogovina. Here enforcement measures were authorized in February 1994 in circumstances where, as was the case in Somalia, the existing United Nations effort had proved both inappropriate and inadequate.[14] They were intended to safeguard civilian 'protected areas' and involved the threat, and eventual execution, of limited air strikes against specified military targets. These were entrusted to NATO forces, acting on behalf of the United Nations, in circumstances where ground forces were operating in accordance with traditional peacekeeping principles. Inevitably this raised fears about the safety of ground forces and highlighted, again, the central contradiction between the legitimation needs of peacekeeping and the credibility needs of coercive collective action.

This was expressed succinctly by a former commander of United Nations forces in Bosnia, Lt. General Sir Michael Rose: 'Patience, persistence and pressure is how you conduct a peacekeeping mission. Bombing is a last resort because then you cross the Mogadishu line'. This last comment, of course, refers to the failure of peace enforcement in Somalia (Guardian 30.9.1994).

In Bosnia, as in Somalia, the introduction of enforcement measures has been the subject of much controversy. It seems evident that in bitter intrastate conflicts, where there is limited military discipline on the part of participants and cease-fire violations are routine but unattributable, there is simply no peace to enforce. In consequence United Nations operations risk losing legitimacy associated with their symbolic character, without compensatory gains in credibility.

## Peacekeeping

'Peacekeeping' is defined in *Agenda for Peace* as 'the deployment of a United Nations presence in the field, hitherto with the consent of the parties concerned' (para. 20). The word *hitherto* suggests a departure from traditional peacekeeping principles, implying that peacekeepers may, in future, encounter opposition. The changed emphasis is intended to facilitate responses by the United Nations in the confused circumstances of intrastate conflicts, where it is not always clear from whom consent must be obtained. This is particularly relevant to situations, such as occurred in Somalia in 1992 and Rwanda in 1994, where there is a collapse of authority.

To increase the organization's capacity to respond rapidly and effectively to conflict situations, the Secretary-General has proposed a range of practical measures in relation to personnel, logistics and funding. These measures, again, require a new level of commitment from member states which does not appear to be readily forthcoming. In addition, the Secretary-General proposed that the possibility of closer cooperation between the United Nations and regional organizations be explored. This has resulted in agreement that organizations such as NATO and the Western European Union (WEU) can be put at the disposal of the United Nations on a case-by-case basis. Both these organizations have been involved in supporting the United Nations operations in Bosnia, while in 1994 the Organization of American States (OAS) was involved in operations in Haiti.

## Peace building

The final category of operation discussed in *Agenda for Peace* is post-conflict peace building. Here the intention is to consolidate and extend a range of activities which have developed over time. Post-conflict measures are potentially very broad in scope – from demilitarization procedures such as supervision of cease-fire agreements and removal of land mines, to reconstruction measures such as development of infrastructure, assistance with the creation of political institutions and supervision of elections. Peace building, in consequence, could involve substantial commitment, which was likened by Douglas Hurd, then UK Foreign Minister, to 'painting a country blue'. United Nations support for post-war reconstruction and institution building in Cambodia is an example of peace building, albeit with mixed success.

Again the proposals necessitate a high level of resource and other commitment from United Nations members. The case of Eritrea, which seceded from Ethiopia in 1991 after twenty-five years of civil war, exemplifies the need for comprehensive peace building measures. However a three-year programme for refugee reintegration and rehabilitation of settlement areas, launched in 1992 and costed at $262 million, had attracted only $32.4 million in pledges by the end of 1993 (Boutros-Ghali 1993a:97–8). In consequence the Secretary-General has expressed disappointment that commentary upon *Agenda for Peace* has given 'little attention' to the concept of peace building (ibid.:96).

Nevertheless the organization is involved in many tasks related to peace building, of which mine clearance is the most urgent. Estimates suggest the presence of at least ten million mines in Afghanistan, five million in Cambodia and two million in Mozambique, and in each case there is UN involvement in coordinating and funding mine clearance and in training mine clearers. In addition the organization has been increasingly involved in the provision of electoral assistance since the end of the Cold War – in 1993 the newly established Electoral Assistance Unit was involved, in a variety of ways, in thirty-four states.

## Summary

The proposals contained in *Agenda for Peace* have far-reaching implications. Emphasis on the fundamental relationship between peace, development and democracy underlines the notion that security is indivisible and hence a global issue. This approach is reflected in the proposals for preventive measures, amelioration and post-conflict peace building. All of these proposals accord with our concern to emphasize the many sources of insecurity.

Responses to *Agenda for Peace*, however, have focused almost exclusively upon proposals to enhance the United Nations' ability to respond to immediate rather than fundamental sources of conflict. These proposals suggest a major role for the organization in conflict between and within states, and new mechanisms for carrying out that role. In particular the proposed new categories of military operation – preventive deployment and peace enforcement – represent a major departure from traditional peacekeeping. They clearly envisage a more muscular response to conflict situations, with increased recourse to enforcement measures.

In situations of intrastate conflict, the proposals contained in *Agenda for Peace* have considerable implications for state sovereignty and the principle of non-intervention in the domestic affairs of states. This raises questions, which were not addressed in *Agenda for Peace*, about the moral and legal as well as the political and military implications of the Secretary-General's proposals; of their desirability as well as their feasibility. Failure to discuss the politics of collective action is understandable given the Secretary-General's position as an international civil servant. Failure to discuss the moral, and indeed legal, questions concerning the circumstances in which collective action is appropriate is, perhaps, a little surprising. Apparently the Secretary-General sees no need to question the legitimacy of the highly proactive role he envisages for the United Nations in the future.

## Collective Intervention in Intrastate Conflict

External, usually uninvited, interference in the domestic affairs of states was a common practice of both superpowers during the Cold War. Nevertheless, the norm of non-intervention in matters within the domestic jurisdiction of states has remained entrenched in international law. It is closely linked to the principle of sovereignty and applies equally to international organizations and to their members. In consequence it is at the heart of the contradiction between the social and humanitarian aims of the United Nations Charter, and the means of achieving these aims. It is central, also, to consideration of new approaches to security and insecurity.

The ending of the Cold War has removed many incentives for competitive, self-help intervention and shifted the focus of debate from realist justification of intervention on national security grounds, narrowly conceived, to liberal internationalist speculation concerning the potential for intervention in the interests of international security, broadly defined. Here, arguments centre upon the circumstances in which, if at all, intervention can be justified on humanitarian grounds.

### *Humanitarian intervention: the moral dimension*

Concern, here, is with the relationship between peace and justice or, more precisely, whether justice should be prioritized over peace. This debate engages liberal internationalists in particular: for realists the principal criterion guiding the practice of intervention remains pragmatic assessment of self-interest.

The norm of non-intervention was formulated in the interest of peace and is intended to reduce the incidence of interference by states in the domain of their neighbours. It has a moral dimension, none the less, in that it recognizes and respects, in principle, the rights of peoples to observe customs and practices in accordance with their distinctive cultural traditions. Herein, however, lies a dilemma: the non-intervention norm has all too frequently been invoked by regimes involved in systematic persecution or slaughter of sections of their populations. Consequently, bitter conflicts and repressive policies within states have been allowed to continue in the interest of averting interstate conflict and maintaining the reciprocity of the non-intervention norm. Indeed, on occasions where governments might well have sought to justify an intervention on humanitarian grounds, they have not done so. In one such case, the intervention by Indian forces in Pakistan which led to the secession of Bangladesh in 1971, the Indian government did refer to humanitarian grounds in justification of its action. However this reference was later deleted from the records of the Security Council and replaced by the claim that the intervention was an act of self-defence (Akehurst 1984:96). Later, in 1979, the Vietnamese government denied its role in the overthrow of the odious Pol Pot regime in Cambodia, while many governments – including those of the United Kingdom, the United States and a number of non-aligned countries – condemned the Vietnamese action. These, and other, examples led Akehurst to conclude in 1984 that 'there is now a consensus among states in favour of treating humanitarian intervention as illegal' (ibid.:99).

This consensus remained until the end of the Cold War but was subsequently challenged by events in the aftermath of the Gulf conflict. Following the defeat of Iraq, and encouraged by the rhetoric of western political leaders (notably US President George Bush) Kurdish and Shiite minority groups rebelled against the Iraqi regime. The brutal suppression of these rebellions and the subsequent flight of Kurds towards the Turkish border attracted considerable media coverage and public opinion was outraged. Eventually the western allies took action, sanctioned by the United Nations, to create 'safe havens' within Iraq for the Kurdish people. This intervention was justified by the Security Council in terms of 'threat to international peace and security' and must, in any event, be seen in the context of other intrusive measures imposed following the defeat of Iraq. Consequently Operation Provide Comfort was considered unlikely to have created a precedent for humanitarian intervention in the future (Mayall 1991:426).

To some extent this assessment was premature. During the years following the Gulf War there have been a further three cases where humanitarian interventions have been mounted by the United Nations at the behest of its members – in Bosnia, in Somalia and in Rwanda – while in 1994, with United Nations approval, a multi-national force dominated by the United States intervened for similar reasons in Haiti. In each of these cases the intervention followed extensive media coverage depicting the horrific effects of intercommunal conflict. The very mixed success of these interventions has added new urgency to debates concerning justice and the use of military means: transposed, in contemporary terms, to discussion of the circumstances in which collective intervention may be justified.

Positions in this debate range between two extremes – Gandhian pacifism, which maintains that use of military means is unacceptable in any circumstances; and deeply felt demands for urgent action regardless of the niceties of non-intervention norms. This view has been expressed by Hella Pick: 'Compassion, conscience, anger, passion itself are part of the equation for me, and surely also for countless others, as they see flitting across their television screens the suffering etched in the faces of innumerable anonymous people, so many of them children' (Pick 8.11.1992). Between these positions lie attempts to judge the rightness of collective intervention by applying the principles of the Just War tradition (Walzer 1980; Dunn 1994; Smith 1994). According to this tradition military action is subject to a number of criteria, some of which apply to the justice of the resort to military means, others to its conduct.

The criteria for the initiation of intervention demand that there must, firstly, be justice in the authority. In the contemporary cases of collective intervention with which we are concerned, formal authority has lain with the Security Council of the United Nations. Given the special status of permanent members within that body, it is necessary to question whether the United Nations possesses moral authority superior to that of states acting alone. For some commentators the answer is emphatically negative (Walzer 1980:107); the view of others is more nuanced (Smith 1994:139). Reform of the Security Council might, perhaps, enhance the moral authority of the UN.

The second and third criteria demand that there be justice in the cause of the intervention and the intention of those intervening. Insofar as humanitarian interventions are undertaken in defence of others with the intention of relieving suffering and promoting peace, these criteria may seem relatively unproblematic. Difficult questions arise, nevertheless, concerning the extent and degree of suffering which might justify coercive intervention in cases which fall short of genocide or mass starvation. This problem is intensified by partial media coverage and inconsistent action by governments and international organizations, as evidenced by the failure to respond to the persecution of the East Timorese people. If intervention is to be justified on moral grounds it must be practised impartially.

In addition, recourse to military means must be a last resort, a condition which implies the exhaustion of alternative measures and is notoriously difficult to assess. Moreover the need to respond militarily to situations aggravated by mass starvation, which has clearly developed over time, suggests the inadequacy or absence of ameliorative or preventive measures; indicating, again, a focus upon the effects rather than the causes of insecurity.

According to the Just War tradition the means employed must be proportional to the ends, a criterion which demands that the benefits of intervention outweigh the harm caused. In the case of the intervention in Somalia, for example, the loss of life of United Nations personnel and of innocent civilians, and the loss of credibility of the organization, must be weighed against any benefits achieved in reducing starvation – an impossible calculation. Finally, there must be reasonable hope that the operation will be successful, again a problematic criterion. Experience during the past three years suggests that, unless its aims are very modest, coercive intervention in civil conflicts is unlikely to achieve success.

The criteria governing the conduct of operations also raise some difficult issues. In particular the requirement for protection of non-combatants is highly problematic in circumstances of intercommunal conflict, where combatants and non-combatants tend to be indistinguishable. During the Somali operation considerable disquiet was expressed over the apparently indiscriminate use of force by United Nations troops. According to Amnesty International, 'Some of the civilians killed by UN or US troops seem to have been victims of the use of lethal force in breach of human rights and international humanitarian law obligations' (cited in Thakur 1994a:401). In these circumstances it is essential to establish that United Nations forces are subject to the constraints and processes of international law, an issue which was not addressed in *Agenda for Peace*.

Debates concerning the justice of collective intervention raise issues deserving careful consideration. Ultimately, however, arguments for intervention cite a moral imperative which rationalizes Hella Pick's plea for action, that is 'the most fundamental interpersonal claim of justice between human beings: the duty to preserve the other members of our species . . . as far as we readily can' (Dunn 1994:261). Arguments against intervention are more likely to be based upon the prohibitions of international law[15] or upon concerns about the feasibility of intervention. It is to these latter that we now turn.

## The feasibility of collective intervention

Here debate centres upon the interconnected political and military factors which may impede or undermine the practice of collective intervention. These link with the key concepts of legitimacy and credibility.

Legitimacy rests upon acceptance of the authority of the United Nations and, in situations of coercive collective intervention, it is the legitimacy of the Security Council which is at issue. The domination of this body by five powerful states with privileged status ensures that its decisions are selective and essentially status quo oriented. This contrasts with the position of the General Assembly, which is dominated numerically by Third World states and emphasizes distributive justice before order. As presently constituted, the Security Council reflects neither the membership nor the interests of the General Assembly and, in consequence, lacks legitimacy. Minor reforms such as accordance of permanent Security Council status to Japan and Germany would not resolve the problem of representational legitimacy; nor would they address the related issue of the permanent member veto, which further delegitimizes the Security Council's decisions. However the ability to take unilateral action without interference or even formal censure by the Security Council is unlikely to be relinquished by permanent members. The Russian government, for example, will wish to retain the ability to respond unilaterally to secessionist movements in the Caucasus and possibly, also, to instability in the 'near abroad' of the former Soviet republics. Consequently, the operations sanctioned by the Council are regarded in many Third World states as an expression of neo-imperialism; intervention by the strong in the affairs of the weak.

Credibility is a function of effectiveness which, in turn, depends upon political will. Here, while the Security Council has acquired a new ability to authorize action since the end of the Cold War, member states have shown reluctance to commit the financial resources and personnel necessary for implementation. There are a number of reasons for this. Interventions in civil wars are dangerous, uncertain of success and tend to involve high levels of commitment, over a long period of time. This places a heavy financial burden upon member states and causes problems where, as in the case of the United States, deployment of forces is contingent upon the maintenance of domestic support. The loss of American lives in Somalia in 1993 had considerable impact, and the United States government is unlikely to commit ground forces to United Nations operations in the foreseeable future. Indeed the new Republican majority in Congress attempted in February 1995, only a month after taking office, to gain control of policies related to commitment of resources to the United Nations, with the intention of impeding any future United States involvement in UN operations.

A number of additional factors associated with the management and execution of United Nations operations have also impinged upon the credibility of the organization. At the management level there is insufficient capacity or expertise for coordination of operations or for logistics planning. Moreover, since the UN lacks stocks of even the most basic equipment, procurement in the field tends to be a complicated and lengthy process.[16] While these problems might be addressed by administrative reform and more generous funding, others may be an inevitable result of multi-force operations. In particular, the considerable differences between military traditions and levels of training make cooperation difficult and reduce efficiency and effectiveness. In addition there is a tendency, for example among British and French forces, for individual contingents to refer orders from UN field commanders to their national headquarters for confirmation. This places in doubt their loyalty to commanders in the field and delays implementation of orders (Berdal 1993:70). These operational difficulties further erode the political will of member states to support United Nations operations. Where costs are high and benefits, in terms of achieving a successful outcome to the intervention, are uncertain, the incentives to free riding are strong.

Two remedies to the operational deficiencies of United Nations efforts were proposed in *Agenda for Peace*. The first, that dedicated and specifically trained forces and the necessary equipment be made available to the organization by member states, has provoked little practical response. The second, the utilization of regional organizations in support of UN operations, has already been attempted in Bosnia and elsewhere. There are a number of positive elements to this solution, in particular the availability of organizations such as NATO which satisfy two basic criteria – that is, having established procedures for multinational cooperation and sophisticated planning and logistics capabilities. In practice, however, there are few organizations other than NATO which meet the first of these criteria, and none which meet the second. The record of interventions by regional organizations suggests that, in addition to lack of capacity, the intervenors experience difficulty in maintaining impartiality and cohesion in situations where they tend to have close, prior links with the combatants. This was the case both with the European Community intervention prior to the dissolution of the Yugoslav Republic and the Arab League and Islamic Conference efforts in Somalia. In both cases United Nations intervention was requested following unsuccessful action by the regional organizations (Rivlin 1992:104).

While NATO may appear to be the organization best equipped to play a regional collective security role, the Bosnian operation has revealed many difficulties. NATO officers and officials have been impatient of United Nations procedures and divided over the wisdom of adhering to the UN method, based on impartiality and consensus building between parties to the conflict. Divisions between the United States and European NATO members over the conduct of the operation have been damaging to the alliance and call into question the likelihood of NATO forces operating under UN command in the future.

It is possible, however, that these problems of command and control and lack of capacity can be overcome, and that collaboration with regional organizations may, in the long term, help to address the lack of legitimacy and credibility suffered by the United Nations. This is certainly the hope of the Secretary-General, who argues that 'regional organizations must be helped to carry a larger share of the burden in peacemaking as well as peace keeping. Their involvement will in turn serve to promote the democratization of international relations' (quoted in Rivlin:110). These words encapsulate hopes that global problems of security and insecurity may one day find global solutions.

## Conclusion

The end of the Cold War brought hopes that the concept of national security, with its emphasis upon military rivalry between states, might be replaced by a universal concept of human security based on the understanding that much of the time, for most people, feelings of insecurity derive from the uncertainties of daily life. While the concept of security is increasingly used to refer to these broad issues, there is a danger that it may be irredeemably contaminated by its historical use in relation to national security. Consequently we have found it fruitful to refer, in addition, to the concept of insecurity.

The end of the Cold War brought hopes, also, that global solutions could be found, through a reformed and invigorated United Nations organization, to problems of insecurity deriving from a multitude of sources – economic, environmental, the practice of sexual or racial discrimination, the spread of infectious disease, or the outbreak of war. However our discussion of the moral arguments and practical problems associated with proposals intended to give substance to these hopes has identified a number of difficulties. In addition the record of post-Cold War UN operations has been discouraging.

Two sets of issues are troubling. Firstly, several of the proposals in *Agenda for Peace* are problematic. In particular the new measures intended to strengthen the enforcement capacity of the United Nations – preventive deployment and peace enforcement – confuse the principles of peacekeeping and collective security–deterrence. The difficulties caused by this have already been experienced in Bosnia and Somalia, with tragic results that have compounded the problems of legitimacy and credibility suffered by the United Nations. Moreover the climate of mutual recrimination which has attended failed peace enforcement deployments is not conducive to reasoned discussion of alternatives. Consequently, although the possibility of learning from past and present mistakes should not be dismissed, the present pattern of confused, tardy and *ad hoc* response to crises seems likely to continue for some time.

Secondly, and more fundamentally, the proposals for reform continue to prioritize immediate sources or manifestations of conflict over fundamental sources of insecurity. Moreover the continuing, and related, trends of economic liberalization and globalization militate against any reversal of this prioritization. While the application of some form of global Keynesianism may, in the future, provide solutions to some aspects of social and economic inequality (Murphy 1994:269), the deteriorating situation in Sub-Saharan Africa, for example, requires urgent attention. As yet there is little evidence of the political will necessary to deal with humanitarian crises of this magnitude; indeed governments and peoples in affluent regions are increasingly preoccupied with domestic issues. At present there appears to be little awareness that 'today there is no longer any such thing as someone else's problem' (Boutros-Ghali 1993b:96). In the long term, however, the insecurities generated by an increasingly complex and interlinked range of global issues may provide the impetus to seek fresh collective approaches to security, based upon a fundamental reformulation of its meaning and an appreciation that security is truly indivisible.

## Notes

1   This debate can be followed in the Journal of Peace Research. It was initiated by Johan Galtung's 1969 article 'Violence, Peace and Peace Research', to which Kenneth Boulding (1977) replied in strong terms.
2   This is demonstrated by the activities of the western peace movement during the Cold War, which were aimed exclusively at the security policies of individual western governments or of the western alliance.
3   'New Dimensions of Human Security' is the theme of the 1994 *Human Development Report* of the United Nations Development Programme. The concept of human security is expounded in chapter two of that Report.
4   The text of Article 1,3 reads as follows: 'To achieve international cooperation in solving international problems of an economic, social, cultural, or humanitarian character, and in promoting and encouraging respect for human rights and for fundamental freedoms for all without distinction as to race, sex, language, or religion.'
5   The intervening Principles (2 to 6) require the member states to abide by the terms of the Charter in the conduct of their relations with one another and with the organization.
6   The permanent members of the Security Council comprise The Republic of China, France, Russia (replacing the Union of Soviet Socialist Republics), the United Kingdom and the United States of America. The continuing dominance of the Security Council by these states has increasingly been contested in recent years – by liberal internationalists seeking

to reform and democratize the UN system and by governments of states such as India, Brazil, Germany and Japan seeking to attain permanent member status.

7   For a discussion of the 'extraordinary financial irresponsibility' of member states, see Higgins (1993:475–9).

8   For an interesting discussion of the use of the veto by Security Council permanent members see Morphet (1990).

9   For a full discussion of the Gulf War, accompanied by informative appendices, see Ken Matthews (1993) *The Gulf Conflict and International Relations*.

10  For a detailed discussion of peacekeeping operations see James (1990); alternatively a concise summary is provided by Goulding (1993).

11  These characteristics broadly follow those set out by Marrack Goulding, former United Nations Under-Secretary-General for Peacekeeping Operations, as the criteria of 'traditional peacekeeping' (Goulding 1993).

12  This was the position taken by Major-General Lewis Mackenzie, former UN commander in Sarajevo. He argued that, unlike the situation in Bosnia, enforcing peace in Somalia was a relatively easy military task and hence a suitable opportunity for a demonstration of the United Nations' credibility (cited in Thakur 1994a:396).

13  Relations between United States and United Nations officials quickly became strained during the Somali operation. By 1994 United States officials were describing the Secretary-General as 'egocentric, lacking in political and management skills, effective neither as a leader nor a bureaucrat' (cited in Thakur 1994a:408).

14  The mandate of the United Nations operation in Bosnia–Herzogovina (UNPROFOR II) is covered by several Security Council Resolutions and is multi-faceted and imprecise. It includes patrolling functions, securing Sarajevo airport, ensuring the safe movement of humanitarian aid, protecting convoys of detainees and monitoring compliance with a ban on military flights over Bosnia–Herzogovina. As has been pointed out, this mandate is totally unrealistic in a bitter civil war where there is no cease-fire agreement in place (Higgins 1993:469).

15  The legal position was briefly discussed in relation to the provisions of the United Nations Charter. The contradiction between humanitarian law and the principle of state sovereignty has been differently interpreted by international lawyers, however, and in recent years has been the subject of intensified debate. See, for example, Damrosch, L. F. and Scheffer, D. J. (eds) 1991, *Law and Force in the New International Order*.

16  For a detailed discussion of the operational difficulties experienced in Bosnia by UNPROFOR II see Berdal 1993.

# Part II

# Globalization:
# Issues and Processes

# 7

# Change and Development in the Global Economy

## Chris Mulhearn

Let us begin with some reflections on the meaning of the term 'global economy'. In theoretical terms, an economy – local, regional, national or international – is simply a level at which a number of important economic relationships are articulated. The economies of advanced states, for example, are characterized by relatively open labour, goods and capital markets. People with the necessary qualifications and experience are able to move fairly easily from job to job; there are few restrictions on what and at what price individuals can buy and sell to one another; and savings and investment opportunities are similarly unconstrained. These different markets are themselves regulated and controlled by legal, institutional, social and cultural frameworks. Thus, one simple 'test' for globalization might be the extent to which such conditioned but otherwise relatively open relationships now obtain at the global level: is the world economy becoming as coherent an entity as an advanced national economy?

There are, however, several problems with this rather blunt approach. In the first place, it is possible to argue that global economic reach is not a particularly *new* phenomenon: witness claims that the second half of the nineteenth century was the 'golden age' of capitalism. During that period, the development of international trade, capital and labour markets facilitated unprecedented economic expansion in what were to become the advanced industrial nations, as well as the rapid growth of a large number of primary commodity exporters (Williamson and Milner 1991). World markets clearly have an established history.

Secondly, it is important to recognize that while some features of a global economy are in place, there is a very real unevenness inherent in the globalization process. At one level this means that some states, societies or communities may be relatively or absolutely impoverished by their integration into the global network; consider, for example, the disruption and dislocation experienced in less developed societies by agricultural populations as a result of rapid industrialization. Equally significant, the reaction of threatened interest groups to actual or perceived global threats may serve to impede further integration. For example, the spectacular growth rates achieved by the newly industrializing countries (NICs) such as Taiwan since the 1960s have in part rested on the competitive advantage bestowed by their looser (that is cheaper) labour markets. In the industrial countries, the price of so-called 'shifting comparative advantage' has been paid by displaced labour and capital in industries such as clothing and footwear. This in turn has led to the emergence of new forms of protection in the advanced economies which actually serve to restrict the process of globalization. It is apparent, then, that global processes are not unfolding in a simple linear fashion, without controversy; they are subject to a range of countervailing tendencies and pressures.

Thirdly, the major international economic institutions which emerged in the aftermath of World War Two, and upon which much global economic momentum rests, continue to be subject both to episodic crises and secular forms of decay. The 1986–94 struggle to settle the Uruguay Round of the General Agreement on Tariffs and Trade (GATT) provides a recent example of global institutional weakness. Although the round has been hailed, ultimately, as a success, it leaves unresolved the most important issues of trade liberalization upon which it had intended to focus (see section below on GATT). These have critical implications for future global integration. Similar questions remain over the future of the Bretton Woods institutions and the unwelcome drift of the international monetary system (see section below on the Bretton Woods system). Can strong claims be made for globalization when its institutional framework is clearly in some difficulty?

Fourthly, there is an apparent tension between the expressed interests of governments and the growing economic powers and capacities of international capital, both financial and industrial. As in the case of recent protectionist sentiment, this does not deny the acceleration of the shift to the global, but it again suggests that the process can be a contentious one. The Exchange Rate Mechanism (ERM) crisis of 1992, which saw sterling's membership of the fixed currency system suspended and other major currencies, notably the French franc, come under severe pressure, arose because of the existence of huge rootless concentrations of *finance capital* which were used to 'target' selected currencies. In sterling's case, the combined resources and political will of the member states of the European Community proved insufficient to mount an effective defence. The objectives of global *industrial capital* may also clash with the interests of nation-states. For example, the growing investments in less developed countries (LDCs) by trans-national corporations (TNCs) are often claimed to be exploitative rather than developmental, transferring few skills, technologies and relatively little income to the peripheral parts of the globe (Brandt 1980).

These issues complicate rather than deny the process and level of modern economic globalization. Evidence cited below will demon-strate that economic activity *is* increasingly coordinated on a global basis. Moreover, given the integration of virtually all the former planned communist economies into the western market system, global integration is likely to accelerate beyond the millennium. However, the discussion thus far suggests that globalization is an uneven, contested and unstable process. It is certainly one which has benefited some economic agents more than others and as such it is, simultaneously, the focus of affirming action by those who would gain from it, and attempts at denial and limitation by those who might lose. The instability of the globalization process has arisen both from purposeful attempts to constrain it on the part of those who perceive some aspect of it as threatening and from the decay of those international institutions which have promoted and conditioned its progress.

Let us turn, then, to description and analysis of the global economy. Notwithstanding the claims of earlier times, this chapter will concen-trate on the post-war period as the focus of three major developments:

1  unprecedented growth and change in increasingly integrated world markets;
2  the emergence for the first time of global economic institutions;
3  the emergence, again for the first time, of large numbers of globally oriented industrial and financial firms.

## Change and Development in the Global Marketplace since 1945

An unprecedented amount of goods and services has been produced and traded in the world economy during the post-war period. Both output and export growth during the post-war boom were at least twice as fast as had been achieved in any earlier industrial period (Armstrong, Glyn and Harrison 1991). Many economists claim a causal link be-tween trade and growth: it is the new markets for goods and services which stimulate increases in production; see, for example, Kenwood and Lougheed (1992) and Grimwade (1989). This argument implies that a more open and integrated world economy will also necessarily be a materially wealthier one.

However, while this appears to be the case in aggregate, post-war economic expansion has followed a much more complex course when particular countries and groups of countries are considered. This applies also to the changing nature of what is traded. For the most part, the more affluent countries have retained their elevated positions, though there have been some notable changes within this group: the rise of Japan and Germany in particular and the relative weakening, amongst others, of the United States and the UK. The poorer countries on the other hand, again with a small number of important 'newly industrializing' exceptions, have remained relatively impoverished. The key to progress in the developing post-war global economy appears to be participation in the growing global market for manufactured goods or, to a lesser extent, the possession of oil. Specialization in the production and exchange of primary commodities and food makes at best for very modest economic development, given the long-term stagnation of the markets for this kind of output.

Table 7.1 illustrates the conventional relationship between trade and economic growth. In each period, it is the growth in trade which has 'led' production. Note, however, the slowdown in the expansion of world trade in the 1970s and 1980s and the concomitant slackening of output growth. The average rates of growth for the 'boom' years – between 5 and 6 per cent – compare very favourably with the equivalent figures for earlier periods. Thus for 1870–1913, the noted 'golden age' of industrial capitalism, output growth averaged 2.6 per cent per

**Table 7.1** Growth of world output and merchandise trade, 1960–1993[a] (annual average % change in volume)

|  | Output | Trade |
|---|---|---|
| 1961–1970 | 6 | 8.5 |
| 1971–1980 | 4 | 5.0 |
| 1981–1987 | 2 | 2.5 |
| 1988–1993[b] | 2.5 | 5.6 |

[a] Note that international trade data may contain some valuation discrepancies and other inconsistencies. For a brief discussion see GATT (1987) pp. 148–52.
[b] 1993 IMF estimate
*Sources*: GATT (1987), IMF (1992)

**Table** 7.2 Average rates of annual growth of national income 1951–1969

|                    | %  |
| ------------------ | -- |
| Six EEC Countries* | 5  |
| Japan              | 10 |
| UK                 | 3  |
| USA                | 4  |

* Belgium, France, West Germany, Italy, Luxembourg, Netherlands
*Source*: Dalton (1974)

annum; while for 1913–50 the average rate was only 1.9 per cent (Kenwood and Lougheed 1992).

The most buoyant phase of post-war expansion – the 1950s and 1960s – was associated with uniformly higher rates of growth in the advanced industrial countries than anything previously experienced (see table 7.2), together with 'full employment' but without the now commonplace attendant inflationary difficulties. By the early 1970s output in the leading economies was almost three times as great as it had been in 1950 (Armstrong, Glyn and Harrison 1991). In terms of the growth and integration of markets, the years 1950–70 can be conceived of as a period of *global foundation*. The *dis*integration of the world economy which took place during the 1930s presented the architects of the post-war economic environment with an enormous task. The mutually destructive isolationism and protectionism of the later inter-war years had to be replaced with a framework conducive to growth, prosperity and full employment. The structure which emerged provided for an increasingly open and integrated nexus of markets which would rapidly mature at the global level. While it is true that the post-1970 period has been one of slower growth and a more fitful evolution of these markets, this still represents growth and evolution from the plane of the most intense and dynamic period of economic development in human history. Hence the interpretation of the post-war boom as the foundation of the global economy.

Let us now begin to consider the performances of individual industrial countries in this shift to the global. Although the Japanese economy can be seen from table 7.2 to have grown at a quite phenomenal rate, it is useful to look first at what is still the world's largest economy: the United States.

Although it grew relatively slowly during the post-war boom in comparison to some other countries, the United States began the period in a position of enormous absolute economic strength with over half world GDP and two-thirds of the world's gold reserves. Such a huge initial advantage allows a primary position to be sustained even with moderate income growth: a modest expansion of a massive income is still a significant absolute increase. Moreover, although its share of world income has been trimmed since 1945, the United States remains economically almost twice as large as Japan, its nearest rival, and its economy is bigger than all the 138 developing countries, as defined by the IMF, put together. Table 7.3 provides the relevant details. The table also illustrates the significance of Japanese economic progress and the pre-eminence of Germany in relation to the other European countries.

The success of both Japan and Germany during this period can be linked to their striking ability to compete in the burgeoning global market. For example, between 1963 and 1973 world trade increased almost threefold, but Japanese exports increased in value by a factor of six (GATT 1987).

In fact, it is possible to understand the post-war fortunes of most countries by reference to their ability to compete in world markets. Table 7.4 shows the changing 'network' of world trade between 1963 and 1986. Notice first the relative stability of the shares of the three major country groups during this period. The developed countries increased their share of the world market by approximately 2.5 per cent

**Table 7.3** Shares in world GDP, selected countries and groups 1987–1989

|  | *No. of countries* | *Share of world GDP %* |
|---|---|---|
| United States |  | 27.1 |
| Japan |  | 15.3 |
| Germany |  | 6.6 |
| France |  | 5.2 |
| Italy |  | 4.6 |
| UK |  | 4.4 |
| Canada |  | 2.7 |
| Other industrial countries | 16 | 10.5 |
| Industrial Countries | 23 | 76.4 |
| Developing countries | 138 | 23.8 |
| WORLD | 161 | 100.0 |

*Source*: IMF (1991)

(i.e. from 67.1 to 69.6 per cent), while the shares of the developing countries and the old Eastern bloc fell by approximately 1.25 per cent each.

However, when we begin to look at the finer details, some striking patterns begin to emerge. The Japanese share of world trade has virtually trebled, while that of South and East Asia has almost doubled. The latter increase helps to explain the consistently rapid economic growth of what the IMF refers to as 'newly industrializing Asian countries' which comprise Hong Kong, Korea, Singapore and Taiwan. The other, albeit more modestly successful, areas are Western Europe, to which the German contribution is significant; and the oil-rich Middle East. The regions which have had their shares of world trade eroded are North America; Latin America; Australia, New Zealand; South Africa and Africa. Though, because of its size, the United States is less trade dependent than many other countries, its declining share of world GDP – from 50 per cent in 1945 to 27 per cent in 1989 – is in part explained by its inability over the post-war period to maintain competitiveness in world markets.

Among the developing countries, the considerable unevenness in performance requires some explanation. Taking the post-war period as a whole, these countries have generally experienced faster GDP and GDP per capita growth than the developed countries (Kenwood and Lougheed 1992). Unfortunately, however, strong average growth arises from the exceptional performance of a very small number of NICs combined with weakness elsewhere. Again the key to what has happened appears to lie in trade performance. Table 7.4 illustrates the singular achievements of Japan in securing ever larger slices of the global market, but even Japanese success is put into perspective by the individual performances of the four newly industrializing Asian economies. For the period 1970–86, world exports grew on average by 4 per cent per annum, compared with the Japanese figure of 8 per cent. The Asian economies on the other hand all performed better. The relevant figures are: Hong Kong, 10 per cent; Singapore, 12 per cent; Taiwan, 16 per cent; and Korea, 19 per cent (GATT 1987).

The post-war development of these economies is quite spectacular. Between 1965 and 1989 each grew at an annual average per capita income rate of about 7 per cent (Chowdhury and Islam 1993). In 1960, Korean per capita income had been 5 per cent of the US level; by 1992 it had risen to 29 per cent: almost on a par with the more peripheral members of the European Union (OECD 1994). Table 7.5 compares the Asian NIC per capita growth rates with those of other groups.

If success in a growing world market explains the new-found economic strength of the Asian NICs, what underpins their export competitiveness? This is a crucial question, not least because the apparent

**Table 7.4** World merchandise trade, 1963, 1973 and 1986 $bn and percentage shares

|  | 1963 | | 1973 | | 1986 | |
|---|---|---|---|---|---|---|
|  | $ | % | $ | % | $ | % |
| North America | 29.6 | 19.2 | 95.5 | 16.6 | 288.9 | 13.6 |
| Japan | 5.5 | 3.6 | 36.9 | 6.4 | 209.1 | 9.9 |
| Western Europe | 64.2 | 41.7 | 258.8 | 45.1 | 939.3 | 44.3 |
| Aus. N.Z. & S. Africa | 4.3 | 2.8 | 15.4 | 2.7 | 37.8 | 1.8 |
| DEVELOPED COUNTRIES | 103.6 | 67.3 | 406.6 | 70.8 | 1,475.1 | 69.6 |
| Latin America | 11.3 | 7.3 | 29.5 | 5.1 | 89.5 | 4.2 |
| S. & E. Asia | 8.4 | 5.5 | 31.6 | 5.5 | 194.0 | 9.2 |
| Middle East | 5.3 | 3.4 | 27.5 | 4.8 | 78.5 | 3.7 |
| Africa | 6.6 | 4.3 | 20.9 | 3.6 | 50.0 | 2.4 |
| DEVELOPING AREAS[a] | 31.6 | 20.5 | 109.5 | 19.0 | 412.0 | 19.5 |
| EASTERN BLOC | 18.7 | 12.1 | 57.2 | 10.0 | 229.5 | 10.8 |
| WORLD | 153.9 | 100.0 | 573.3 | 100.0 | 2,116.6 | 100.0 |

[a] Includes developing countries and territories which do not belong to the four geographic areas indicated.
*Source*: GATT (1987)

**Table 7.5** Average annual growth of GNP per capita 1965–1990

|  | % |
|---|---|
| Asian NICs | 7.0 |
| Japan | 4.2 |
| OECD | 2.4 |
| South Asia | 1.9 |
| Latin America & Caribbean | 1.8 |
| Sub-Saharan Africa | 0.3 |

*Source*: OECD (1994)

success of these economies suggests the prospect of similar participation in the global economy for other developing countries. According to Singer and Ansari (1988), if the developing countries grew at an annual rate of 5 per cent for 50 years, they would attain *current* developed country income and output levels. The experience of the Asian NICs – faster growth over a shorter period – suggests this is possible. Nevertheless, the question remains; in the modern global context, is this a general possibility?

The progress of the Asian NICs in world markets has been, and remains, crucially dependent on their capacity to successfully develop manufacturing industry. Table 7.6 shows the long-term growth in world trade and output, 1960–86, disaggregated by major product group. While both trade and output growth slackened after 1970, it can be seen that, over the period as a whole, manufacturing remained the most consistently dynamic sector. Consequently, its *share* of trade also increased (see table 7.7).

Agricultural production has been relatively stable over the entire period, with some recent slackening of trade. This sector is constrained by income inelastic demand, which means that, as world incomes rise,

**Table 7.6** Growth in world trade and output by sector, 1960–86 (Annual average percentage change)

|  | *1960–70* | *1971–80* | *1981–86* |
|---|---|---|---|
| EXPORTS |  |  |  |
| Agriculture | 4.0 | 4.5 | 1.0 |
| Mining | 7.0 | 1.5 | −1.5 |
| Manufacturing | 10.5 | 7.0 | 4.5 |
| TOTAL TRADE | 8.5 | 5.0 | 3.0 |
| PRODUCTION |  |  |  |
| Agriculture | 2.5 | 2.0 | 2.5 |
| Mining | 5.5 | 2.5 | −1.5 |
| Manufacturing | 7.5 | 4.5 | 2.5 |
| TOTAL OUTPUT | 6.0 | 4.0 | 2.0 |

*Source*: GATT (1987)

**Table 7.7** Development of world merchandise exports 1980 and 1986

|  | *1980* | | *1986* | |
|---|---|---|---|---|
|  | *$bn* | *%* | *$bn* | *%* |
| Agriculture | 299 | 15 | 298 | 14 |
| Minerals | 567 | 29 | 345 | 17 |
| Manufacturing | 1,095 | 55 | 1,431 | 68 |
| TOTAL | 1,990 | 100 | 2,119 | 100 |

*Source*: GATT (1987)

the demand for food increases at a slower rate. Extra income is used instead for the purchase of manufactured goods and services. The performance of the mining/minerals sector is heavily conditioned by the market for oil. The major oil price rises of 1973–4 and 1980 partly explain the recorded fall in trade and output in this sector, though the subsequent oil price decline over most of the 1980s allowed trade and output to recover somewhat after 1986.

The overwhelming conclusion emerging from these data is that to successfully compete in the global economy and to enjoy the high growth that results it is necessary, in the absence of oil, for a country to specialize in the production of manufactures. As we shall see, this is precisely what the Asian NICs have done.

Table 7.8 shows the origin and destination of manufacturing exports for the developed, developing and eastern trading areas between 1963 and 1986. A number of important changes in the patterns of manufacturing trade are evident. Note first, however, that manufacturing production and consumption remains largely a developed country phenomenon. In 1963, the developed countries produced approx-

**Table 7.8** World exports of manufactures by main areas in 1963, 1970, 1973, 1979 and 1986, $bn and %

| Destination → <br> Origin | | Developed | | Developing | | Eastern | | World | |
|---|---|---|---|---|---|---|---|---|---|
| | | Value | Share | Value | Share | Value | Share | Value | Share |
| Developed | 1963 | 47.7 | 58.8 | 16.9 | 20.8 | 2.2 | 2.7 | 66.8 | 82.3 |
| Area | 1970 | 121.9 | 63.9 | 32.1 | 16.8 | 6.3 | 3.3 | 160.3 | 84.0 |
| | 1973 | 221.5 | 63.8 | 54.5 | 15.7 | 12.7 | 3.6 | 288.7 | 83.1 |
| | 1979 | 551.6 | 58.4 | 186.9 | 19.8 | 38.0 | 4.0 | 776.5 | 82.2 |
| | 1986 | 874.6 | 61.1 | 211.9 | 14.8 | 52.2 | 3.6 | 1,138.7 | 79.6 |
| Developing | 1963 | 2.0 | 2.4 | 1.4 | 1.8 | 0.1 | 0.1 | 3.5 | 4.3 |
| Area | 1970 | 6.4 | 3.4 | 3.4 | 1.8 | 0.4 | 0.2 | 10.2 | 5.4 |
| | 1973 | 16.3 | 4.7 | 6.9 | 2.0 | 0.8 | 0.2 | 24.0 | 6.9 |
| | 1979 | 53.7 | 5.7 | 30.5 | 3.2 | 1.8 | 0.2 | 86.0 | 9.1 |
| | 1986 | 118.2 | 8.3 | 41.8 | 2.9 | 9.1 | 0.6 | 169.1 | 11.8 |
| Eastern | 1963 | 1.1 | 1.4 | 1.6 | 1.6 | 8.1 | 10.0 | 10.8 | 13.3 |
| Trading | 1970 | 3.0 | 1.6 | 2.9 | 1.6 | 14.3 | 7.5 | 20.2 | 10.6 |
| Area | 1973 | 5.6 | 1.6 | 4.6 | 1.3 | 24.5 | 7.0 | 34.7 | 10.0 |
| | 1979 | 15.6 | 1.7 | 13.7 | 1.5 | 53.2 | 5.6 | 82.5 | 8.7 |
| | 1986 | 23.4 | 1.6 | 22.4 | 1.6 | 77.8 | 5.4 | 123.6 | 8.6 |
| WORLD | 1963 | 50.8 | 62.7 | 19.9 | 24.6 | 10.4 | 12.8 | 81.1 | 100.0 |
| | 1970 | 131.3 | 68.8 | 38.4 | 20.1 | 21.0 | 11.0 | 190.7 | 100.0 |
| | 1973 | 243.4 | 70.1 | 66.0 | 19.0 | 38.0 | 10.9 | 347.4 | 100.0 |
| | 1979 | 620.9 | 65.7 | 231.1 | 24.5 | 93.0 | 9.8 | 945.0 | 100.0 |
| | 1986 | 1,016.2 | 71.0 | 276.1 | 19.3 | 139.1 | 9.7 | 1,431.2 | 100.0 |

*Source*: GATT (1987)

**Table 7.9** World's leading exporters of manufactures in 1970, 1980 and 1986

|  | *1970* | | *1980* | | *1986* | |
|---|---|---|---|---|---|---|
|  | *$bn* | *%* | *$bn* | *%* | *$bn* | *%* |
| Germany | 29.9 | 15.7 | 162.1 | 14.8 | 213.0 | 14.9 |
| Japan | 17.9 | 9.4 | 122.7 | 11.2 | 201.9 | 14.1 |
| USA | 28.4 | 14.9 | 139.5 | 12.7 | 147.3 | 10.3 |
| France | 13.1 | 6.9 | 81.2 | 7.4 | 90.2 | 6.3 |
| Italy | 11.0 | 5.7 | 61.5 | 6.0 | 85.2 | 6.0 |
| UK | 15.5 | 8.1 | 81.8 | 7.5 | 77.7 | 5.4 |
| Canada | 8.2 | 4.3 | 30.4 | 2.8 | 53.1 | 3.7 |
| Belgium-Lux. | 8.6 | 4.5 | 44.4 | 4.1 | 50.1 | 3.5 |
| Netherlands | 6.6 | 3.5 | 37.0 | 3.4 | 45.6 | 3.2 |
| Taiwan | 1.1 | 0.6 | 17.4 | 1.6 | 36.2 | 2.5 |
| Switzerland | 4.6 | 2.4 | 26.6 | 2.4 | 35.0 | 2.5 |
| Hong Kong | 2.3 | 1.2 | 18.0 | 1.6 | 32.4 | 2.4 |
| Korea | 0.6 | 0.3 | 15.6 | 1.4 | 31.9 | 2.2 |
| Sweden | 5.1 | 2.7 | 24.0 | 2.2 | 30.8 | 2.2 |
| USSR | 5.0 | 2.6 | 19.5 | 1.8 | 25.0 | 1.7 |
| Spain | 1.3 | 0.7 | 14.9 | 1.4 | 20.5 | 1.4 |
| Austria | 2.3 | 1.2 | 14.5 | 1.3 | 19.7 | 1.4 |
| China | 0.3 | 0.2 | 3.0 | 0.3 | 13.6 | 1.0 |
| Singapore | 0.4 | 0.2 | 9.0 | 0.8 | 13.3 | 0.9 |

*Source*: GATT (1987)

imately 82 per cent of the world's manufactures and consumed 63 per cent of world manufacturing output. By 1986 the equivalent figures were 80 and 71 per cent respectively.

The most significant change revealed in the table concerns the production of manufactures in the developing area (which includes the Asian and other NICs). This jumped from 4.3 per cent of total world output in 1963 to 11.8 per cent in 1986. The share of developing country consumption over this period, on the other hand, actually fell from 24.6 to 19.3 per cent, though it increased in absolute terms. Since both production and consumption shares in the eastern area fell by roughly 5 and 3 per cent respectively, it is possible to argue that there was a shift in the share of manufacturing production from the developed and eastern trading areas to the developing area; and a shift in the opposite direction in terms of the share of consumption.

Tables 7.8 and 7.9 demonstrate the extremely polarized form that developing country industrialization has assumed over the last twenty-five years. Table 7.9 depicts a hierarchy of the world's leading manufacturing exporters, delineated according to the share of total manufacturing trade in 1986. The sharp pace of industrialization in the four Asian NICs is apparent. For example, the Korean share of manufacturing trade had increased from 0.3 per cent in 1970 to 2.2 per cent by 1986. The value of Asian manufacturing exports in 1986 was 113.8$bn out of a total for the developing countries as a whole (from table 7.8) of 169$bn. In other words, fully 67 per cent of developing country exports was accounted for by the Asian economies. This means that the new found manufacturing presence of the developing countries in the global economy must be largely attributed to the NICs.

Two issues now arise: how did the Asian economies succeed in developing highly competitive manufacturing capacity and can this pattern of economic maturation be emulated by other developing countries? Greenaway (1983) argues that the Asian and other NICS initially took advantage of a shifting comparative advantage in the production of labour-intensive manufactures; essentially they were able to produce such goods more cheaply because of lower labour and other costs. More recent analyses contend that the Asian economies in particular are rapidly increasing the sophistication of what they produce and how they produce it (see, for example, Chowdhury and Islam 1993).

More important, from the perspective of globalization, is the issue of emulation. We know from tables 7.8 and 7.9 that the NICs are very few in number and that they account for most of the developing area's manufacturing exports. Moreover, any increase in NIC manufacturing output, whether from existing or new NICs, must find developed area markets – between 1963 and 1986 developing area consumption of its own manufactures increased by only 1 per cent. Are the developed area markets likely to be open and available? Despite the sixteen-fold increase in manufacturing trade over the post-war period (Grimwade 1989), the outlook is officially recognized to be poor (United Nations 1987). Table 7.6 quantified the slowdown in world manufacturing trade and output over the 1970s and 1980s. This does not augur well for further industrialization in the developing area. Moreover, this problem is compounded by reaction in the developed countries to slower growth and greater import penetration from the NICs.

A more detailed treatment of trade liberalization in the post-war period is included in our discussion of GATT later in this chapter. Nevertheless, a few initial points may usefully be made. Greenaway (1983) demonstrates the way in which, during the 1960s and 1970s, the NICs were able to exploit their capacity for relatively low cost production in labour-intensive manufacturing such as textiles and clothing, footwear, toys and sports goods. This allowed these countries to shake off old dependencies on primary products – foodstuffs and raw materials. But the development of manufacturing capacity had production and consumption implications for the advanced countries where most of the new output was to be sold (see table 7.8). On the one hand, western consumers benefited from the availability of a new source of attractively priced commodities but, on the other, western capital and labour employed in these industries were clearly threatened by a new and effective form of competition. While consumers tend not to act collectively in the promotion of their interests, capital and labour clearly do. There consequently arose in the West an effective lobbying system designed to protect threatened industries from 'cheap foreign imports'.

It is important to be aware that these developments were taking place in the context of a rapidly emerging liberalized trading environment actively promoted by GATT (and in particular its western contracting parties) which made traditional forms of protectionism – tariffs and quotas – either illegal or difficult and costly to implement. The response of the advanced countries has been to create separate trade agreements for some goods or, more generally, to indulge in wholly new forms of protectionism outside the GATT framework. In the former case, for example, the Multifibre Agreement permits GATT-illegal quotas against cotton, woollen and synthetic textile products from the developing nations. Elsewhere the developed nations have introduced a panoply of non-tariff barriers to trade (see section below on GATT) which, though initially aimed at the NICs, have become much more pervasive, even to the extent that no one class of countries appears unwilling to apply them.

This, the so-called *new protectionism*, is significant at two levels. First, it is an implicit attempt on the part of the developed countries to control the new international division of labour. This term refers to the shift in certain forms of manufacturing capacity from the developed area to the NICs, together with the associated reduction in primary production in the NICs. The suggestion is that the traditional specialization and trade relationships between the developed and the developing areas are being recast: century-old certainties over who does what in the world economy no longer apply. The extent of the shift away from primary production among selected NICs is detailed in table 7.10.

For some of the advanced countries, the NIC threat and new-found manufacturing weaknesses pose difficult questions of accommodation. For example, table 7.9 demonstrated the significant loss of manufacturing market share by the USA and UK since 1970. Notice that every country in the top ten of manufacturing exporters, except for Japan, Italy and Taiwan, has also lost some market share. It is in this context that the rise of the new protectionism can be understood and its implications for the process of globalization noted. The advanced

**Table 7.10** Commodity composition and growth of merchandise exports for selected NICs

| | Average % change p.a. 1970–8 | % shares of merchandise exports | | | | | |
| --- | --- | --- | --- | --- | --- | --- | --- |
| | | Primary commodities | | Textiles & clothing | | Other manufactures | |
| | | 1960 | 1977 | 1960 | 1977 | 1960 | 1977 |
| Hong Kong | 4.8 | 20 | 4 | 45 | 46 | 35 | 50 |
| Korea | 28.8 | 86 | 15 | 8 | 32 | 8 | 53 |
| Philippines | 5.4 | 96 | 75 | 1 | 5 | 3 | 20 |
| Singapore | 9.8 | 74 | 56 | 5 | 5 | 21 | 39 |

*Source*: Greenaway (1983)

countries clearly perceive the new international division of labour to be a threat: to *their* growth, income and employment prospects. Their reaction, over a long period, has been to try to constrain and limit this threat; axiomatically, globalization is also constrained. It is important not to overstate the significance of such countervailing tendencies to global integration at their current level of intensity, but their potential to develop further momentum should not be ignored.

This brings us to the second issue raised by the emergence of the new protectionism. While it is true that this phenomenon initially characterized developed/developing area relations, it has since become a more generalized problem. The slowdown in world trade and economic growth since the early 1970s, and the associated structural unemployment problems in the West, have prompted the advanced countries to implement protectionist measures against one another as well as against the developing area countries. The main danger here is the possibility of the revival of more open and widespread protectionism, perhaps on a scale reminiscent of the early 1930s when the consequent collapse in world trade led to the deepest crisis ever faced by the capitalist system. While guarding against overstatement, should spiralling protectionism re-emerge it is impossible to know in advance how, when and at what cost a halt could be called.

Having discussed the new forms of global integration involving the developed countries and the NICs, we must consider the implications of globalization for two remaining groups of developing countries: the oil exporting nations and the poorer, often debt-ridden, African and Latin American countries.

It has, perhaps, become a commonplace that the possession of oil resources is a guarantee of national prosperity. Certainly, during the

1970s, the oil exporting countries recorded the highest rates of growth in the developing area. This resulted from two major oil price rises and the highly price-inelastic demand for oil evident at this time. However, reactions to these price rises among the oil importing countries radically altered the picture during the 1980s. The Organization for Economic Cooperation and Development (OECD) countries – the biggest net oil importers – introduced a series of energy efficiency and fuel switching measures which led to a fall in oil consumption over the first half of the 1980s (GATT 1987). Subsequent reductions in the price of oil helped, in part, to reverse this trend (IMF 1991) but high growth trajectories for the oil exporters have yet to re-emerge. Between 1973 and 1982, fuel exporting countries achieved an average annual growth rate of almost 5 per cent, compared with only 1 per cent from 1983 to 1991 (IMF 1991). In terms of the developing countries as a whole, the leading NICs had, by 1986, assumed a greater share of merchandise exports (including oil) than the OPEC (Organization of Petroleum Exporting Countries) countries (see table 7.11).

The shifting fortunes of the oil exporters are particularly interesting when set within the context of globalization. There can be no doubt about the global impact of the oil shocks of 1973–4 and 1980, but the evidence suggests that global adjustment and accommodation processes are also well developed. As in the case of the new protectionism, where new economic forces threaten to unsettle established patterns of development, limiting countervailing pressures are soon evident. However, notice that the 'problems' in both these instances impact negatively upon the developed area. Aspects of global economic change which have negative implications for the less developed area itself are treated with markedly less alacrity. The developing area's debt crisis, for example, often appears to become a significant focus for attention only when default threatens the integrity of the western banking system. It is to an examination of the implications of globalization for the debt-ridden Latin American and African economies that we now turn.

**Table 7.11** Merchandise exports of the developing area by selected group, 1980 and 1986

|  | %<br>1980 | %<br>1986 |
|---|---|---|
| OPEC | 54 | 29 |
| Six NICs | 20 | 41 |
| Other developing countries | 26 | 30 |

*Source*: GATT (1987)

## The Problem of Debt

The debt problem is a spectacular example of modern global linkage. Its origins lie in the huge balance of payments surpluses accumulated by the oil exporting nations after the first major oil price shock. The corollary of external surplus for oil exporters was, of course, external deficit for oil importers; the question then posed was how to pay the inflated fuel bills. At this time a number of factors conspired to make borrowing by the non-oil producing developing countries attractive, and the oil country surpluses were duly lent on to them. The new debtors were viewed as good risks because of the strength of their primary commodity prices and the strong demand for these goods (Thirlwall 1994). Export led growth would be the means by which the loans were repaid. Unfortunately, however, slower growth and higher interest rates in the advanced countries at the start of the 1980s undermined primary commodity markets and the prospect of long-term debt emerged as a direct consequence.

The general implications of the debt problem for the debtor countries can be briefly stated. Given poor export earnings, they lack the ability to generate sufficient foreign exchange with which to repay the debt and the interest thereon. In such circumstances, these countries may be forced to sacrifice imports – necessary for growth or for immediate consumption needs – in order to meet debt obligations. Some notion of the kind of sacrifice that might be necessary is given by the debt-service ratio. This indicates the proportion of export earnings upon which debt obligations have an effective prior claim. In the mid-1980s the debt-service ratio for all developing countries reached 25 per cent but fell back to 20 per cent by 1990, partly because of debt rescheduling (Thirlwall 1994).

Debt-service problems have been particularly acute in Africa. GATT (1987) estimates that the debt-service ratio for Sudan in 1986–7 was actually 300 per cent; in other words, Sudan needed to treble its exports in that year solely to meet its debt obligations. In the mid-1980s, eighteen other African countries were in a position at least as difficult, and three of these had ratios in excess of 1,000 per cent (GATT 1987). Labouring under such burdens, it would be surprising if growth had been anything other than what the IMF refers to as 'sluggish'. In fact, average annual GDP growth in Africa was only 1.9 per cent between 1982 and 1991 compared with 2.9 per cent between 1973 and 1982 (IMF 1991).

In Latin America, similar problems are compounded by the much larger scale of indebtedness. Thirlwall (1994) notes that the debt-related transfers now expected from this region are greater, as a proportion of total output and trade, than the war reparations imposed on Germany after 1918. The consequent debt-servicing difficulties have inhibited Latin America's capacity to import investment goods: consequently its medium-term growth prospects are considered to be poor (GATT 1987). Similarly the United Nations (1990), in assessing possible development trajectories for the world economy to the end of the century, concedes that the economic constraints imposed by debt in Latin America, and Africa especially, will impede investment and productivity growth and, therefore, the wider economic performance of these regions.

Given the significance of the debt crisis for a large number of countries – including many in the liberalizing former eastern bloc – what measures have been taken to tackle it? Since it first emerged in 1982, the general approach has been to deal with the crisis on a piecemeal basis, usually involving combinations of debt forgiveness and rescheduling, negotiated with individual countries (Thirlwall 1994). While the latter option might alleviate acute debt-servicing difficulties, it can actually increase the overall level of debt as arrears accumulate. Thus, for example, total net borrowing by the net debtor countries in 1990 climbed back to its 1983 level, partly because of such 'exceptional financing' (IMF 1991).

That debt policy should reduce to a series of *ad hoc* measures rather than a more imposing strategic approach is itself interesting. The debt problem has been characterized as: 'a vast charade of money being recycled from creditors to debtors and back again to the creditors, while the total volume of debt grows and the pressure on debtor countries to adjust – a euphemism for deflation – increases' (Thirlwall 1994:321). Clearly, Thirlwall doubts the efficacy of the piecemeal approach. Instead he argues for 'bold, imaginative, global schemes of debt relief' (ibid.:322). For the moment, none are in prospect and it may be illuminating to reflect upon why the *ad hoc* is preferred. Defaults by any of the larger debtors would certainly have serious consequences for creditors in the western banking system and possibly the system as a whole; some smaller American banks did actually come near to collapse in the 1980s (Colman and Nixson 1986). Approaching debt on a case-by-case basis reduces the risk of any particular default, while preserving debtor obligations on interest and amortization (clearing debt). It also minimizes the resource commitments of the developed area in addressing the issue while militating against concerted action by the indebted.

Global problems, like the globalization process itself, appear to have a characteristic unevenness: in this case in terms of the commitment to deal with them. Where the interests of the developed area are threatened, reactions are sharper and more focused; where developing area interests are at issue the response appears more muted. Perhaps the issue is not so much *is* there a global economy as *whose* global economy?

## Summary

This section has attempted to demonstrate that, in terms of the emergence of a highly integrated trading environment, the notion of a global economy is a reasonable one. The twenty-five year period following the end of the Second World War was the most dynamic in human history and was characterized by trade-led economic growth. Even though the 1970s and 1980s witnessed more sedate progress, this necessarily developed upon the global foundation laid down during the post-war boom.

It must be emphasized, however, that globalization through trade has been an inherently selective process. The chief participants and beneficiaries have been the developed countries. Admittedly, some of these have experienced problems with long-term competitiveness but their absolute economic strength at the beginning of the period has continued to underwrite their advanced standing. Among the developing countries, a small number have achieved the decisive shift into manufacturing production and exchange. This has enabled a modest restructuring of the international division of labour and some closure of the gap between these countries and those in the developed area. Among the remaining developing countries, a further select group is dependent upon the vicissitudes of the international oil market but most are largely confined to the stagnant market for non-oil primary commodities. Here, the chief 'global' experience has perhaps been the shouldering of debt.

We have also seen that such global unevenness is not simply a reflection of unequal starting positions and different resource endowments. The advanced countries have perceived the limited industrial progress of the developing area as a significant threat to their economic interests and have responded with various forms of protectionism. Moreover, protectionist sentiment and policy has since become a generalized threat to world trade. It is in this sense that globalization can be seen to be subject to continuing forms of countervailing pressure.

While the integration and recasting of markets has thus far been described in terms of competition between national economies, it is also important to stress the institutional context in which post-war global processes have been situated. The international economic institutions of the post-war period – the Bretton Woods System and GATT in particular – have had an important role in fostering globalization. Paradoxically, the progress of globalization itself raises questions concerning the continuing usefulness and validity of these institutions. The following section explores these issues.

## Globalization: The Institutional Framework

An account of the origins and objectives of the major international economic institutions of the post-war period must begin some years earlier – in the early 1930s, with the Great Depression. The essentially isolationist and inward-looking positions adopted in most countries at this time had served only to extend and deepen the depression. Accordingly, the architects of the post-war institutional framework resolved that stability, openness and multilateralism rather than unilateralism or bilateralism (exclusive agreements between two countries) would in future characterize economic dealings between states: there was to be no return to the 1930s.

Immediate reactions to the Depression took two broad forms: tariff protection in goods markets and competitive devaluations in international money markets. Tariffs raise the price of goods imported from abroad and thus, other things remaining the same, improve the price competitiveness of domestic goods; while currency devaluation lowers the overseas price of exports and raises the home currency price of imports. In both cases the protecting country expects to enhance its international competitiveness. Clearly, however, if *many* countries initiate this type of policy simultaneously, there will be few, if any, winners. Indeed, because markets become increasingly less accessible – world trade fell by two-thirds during the Depression – most economies end up worse off as demand begins to contract. Protectionism of this form helps to account for the length and severity of the slump. Table 7.12 shows the effects of the Depression upon the United States economy, the world's largest.

**Table 7.12** The United States economy during the Great Depression

| Year | GNP ($bn current prices) | Unemployment (%) |
|------|--------------------------|------------------|
| 1929 | 103 | 3 |
| 1930 | 91 | 9 |
| 1931 | 76 | 16 |
| 1932 | 59 | 24 |
| 1933 | 56 | 25 |

*Source*: Dalton (1974)

Because the problems of the inter-war period had been exacerbated by competitive devaluations and unilateral tariff intervention, the post-war priority was to construct an institutional framework which would make protectionism of either sort difficult to implement. The Bretton Woods institutions were intended to provide stability in international currency markets and, after some hesitancy, the General Agreement on Tariffs and Trade emerged as the agency of trade liberalization.

## The Bretton Woods system

In July 1944, representatives from the United States, Britain and other western countries met at a hotel in Bretton Woods (a picturesque mountain resort in the state of New Hampshire) in order to decide upon a monetary system which would, to mutual advantage, bind their economies together in the coming peace. The intention was to introduce a system of fixed exchange rates which would prevent the kind of rival unilateral currency devaluations which had punctuated and underpinned the Depression.

The system agreed at Bretton Woods centred on the US dollar, which was linked to gold at 35$ an ounce. All other participant currencies were fixed against the dollar (or gold) so that par values for each currency in terms of all others could be established; for example, the pound was pegged at $4.03. Each country's central bank was then obliged to defend its par value or exchange rate within a margin of 1 per cent above or below parity.

The system was characterized by a commitment to exchange rate stability and, as a corollary, an aversion to the kind of competitive devaluations witnessed in the previous decade. The pivotal role played by the dollar reflected the overwhelming economic power of the USA at the end of the Second World War. As noted, at this time half the world's output was produced by the USA and, therefore, the dollar was in high demand on the foreign exchanges as the currency needed by non-US residents to buy American goods and services. Moreover, under Bretton Woods, the dollar was to be convertible into gold. This was possible because the US Federal Reserve held 67 per cent of the world gold stock; and desirable because, in theory, it would act as a bastion against inflation by inhibiting unwarranted expansion of the American money supply: dollars could not simply be printed by the US authorities, they had to be backed by gold.

The maintenance of currencies at agreed rates was to be achieved by central bank intervention in the foreign exchange markets. In the absence of government intervention, an exchange rate, simply the price of a currency expressed in terms of another, is determined by the supply of and demand for that currency. For example, UK residents supply sterling in order to obtain foreign currency to buy imports or invest abroad, whereas demand for sterling by overseas residents arises from their purchase of UK exports, or investments they make in the UK economy. Left to market forces the exchange rate would fall when there was an excess of supply over demand and rise when demand outstripped supply. To prevent a fall in the exchange rate the Bank of England would have to intervene in the foreign exchange market and buy up the excess supply of pounds using other 'reserve' currencies. In this way sterling's supply and demand would remain equal and the pound would not change in value. In the case of an excess demand for the currency and a rising exchange rate, the process of central bank intervention is reversed: an excess demand for sterling would be met by the Bank of England as it acquired other reserve currencies in exchange for pounds.

Because a fixed exchange rate system of this sort is underpinned by central bank intervention in the foreign exchange markets, it is clearly important that central banks have sufficient reserve currency resources to maintain their currencies at agreed levels. The Bretton Woods agreement established a new institution, the International Monetary Fund, partly to ensure that this 'liquidity' requirement was met. System members had to provide the Fund with a quota of gold and dollars which was calculated on the basis of shares in world trade: the bigger a country's share, the larger its quota. In turn, each member could borrow from the Fund in order to stabilize its currency should the need arise.

As noted, currency instability arises when balance of payments disequilibria create mismatches between the supply of a currency and the demand for it. The Bretton Woods system envisaged that IMF loans would allow members to maintain the par values of their currencies, particularly in the face of temporary balance of payments deficits. However, if a country faced a longer-term deficit, or fundamental disequilibrium, then it would be permitted to devalue its currency in order to bring about balance of payments adjustment. If the devaluation was less than 10 per cent the country did not need IMF approval for its action but bigger devaluations had to be IMF sanctioned. In this way, the IMF was to 'police' as well as resource the Bretton Woods system. Note also that the provision for devaluation where circumstances warranted it made the system, at least in theory, fixed but adjustable. The chief architects of Bretton Woods, Harry Dexter White for the USA and John Maynard Keynes for the UK, certainly envisaged that currency par values would need to be adjusted from time to time (Scammell 1987). If they were not, the downward pressures on deficit country currencies might fatally rupture the system.

Finally, the Bretton Woods currencies were intended to be fully convertible, that is there were to be no restrictions on the capacity of economic agents to move out of one currency and into another. During the inter-war period some countries, notably Germany, had imposed exchange controls which constrained the ability of domestic residents to use their own currencies to buy others (Chacholiades 1990). This, of course, is simply another form of protectionism: if domestic residents cannot obtain foreign currencies, they cannot buy imports. Convertibility was to be a further bulwark against unilateralism.

To briefly summarize, the architects of Bretton Woods envisaged a system of fixed but adjustable exchange rates and freely convertible currencies, presided over by a pluralistic international institution which would both provide the resources necessary to lubricate the system and the authority essential to the maintenance of harmony and good order.

So much for the plans of White and Keynes. In Scammell's (1987) view, their ambitions eventually foundered upon the narrower horizons of those charged with their implementation. While the Bretton Woods system was associated with the remarkable general economic growth of the early post-war period, it did not develop in the way its creators intended. The objective of exchange rate stability was certainly met – indeed, as we shall see, exchange rates were perhaps *too* stable – but the system proved in the end critically deficient in other ways.

The central problem was the role of the International Monetary Fund. In the immediate post-war period the US government agreed to underwrite reconstruction in Europe on the understanding that the beneficiaries of its Marshall Aid programme did not simultaneously borrow from the IMF (Burk 1991). At the same time, because they were much less attractive than the dollar, most major European currencies were made temporarily non-convertible. In these circumstances, the scope for management of the international monetary system by the IMF proved to be limited. Perversely, however, it did pressure members to refrain from currency realignments which they might otherwise have made (Scammell 1987). Crucially, this robbed the system of an adjustment mechanism: deficit countries often failed to devalue, initially because of IMF strictures but later because devaluation was held to be a sign of economic and political weakness; surplus countries were naturally reluctant to revalue for fear of damaging their export-led growth prospects.

However, for a long time these problems lay dormant. While the IMF could not provide the reserve currency liquidity necessary to support the fixed exchange rate regime now in place, the United States proved able and willing to undertake this task. At first this was achieved via the provision of Marshall Aid and then later, towards the end of the 1950s, by the emergence of significant US balance of payments deficits. These provided a growing pool of dollars outside the United States which became the necessary reserve lubricant of the fixed exchange rate system. At about the same time, after more than a decade of post-war reconstruction, convertibility of all major currencies was achieved and the system was judged to be fully functioning.

Unfortunately, however, because of the constrained role of the IMF and the alternative liquidity supplied by the US balance of payments deficit, Bretton Woods was now possessed of a fundamental flaw which was to be at the heart of its destruction a little over a decade later, at the start of the 1970s. The problem centred on the scale of the dollar pool and international confidence in the dollar as the linchpin of the system. While the US deficit remained within tolerable limits, dollar confidence would be maintained and the dollar pool could perform its new-found role without difficulty. However, should the deficit become too large, dollar confidence could be undermined as holders of dollars elected to exchange them for gold (recall that the US Federal Reserve was obliged to meet any such requests from other central banks). Now, as the economist Triffin (1960) famously anticipated, the continued and unprecedented expansion of world trade would actually *require* the liquidity-bearing dollar pool – and thereby the deficit – to increase. Clearly, there was a contradiction here: the growth in world trade demanded an expansion of the liquidity provided by the dollar pool but, as the US deficit and dollar pool expanded, dollar confidence would be undermined and the whole system threatened. In acknowledgement of the work of its discoverer, this problem became known as the 'Triffin dilemma'.

The manageable deficit of the late 1950s grew at a rate sufficient to threaten the Bretton Woods system over the next decade, principally because of the influence of America's growing involvement in the Vietnam War. The burgeoning US deficit was matched by growing balance of payments surpluses in Japan and Germany, and there was consequent speculation against the dollar and in favour of the yen and mark as well as other currencies. Ultimately, the scale of central bank intervention required to maintain the fixed exchange rate parity grid proved too large. In addition, the Federal Reserve's stock of gold had fallen rapidly as it attempted to prop up the ailing dollar. In August 1971 President Nixon formally ended the Bretton Woods system by breaking the link between the dollar and gold.

### After Bretton Woods: 'non-system' or new system?

Triffin clearly demonstrated that hindsight was not necessary to detect the fundamental flaws which would ultimately wreck Bretton Woods. Given its innate contradictions and ignominious end, now fully a quarter century away, questions might reasonably be asked about the system's continued relevance. If the performance of the world economy had been poor or merely adequate over the lifetime of Bretton Woods, little nostalgia or approbation would attach to it. It is the startling pace of growth during this period which gives rise to debate about a revival of Bretton Woods or some similar arrangement. The defenders of fixed exchange rate systems claim that the stability they offer greatly encourages trade and growth.

Fixed exchange rates necessarily imply the absence of the kind of currency turbulence which brings uncertainty to export and import prices and therefore discourages trade. However, others dispute the purported advantages of exchange rate fixity, claiming that Bretton Woods was merely associated with the post-war boom rather than a cause of it. The preference, here, is for exchange rates to be freely floating according to the dictates of the market. Since the end of the Bretton Woods system there has, indeed, been a general return to floating exchange rates (the so-called 'non-system') but currencies have still been subject to central bank management of varying degrees of intensity. Space constraints prevent a full elaboration of the range of positions in this debate, but a few key points may usefully be summarized here, using the evolution of the 'non-system' as a context.

One general point of agreement between the fixed and flexible exchange rate 'camps' is that the re-emergence of high and varying rates of inflation in the world economy during the 1970s made the medium-term restoration of a fixed system unlikely. Widely divergent inflation rates between countries usually necessitate currency adjustments so that significant gaps in international price competitiveness do not emerge. For example, the relatively high rate of inflation in the UK during the 1970s – an annual average of 13 per cent – was associated with a fall in the value of the pound against the currencies of lower inflation countries such as West Germany (with annual average inflation rate 4 per cent over the same period). If the pound had not fallen against the currencies of low inflation countries, UK goods would have lost price competitiveness *vis-à-vis* the goods produced in these countries, with a consequent worsening of the balance of payments difficulties experienced by the UK at the time.

It is important to emphasize that the end of the Bretton Woods system did not usher in a market-led, perfectly flexible exchange rate framework. Although exchange rates were now free to move – and in the new inflationary climate they needed to – central banks continued to intervene in the currency markets. Indeed, one legacy of Bretton Woods was that they now did so collectively (Sodersten 1980). Moreover, although there were significant short-term currency swings up to the mid-1970s, thereafter the 'non-system' became more stable for a time, as central banks accumulated skills in managing flexibility (Milner and Greenaway 1979). Reflecting upon the development of the 'non-system' up to the mid-1980s, Scammell (1987) goes so far as to claim that it showed some signs of working in the way Bretton

Woods was intended. He argues that, in the short run, balance of payments deficits were financed by running down currency reserves and/or borrowing; whereas over the longer term they were corrected by exchange rate realignment. This approach both facilitated adjustment – crucially absent from Bretton Woods – and moderated currency movements. Nevertheless, in common with some other economists, Scammell concedes that the present 'non-system' should be replaced by some formal mechanism of exchange rate fixity. What are the perceived shortcomings of the 'non-system' which prompt such a view?

The primary difficulty is foreign exchange market misalignment and volatility. The main example of the former during the 1980s was the overvaluation of the dollar in relation to the burgeoning US balance of payments deficit. This was a problem both for the US government, which found adjustment elusive, and for the global economy generally as it faced a rising tide of protectionist sentiment in the USA. In 1985 the leading industrial nations – the USA, Japan, Germany, France, and the UK, collectively known as the G5 – agreed to orchestrate a gradual decline in the value of the dollar. This response, the Plaza Agreement, was an explicit recognition that the 'non-system' was producing perverse key currency movements. Theoretically, the dollar should have depreciated automatically given the burgeoning American balance of payments deficit; its gradual appreciation threatened to make the deficit worse and US trade policy more defensive. The Plaza Agreement, at least for a time, averted this damaging possibility.

The 'non-system' was also the focus of unwelcome bouts of currency instability in the 1980s. The movement of sterling during the first half of the decade provides a good example. From an exchange rate in the early 1980s of £1 to almost 2.50$, the value of sterling plunged virtually to dollar parity (£1:1$) in the sterling crisis of early 1985. Such wild swings appear relatively unrelated to developments in the real economy and clearly hinder medium-term business planning. The 1987 Louvre Accord was a collective attempt by the G7 (the G5 plus Italy and Canada) to prevent such oscillations. The Accord tied the G7 currencies together in undisclosed 'target zones' which were then to be policed by the G7 central banks. The element of secrecy surrounding the zones was generated by a desire not to provide private actors in the foreign exchange markets with information which might facilitate destabilizing speculation in favour of, or against, particular currencies. Finally, Louvre reflected the G7 view that the exchange rates prevailing at the time were justified by real economic conditions (Sodersten and Reed 1994).

While a number of influential commentators remain implacable opponents of exchange rate fixity – see, for example, the recently expressed views of Milton Friedman (in Snowdon, Vane and Wynarczyk 1994) which confirm his classic (1968) case for flexible exchange rates – the cautious movements towards more determined forms of key currency management have prompted calls for a formal end to the 'non-system' (for a review of some options see Krugman and Obstfeld 1994). Circumstances are now judged to be especially propitious given the apparent easing of global inflationary pressures during the 1980s.

Differences over the form and desirability of change in the international monetary system are matched by differences over whether such changes are likely to occur in the near future. For example, Williamson and Milner (1991:396) consider that the 'G7 has established arrangements for policy coordination that could provide the basis for a restored world system'; while Sodersten and Reed (1994:678) argue that 'It seems safest to conclude that floating exchange rates, perhaps intermingled with currency blocs, will continue, at least until the next major crisis'. The latter view is interesting in that it implicitly considers the present 'non-system' to be crisis free. This might not be a sentiment widely shared in debt-ridden Africa and South America where the IMF writ is heavily criticized (see Christian Aid, undated). Once again the question of *whose* crisis and *whose* interests appears relevant.

## The General Agreement on Tariffs and Trade

The post-war plans for institutional control of the international monetary system were complemented by similar intentions for the international trading environment: stability and multilateralism in both money and goods markets was the ambition. While the IMF was to oversee the former, a separate institution, the International Trade Organization (ITO) would deal with the latter. However, a number of governments advocated progress in trade liberalization in advance of the ITO and, as a result, the General Agreement on Tariffs and Trade was concluded in 1947. The GATT was to have been superseded by the ITO but the ITO itself was compromised by, and ultimately foundered upon, differences between the US and Britain over its powers and responsibilities. This left the GATT as the primary vehicle for trade liberalization. The GATT has since assumed institutional status with a permanent secretariat in Geneva and its membership, or number of 'contracting parties', has grown from 23 countries in 1947 to 125 in 1994.

The central premise of the GATT is that trade liberalization is conducive to generalized economic growth. As such its immediate post-war aim was to prevent a lurch back into the tariff protectionism prevalent in the 1930s. Over the longer term, it has sought to dismantle the barriers to trade erected during that time and to provide a system of rules which favour openness in world markets. In pursuing these objectives, the GATT is generally recognized to espouse three basic principles: non-discrimination, reciprocity and transparency.

Non-discrimination prevents selective forms of trade liberalization, in that it requires trade concessions granted by one country to be extended to all contracting parties rather than a favoured few. Such concessions are also 'bound' (that is made permanent) by the GATT. Note that any new trade restrictions must also be applied in a non-discriminatory manner. This principle ensures that trade policy covered by the GATT is conducted on a multilateral basis. Hence unilateral and bilateral actions – so damaging during the Great Depression – are 'GATT-illegal'.

Reciprocity obliges countries in receipt of trade concessions from their GATT partners to respond in kind. The intention behind this principle is to avoid 'free rider' problems which might arise if some countries were content to benefit from the many trade concessions granted to them as a result of non-discrimination, without themselves granting concessions to others.

Finally, the principle of transparency establishes an important distinction between the tariff and the quota as instruments of protection. A tariff is a tax on a tradable good. The tax raises the price of the good and, other things remaining the same, makes it less attractive to consumers. A quota, on the other hand, is a quantitative restriction on the volume or value of a tradable good. Because it works directly through the price mechanism, the tariff is conventionally recognized to be the clearest and most direct form of market intervention and is therefore preferred to the quota, which may generate more uncertain effects. Following this reasoning, the GATT proscribes the use of quotas unless unusual circumstances apply; generally, then, the only form of protection sanctioned by the GATT is the tariff.

There are several exceptions to these three principles. For example, members of a common market such as the European Union, are exempt from the non-discrimination requirement when granting tariff concessions to their partners; equivalent concessions do not have to be extended to other GATT contracting parties. Similarly, developing countries may find the obligation of reciprocity particularly onerous *vis-à-vis* their developed country counterparts; consequently this principle has been waived for developing countries.

Trade liberalization under the GATT has developed largely in a series of 'Rounds'. These are effectively rolling negotiations, sometimes conducted over several years, which address pre-determined liberalization agendas. The most recently completed round – Uruguay, after the country in which the first meeting took place – was the eighth since 1947. Rather than consider the achievements of each round in turn, it is useful to group them into two periods: those conducted against the background of the post-war boom up to the end of the 1960s and the last two rounds, Tokyo (1973–9) and Uruguay (1986–94), which were conditioned by both a period of slower growth and the important shifts in the pattern of world trade discussed earlier.

Space constraints prevent a detailed review of the first five Rounds: Geneva (1947), Annecy (1949), Torquay (1951), Geneva (1956) and Dillon (1960–1). Generally speaking, the greatest tariff reductions were made in the earliest of these rounds, with slower progress in the last two (for a brief discussion, see Greenaway 1983). The Kennedy Round (1964–7), however, proved to be a decisive reassertion of multilateral trade liberalization. Substantial tariff reductions were agreed on almost 75 per cent of world industrial trade and, according to Williamson and Milner (1991:333), it 'succeeded in dismantling much of the old protectionism'. In other words, the round finally laid to rest a large swathe of the tariff protection established during the Great Depression; as noted, this was one of the longer-term objectives of the GATT.

Although the Kennedy Round is usually heralded as the most successful of all the GATT negotiations, it did leave a number of issues unresolved. For example, it failed to produce agreement on the protection of agriculture, while permitting the continued quota protection by the advanced countries of so-called 'sensitive' textile production. In consequence it left unsatisfied some important LDC aspirations: it has been the task of the Tokyo and Uruguay Rounds to try to deal with such outstanding problems. Unfortunately, changing economic circumstances have conspired to make the post-1970 period a much less propitious time for conducting trade negotiations.

The Tokyo Round made some further progress on tariff reform, although the scope for tariff cuts had been much reduced by the success of the Kennedy Round; consequently, commentaries on the Tokyo negotiations – Greenaway (1983) for example – have tended to highlight their lack of progress on other fronts. Thus, the deadlock over agriculture could not be broken, 'sensitive' items remained sensitive and there was no agreement concerning measures to deal with the rise of new forms of NTB such as the voluntary export restraint (VER). A VER is simply an agreement by an exporter to quantitatively limit the volume or value of output sent to another country. The volume of Japanese cars exported to Europe and the US has been voluntarily limited in this way in recent years. VERs clearly offend the spirit of the GATT yet, since they are implemented by the exporter, the GATT has no claim upon what are highly discriminatory forms of protection. Exporting countries are usually 'persuaded' to agree to VERs for fear of more draconian measures if they do not comply. Boonekamp (1990) notes that VERs have become particularly widespread since the end of the 1970s.

The Tokyo Round thus left a substantial collection of unresolved issues. Some of these had themselves been carried over from the

Kennedy Round while others – such as the proliferation of VERs – have a more recent provenance. It was also apparent that LDC and NIC disquiet persisted at the inability of the GATT to address the burgeoning non-tariff discrimination they were enduring at the hands of the developed countries; an issue which we discuss, also, in chapter three.

It fell to the Uruguay Round, which began in 1986, to confront both the backlog of issues from Tokyo and a possible re-emergence of regional trade discrimination. In one sense, the major achievement of the Uruguay Round is that it was concluded at all. The round was due to be completed in 1990 but dragged on in protracted crisis until 1994. The main reason for this was a bitter dispute between, on the one side, the Cairns[1] group of agricultural producers and the United States, and on the other the European Union (EU). The Cairns group and the US wanted free trade in agriculture and thus an end to EU agricultural subsidies. In the event a compromise allowed the subsidies to be cut but not abolished.

The Uruguay Round also agreed further cuts in tariffs though, again, earlier successes softened the absolute impact of this form of liberalization. Other new measures include the deregulation of trade in financial services and a provision to standardize the way in which patents and copyrights are protected. More controversially perhaps, the round has resulted in an agreement to phase out both VERs and the infamous multifibre quotas which developed countries have imposed on LDCs since the early 1960s. While this kind of outcome appears to be exactly what the GATT needed in order to re-establish its credentials after the Tokyo impasse, some words of caution are in order.

In the first place, the willingness to eliminate VERs comes at a time when, because of depressed market conditions in the advanced countries, exporting countries are often unable to reach their voluntary quotas. Different circumstances might prompt a revival of pro-VER sentiment. Much the same point can be made about the willingness of the US to refrain, for the moment, from the kind of aggressive unilateralism indulged in towards the end of the 1980s. Under a provision of the 1988 Omnibus Trade Bill, the US obliged itself to take retaliatory protective measures against specific countries it judged to be engaging in unfair trade practices. This so-called 'Super 301' action clearly defies GATT principles and yet the Uruguay agreement has permitted the US to retain the option of using it should the need arise; indeed Japan was 'Super 301 targeted' immediately prior to the formal conclusion to the Uruguay Round (*Financial Times*, 5.3.84). Moreover, there have been calls for the EU to introduce its own Super 301 equivalent (*Economist*, 18.12.93). Finally, the multifibre quotas are to be phased out over a period of ten years. The multifibre arrangement was always intended to be a temporary measure to give the developed countries time to adjust to effective LDC competition. Deadlines have been consistently extended, however; by the time the latest deadline runs out in 2004, the quotas will be forty-three years old – perhaps they will live to enjoy a few more birthdays thereafter.

The gains from the Uruguay Round are estimated by the OECD to be of the order of $270 billion by the year 2002, though this figure ignores the social and economic costs of adjustment – such as unemployment – as economies are opened up to new forms of foreign competition. There are also important differences in the way the gains may be distributed. The EU, Japan and the US will together receive almost 60 per cent of the total increase in income, while at the other end of the scale, it is anticipated that Africa will actually lose income as a result of the round's completion.

During the Uruguay Round many commentators raised the spectre of the Great Depression when warning of the possible consequences should the round fail. Though this did not happen, the issue of protectionism is still present in other guises. There is, for example, the threat of the division of the global economy into competitive trading blocs. The EU and the more recent (1993) North American Free Trade Area (NAFTA), which binds together the United States, Canadian and Mexican economies, are already established and Asia–Pacific economic cooperation talks are well advanced. As noted, both the USA and EU have already demonstrated their attachment to various forms of protection when it appears to be in their interest. Even before its inception, notice was given that NAFTA would be raising external barriers to imports of textiles and cars (*Economist*, 13.11.93). The creation in 1989 of the Asia–Pacific Economic Cooperation (APEC) forum, which includes the USA, Japan and Australia as well as a number of the most successful NICs, might also be interpreted as an attempt to rival the anticipated economic power of an enlarged EU. The protracted struggle between the USA and the EU was the most notable feature of the final stages of the Uruguay Round. During this not particularly edifying process, the majority of contracting parties could do little but look impotently on in the hope of a positive outcome. This may be a portent of the pattern of global trade negotiations in the future.

## Globalization and the Transnationals

A transnational corporation (TNC) may be defined as a firm which owns and controls assets in more than one country. On occasion, the definition is narrowed to include only industrial forms of activity; Jenkins (1987), for example, adopts such an approach. One reason for using this narrow industrial definition is the relatively poor availability of data on TNCs specializing in service activities such as banking (Edwards 1985). Here, initially, we concentrate on TNCs engaged in industrial activities, but turn later briefly to consider service TNCs.

While the ownership and control of assets across international borders has consistently featured in TNC definitions, several commentators have noted the emergence, in the 1980s, of new kinds of international linkage between firms (see, for example Dunning 1988; Dicken 1992; OECD 1992). Such linkages include, *inter alia*, joint ventures, subcontracting and licensing between formally independent firms. While economic activity thus organized might not be classified as transnational precisely because of the independence of the parties concerned, Dicken (1992) suggests that developments of this kind call for a wider definition of transnationalism.

Though the TNC is hardly a new phenomenon – many of the world's largest transnational firms have their origins in late nineteenth-century cross-border expansion – it is only in the post-1945 period that such corporations have become a significant force. Indeed, so spectacular has been their recent growth in scale and number that TNCs have been claimed as 'the single most important force creating global shifts in economic activity' (Dicken 1992:47). Total global sales of TNCs are now estimated by the United Nations Conference on Trade and Development to actually outstrip the value of world trade (*Guardian*, 31.8.94). This is possible because a proportion of TNC sales take place *within* the firms themselves (see Grimwade 1989).

The leading TNCs are also, in some respects, financially larger than many nation states. For example, the 1989 sales total of the US car manufacturer General Motors was bigger than the gross national product (GNP) of Belgium. In the same year, Ford's sales exceeded the Austrian GNP. It is also interesting to note that the largest TNC outside the elite group of advanced nations, the South Korean firm Samsung, generated sales in 1989 equivalent to approximately 10 per cent of the South Korean GNP. Given the exceptional progress of the South Korean economy over the last twenty-five years and the apparent contribution made by this one firm, Dicken's claim for the global influence of TNCs appears to have some foundation.

The dominance of TNCs in some world markets is overwhelming. Sales of almost all primary commodities are now controlled by a handful of multi-commodity traders (Lang and Hines 1993). Half of the world market in semi-conductor production – at the leading edge of global technological change – is shared between 10 US and Japanese TNCs, while the market share of the top 21 firms is 70 per cent. In construction, 25 firms account for 45 per cent of contracts awarded abroad; in automotive parts, just 3 firms account for almost 20 per cent of global sales; and even in the relatively diverse chemicals industry, the top 10 firms also enjoy one fifth of all sales (OECD 1992).

It is possible to greatly extend this kind of empirical survey but there is a danger that doing so would cause us to neglect important patterns of TNC development. Accordingly, we will reflect upon the nature and pace of TNC growth over the post-war period, following, initially, a 'stages' approach, variations on which are offered by many writers in the field (see, for example, Edwards 1985; Dunning 1988; Robock and Simmonds 1989; Dicken 1992; OECD 1992).

Even in the immediate aftermath of the Second World War the rate of TNC expansion began to assume entirely new proportions, reaching a level, between 1946 and 1952, 50 per cent higher than its previous peak in the 1920s (Dicken 1992). Thereafter, TNC growth continued to accelerate, in tandem with the post-war boom, up until the beginning of the 1970s. During this period, TNC expansion was dominated by firms of US and, to a lesser extent, UK origin. Thus, at the end of the 1950s, some 55 per cent of all foreign direct investment (FDI) was made by US TNCs, while UK firms accounted for a further 20 per cent; the balance of the remaining 25 per cent came from the Netherlands, Switzerland, Canada and France (Robock and Simmonds 1989).

While general TNC expansion actually slowed for a time in the 1970s, again mirroring the sluggish performance of the global economy over this period, it revived during the 1980s (Dunning 1988). As table 7.13 shows, the newest and most dynamic sources of TNC growth are clearly Japan and West Germany. In terms of the percentage of the world total of outward direct investment, the contribution of these two countries was relatively insignificant even up to the late 1960s. In the Japanese case, this reflected government pressure upon the corporate sector to invest in the domestic economy (Dicken 1992); while Dunning (1988) suggests that the dispossession of the overseas assets of both Japan and Germany in the 1945 armistice also helps to account for the period of relatively low TNC activity in these countries. Finally, table 7.13 illustrates the growth of the LDC originated TNC. The share of this group is clearly still small as yet, but the exceptional growth rates of the NICs in particular suggests that TNCs from this source may become much more prominent in future years.

From the foregoing, it is evident that there is a marked parallel between rates of TNC expansion and wider western economic growth. The post-war boom was mirrored by rapid TNC growth; the world economic slowdown of the 1970s was paralleled by more sedate TNC activity, and the modest recovery in the 1980s has been associated with new TNC expansion. Yet it is important to note that TNCs have generally been more dynamic than their host economies. Table 7.14 compares the respective growth rates of the largest industrial TNCs and their host economies in terms of national industrial production. It

**Table 7.13** National origins of FDI in the world economy

| Country of origin | Percentage of world total of outward direct investment | | |
|---|---|---|---|
| | *1960* | *1975* | *1985* |
| USA | 47.1 | 44.0 | 35.1 |
| UK | 18.3 | 13.1 | 14.7 |
| Japan | 0.7 | 5.7 | 11.7 |
| West Germany | 1.2 | 6.5 | 8.4 |
| Switzerland | 3.4 | 8.0 | 6.4 |
| Netherlands | 10.3 | 7.1 | 6.1 |
| Canada | 3.7 | 3.7 | 5.1 |
| France | 6.1 | 3.8 | 3.0 |
| Italy | 1.6 | 1.2 | 1.7 |
| Sweden | 0.6 | 1.7 | 1.3 |
| Advanced economies | 99.0 | 97.7 | 97.2 |
| Developing economies | 1.0 | 2.3 | 2.7 |
| WORLD | 100.0 | 100.0 | 100.0 |

*Source*: Dicken (1992)

**Table 7.14** TNC growth and national industrial output growth

| | *Average growth rate (in sales) of the largest industrial TNCs (% p.a.) (1957–77)* | *Average growth rate of national industrial production (% p.a.) (1960–77)* |
|---|---|---|
| Japan | 15 | 9 |
| France | 15 | 5 |
| West Germany | 13 | 4 |
| USA | 8 | 4 |
| UK | 8 | 2 |
| Canada | 8 | 5 |

*Source*: Edwards (1985)

is apparent that in each case TNC growth is faster. Moreover, the gap between the two is thought to be increasing; Dicken (1992) cites evidence which suggests that, on average, FDI grew twice as fast as GNP in the 1960s but four times as fast in the 1980s.

The changing pace of TNC expansion and its shifting sources are clear, but what of its geography: which regions are in receipt of most TNC activity? There are two general points to be made here. First, the majority of TNC investment takes place between the advanced countries. Table 7.15 shows that, by the 1980s, the developed countries absorbed three quarters of global FDI leaving one quarter for the LDCs. This is a reversal of the situation prevailing before the Second World War when the LDCs received the balance of investment. The change is explained by the relative decline of FDI in agriculture and minerals in the LDCs and the post-war explosion in cross-border manufacturing investment in the advanced countries. Note, again, that this parallels the very rapid growth in manufacturing trade between the advanced countries discussed earlier.

Second, within the advanced countries, there has been a pronounced shift in the locational focus of FDI over the post-war period. Initially, the dominant group of US TNCs concentrated investment in the advanced economies of western Europe, making this area the primary focus of FDI. The attraction of Europe at this time is partly explained by the creation of the EEC and the European Free Trade Association (EFTA) and the new large markets associated with these developments (Robock and Simmonds 1989). However, the USA has itself since become host to the largest, and still rapidly growing, share of TNC investment. Table 7.16 illustrates the general proportions of this shift. In 1975 the USA claimed just over 11 per cent of global inward investment, compared to Western Europe's 41 per cent. By 1985, the American share had climbed to 29 per cent, fractionally ahead of Europe. It is important to be clear about what is happening here. As we have seen, in absolute terms, US TNCs are still responsible for more investment abroad than firms from any other country, and the volume of US investment abroad continues to increase. However, Japanese and German TNCs in particular have raised their levels of foreign investment at a much faster rate over the 1970s and 1980s (see table 7.13) and much of this, as well as TNC investment from other countries, has gone to the USA. The attraction of the American market lies partly in

**Table 7.15** Distribution of accumulated FDI by area (%)[a]

|                      | 1938 | 1960 | 1973 | 1983 |
|----------------------|------|------|------|------|
| Developed countries  | 34.3 | 67.3 | 72.9 | 75.5 |
| LDCs                 | 65.7 | 32.3 | 27.1 | 24.5 |

[a] Because of the existence of unallocated FDI, the columns need not sum to 100.
*Source*: Dunning (1988)

**Table 7.16** The changing focus of FDI in the global economy

|  | Percentage of world FDI inward investment stock | |
|---|---|---|
|  | 1975 | 1985 |
| United States | 11.2 | 29.0 |
| Western Europe | 40.8 | 28.9 |
| Japan | 0.6 | 1.0 |
| Other developed countries | 23.1 | 17.1 |
| LDCs | 24.3 | 24.0 |

*Source*: Dicken (1992)

its size and affluence but, for Japanese and German TNCs, the weakness of the dollar in the early 1970s was also important as it made American assets relatively cheaper to buy (Robock and Simmonds 1989).

The apparent influence of market size upon TNC investment patterns is worthy of further consideration in the light of recent developments in Europe and North America. The creation of the European single market and its continuing enlargement is expected to revive TNC activity in Europe (Young, McDermott and Dunlop 1991). Similarly, the creation of NAFTA may stimulate further TNC interest in North America from Europe and the Far East. This raises the interesting question of the paucity of TNC investment in Japan. While Japanese TNCs have the fastest growing share of global FDI, the Japanese economy itself hosts remarkably little investment from abroad: for example, just 1 per cent of world FDI in 1985. While a discussion of Japanese trade and industrial policies is beyond the scope of this chapter, their mercantalist (protectionist) character has long been alleged (see Donnelly 1994).

Much of the discussion in this section has been concerned either with industrial TNCs specifically or with transnationalism as a general phenomenon. It remains to consider the transnationalization of service activities. This issue has received less attention in the literature, possibly because of economists' conventional prioritization of industrial matters. However, there is a clear relation between basic industrial production and the financial activities which support it: the transnationalization of industry in the post-war period has been associated with a complementary transnationalization of services.

While a general link between industrial and service TNC growth is to be expected, there are important, additional factors which have prompted service TNC expansion. The contemporary scale of the foreign exchange market provides a good indication of the nature of TNC growth in banking. Foreign exchange dealing is now at a level much greater than that required to service world trade – its nominal purpose. According to Sedgemoor and Skinner (1987), in the mid-1980s only about 20 per cent of foreign exchange transactions were concerned with trade; the bulk of the remaining 80 per cent were speculative investments in financial instruments denominated in particular currencies. The central point, here, is that operations on this scale involve huge concentrations of financial capital and power. How have these emerged? The answer to this question lies in the mutation of the international capital market since the early 1960s and, in particular, the emergence of TNC dominated 'offshore' banking activities.

The Eurocurrency markets are the best known form of offshore banking. They originated from a desire by the Soviet Union in the 1950s to hold dollar deposits (Eurodollars) outside the USA, thus avoiding the possibility that the American government might freeze them. They were lodged instead with European banks (Chacholiades 1990). Eurodollar deposits grew rapidly in the 1960s, reflecting the role of the dollar as the world's key intervention currency and also, crucially, because banks holding dollars outside the USA could escape the regulatory framework imposed by the US monetary authorities on the domestic banking system. Like the Soviet government, banks began to find it advantageous to have dollar holdings beyond the reach of US government interference. Such deposits could then be 'lent on' in highly profitable ways that might not be possible under US banking rules.

The same principle which gave rise to the Eurodollar market has since created a range of offshore markets denominated in other key currencies. Such markets have also promoted growth in transnational banking as banks sought to compete for this new form of business in an increasing number of financial centres. While the European centres such as London, Paris, Frankfurt, Brussels, Milan and Amsterdam originated the Eurodollar market, offshore banking has since spread as far as the Middle East, Asia and the Caribbean. The terms 'Eurodollar' and 'Eurocurrency' therefore actually understate the real geography of this process.

In the 1970s the growth of the Eurocurrency markets accelerated further as a result of the impact of the first oil price shock. As noted earlier, the oil price rises of 1973–4 generated huge balance of payments surpluses for the oil exporting countries, which were then 'recycled' to less developed countries in particular. The Eurocurrency markets were the principal focus of this recycling. In 1980, the second oil price shock provided a new stimulus to offshore banking (Chacholiades 1990).

The Eurocurrency market in the early 1990s was estimated to be of the order of $6 *trillion*, two thirds of which is actually denominated in dollars; the rest in other key currencies. Table 7.17 illustrates the remarkable scale of expansion of the market over the last twenty years. According to Sodersten and Reed (1994), Eurocurrency transactions are now the dominant form of international banking activity, comprising 89 per cent of all international transactions.

There are two central points which arise from this brief discussion of financial TNCs and the Eurocurrency markets in which they are active. First, TNC operations in these markets are not subject to any regulatory control: avoidance of political restraint, as we have seen, was actually the motive for their creation. Second, the markets represent huge accumulations of money, in Jeremy Seabrook's phrase, 'moving noiselessly around the globe' in response to the imperatives of a relatively small group of decision-makers. One clear danger, here, is of financial panic over which the world's banking authorities might have little influence (Williamson and Milner 1991). The world stock market crash of 1987 exemplfies the kind of problem which threatens highly integrated and technologically sophisticated markets. More seriously, perhaps, the advent of large concentrations of globally mobile capital imposes new forms of constraint on governments. Thus the threat of disinvestment or capital flight may serve increasingly to moderate government policy in directions perceived to be appropriate to the interests of the markets (Helleiner 1994). The suspension of sterling from the ERM in 1992, which left the UK government bereft of a credible anti-inflation strategy, was the product of just such a capital flight.

Dunning (1988) has suggested that the territorial spread of TNCs was probably greater before 1914 than it has been in the post-war period. More regions of the world were then open to investment flows

**Table** 7.17 Estimated size of the Eurocurrency market 1963–1990 ($bn)

| | |
|---|---|
| 1963 | 7 |
| 1964 | 9 |
| 1967 | 18 |
| 1970 | 57 |
| 1973 | 132 |
| 1976 | 147 |
| 1979 | 475 |
| 1990 | 6,000 |

*Sources*: Williamson and Milner (1991) and Krugman and Obstfeld (1994)

and there were few restrictions on the forms capitalist activity could assume. Following the collapse of most of the centrally planned economies in 1989, it appears that the territorial claims of the transnationals will widen once again. Thus, in 1993, the liberalizing Chinese economy received a 13 per cent share of total world FDI (*Guardian* 31.8.94). The changing organizational forms of the TNC may also help to accelerate this process. The increasing prevalence of new kinds of TNC alliance noted earlier, coupled with the emergence of new and advanced forms of production organization, will further raise the growth rates of the transnationals (see Bernard 1994).

If TNCs are to possess a greater territorial span, and an even greater economic mass, the problems associated with the threat of capital flight for the advanced countries and 'decapitalization' – taking out more than is put in – for the LDCs may become even more pressing (Colman and Nixson 1986). Strange (1994) argues that such developments call for new kinds of state–firm diplomacy in which, for example, states exhibit a degree of shrewdness in choosing appropriate partners among firms. It might be argued that the UK has already begun to employ this tactic in its successful wooing of Japanese TNCs, which it considers have a natural empathy with the kind of labour market reforms implemented in the 1980s.

While a new state–capital diplomacy might be the best option when confronted with an increasingly powerful transnational reality, there are other examples which starkly illustrate the limits to such processes of accommodation. Ten years after the disaster in the Indian city of Bhopal, in which at least 6,000 people were killed and up to half a million injured by a poisonous gas leak from a TNC run factory, the American firm concerned, Union Carbide, has – in a compensation settlement which values each life lost at $3,000 – renounced any responsibility for the accident (*Observer* 20.11.94). This truly is decapitalization.

## Conclusion

This chapter has offered some reflections on key features of the development of the post-war global economy. Perhaps the most striking feature to emerge from the discussion is the interpenetration and interdependency of notionally separate global processes. Consider, for example, the history of the international monetary system since 1945. Although this was discussed in terms of the achievements, contradictions and ultimate failure of the Bretton Woods system, important processes conditioning developments in the monetary sphere are to be located elsewhere. Thus the critical weakness of the dollar in the early 1970s did not arise out of the ether, it was a reflection of chronic deterioration in the trading performance of the US economy in comparison with the progress being made by Germany and Japan. Moreover, the financial flows which actually broke the Bretton Woods system were partly facilitated by the growth of new offshore capital markets and the burgeoning concentrations of wealth therein.

While the global economy is clearly a highly integrated entity, it is also an enormously uneven one. The advanced economies continue to consume a disproportionate share of world output. With the exception of a relatively small number of NICs and, perhaps, newly liberalizing economies, this pattern shows little sign of disruption. For the impoverished and debt-ridden countries of Latin America and, in particular Africa, continued relative, even absolute, decline is the medium-term prospect.

## Note

1   The Cairns group comprises: Argentina, Australia, Brazil, Canada, Chile, Columbia, Fiji, Hungary, Indonesia, Malaysia, Philippines, New Zealand, Thailand and Uruguay.

# 8

# The Politics of the
# Global Environment

## John Vogler

In the last twenty years there has been a revolution in scientific under-standing of the processes of global environmental change. The actual and potential seriousness of environmental degradation has received widespread, if intermittent, public and political attention. From being the province of a handful of specialists, environmental questions have become part of the subject matter of international politics, a process neatly encapsulated in the title of a recent book by a serving diplomat – *The Greening of Machiavelli* (Brenton 1994). Opinions differ, how-ever, as to the extent to which global environmental issues, whatever their long-term significance, remain peripheral to the traditional preoc-cupations of statecraft (Smith 1993).

In 1972, at Stockholm, the United Nations held its first major gathering to discuss threats to the human environment, the United Nations Conference on the Human Environment (UNCHE). This produced a declaration and a set of principles dealing with such matters as the desirability of cooperative action to preserve the earth's ecology, the responsibilities of states for transboundary pollution, the sover-eignty of states over their national resources and their rights to devel-opment. It is important to recall that, from the outset, there was a close connection between the environmental and development agendas. Indeed one of the key compromises negotiated at UNCHE was embodied in Principle 21, which coupled state responsibility for transboundary pollution with the inalienable right to the exploitation of national resources – as demanded by southern governments. More concrete recommendations urged, amongst other things, the cessation of commercial whaling (finally achieved in 1985, although partly resumed in 1994) and the setting up of the United Nations Environment Programme (UNEP) in Nairobi.

UNEP's activities in stimulating and coordinating scientific activities over the next two decades contributed materially to a developing understanding that environmental degradation was not simply a localized, transboundary, or even regional phenomenon but was occurring on a global scale. Some theorists of climate change had suspected this for a long time, but the concept of global change now gained commonplace acceptance in political and scientific circles. The second great UN conference on the environment (UNCED – United Nations Conference on Environment and Development or more popularly 'the Earth Summit') held in Rio in the early summer of 1992, if it did nothing else, gave high level political salience and saturation publicity to the problems of global environmental change.

It might be argued that, despite the global rhetoric of UNCED, only a few of the physical processes under discussion occur on a truly global scale. The most evident have been stratospheric ozone depletion and the central item on the Rio agenda – climate change. The earth's stratospheric ozone layer (at an altitude of 15–50 km) serves to protect life from the dangerous effects of UV/B radiation. Its depletion leads to increases in the incidence of human skin cancers and eye cataracts and there is even evidence of risk of suppression of the immune system. Malformations in plant and aquatic life also occur. Ozone layer depletion through the action of man-made halogenated chemicals (chiefly CFCs [chlorofluorocarbons] and halons) had been a scientific hypothesis since 1974. However it was only in the mid-1980s that the extent of the actual damage caused by such chemicals to the ozone layer was fully established. Most dramatic was the discovery of the Antarctic 'ozone hole' in 1985 by a British Antarctic Survey balloon experiment: previous data from a highly expensive and sophisticated American Nimbus 7 satellite having been automatically rejected as being so extreme as to be beyond the bounds of probability. Ozone depletion, although most severe at the poles, was a truly global phenomenon – the response, in terms of the Vienna Convention of 1985 and the Montreal Protocol of 1987 (discussed below) has come to be regarded as a model of international cooperation.

The discussion of ozone layer depletion in the late 1980s was overshadowed by concern about climate change. This was, and to an extent remains, an hypothesis; but one of awesome complexity and implication. The idea that changes in the composition of the atmosphere can alter mean global temperatures is one which dates from the nineteenth century. A relatively stable temperature on earth is maintained by the 'greenhouse effect'; that is, the presence of particular quantities of the greenhouse gases – carbon dioxide, methane, nitrous oxide, CFCs and water vapour – in the atmosphere serves to regulate surface temperature by trapping solar radiation. What has been identified as a problem is the 'enhanced greenhouse effect'. Here excessive quantities of greenhouse gases will, it is argued, serve to raise mean global temperatures over the span of the next century – with a range of serious climatic and physical effects, including a predicted and potentially catastrophic rise in global sea levels.

The Intergovernmental Panel on Climate Change (IPCC) scientific assessment concluded that, under a 'business as usual' scenario with no attempt to alter patterns of energy use, there would over the next century be a mean global temperature rise of 0.3 degrees centigrade per decade. This would amount to a temperature change greater than that seen over the past 10,000 years. The consequence, stemming from thermal expansion of the oceans and melting ice, would be a sea level increase of 20 cm by 2030 and 65 cm by 2100 (Houghton 1991:23–4). A rise in sea level of this magnitude would involve the inundation of low lying coastal regions from the Netherlands to Bangladesh and the disappearance of numerous Pacific atolls.

A wide range of other environmental problems – marine pollution, acid rain deposition, desertification and the loss of biodiversity through deforestation – may not, strictly speaking, occur on a global scale. None the less, by the time of UNCED they had come to be seen as interrelated components of a single global system. Here the fundamental point is that even quite specific forms of degradation are conceptualized in terms of global ecology in which the earth is one com-plex system. The interlinkages become particularly evident when climate change is considered. Carbon emissions from worldwide human activity are absorbed by a variety of natural 'sinks' including forests and the oceans. The cutting down of forests alters the balance between sources and sinks and reduces the biodiversity of the planet, with implications for the development of new pharmaceutical and crop strains. Increased mean temperatures and associated changes in rainfall patterns threaten to accelerate the process of desertification.

The general circulation models of climate change are true global models which have begun, imperfectly, to map the complexities of the system. As Skolnikoff (1993:183) observes, climate change does indeed represent the 'apotheosis of the idea that everything is related to everything else'. Although it is impossible to measure such phenomena with any accuracy, this is also a public and political perception. Many of the problems of global change have their roots in technological 'progress' but one such advance – the ability to observe the planet from outer space – has been deeply significant in fostering an holistic image of the earth which has scientific, political and even spiritual dimensions.

## Socio-Economic Causes of Environmental Change

A clear implication of the holistic view, but one which is often neglected by natural scientists, is that socio-economic and political phenomena are at the core of the problem. Global change of the sort which threatens the physical stability of the planet in the immediate future is the result of human behaviour and human institutions. Technological and economic development since the industrial revolution has been on such a scale as to exceed, or threaten to exceed, the carrying capacity of the natural systems and to damage their recuperative capabilities. Sometimes the problem may be avoidable or its solution relatively simple – for example eradication of CFCs or avoidance of ocean dumping of radioactive waste and heavy metals – but the problem of global environmental change is a function of the trajectory of human socio-economic development. It is associated with energy use and resource consumption integral to human society. In consequence it impinges on the right to development of the earth's poorest peoples and involves deeply controversial issues of future population levels and population policy. In the last analysis it is people and their activities that threaten the planet; environmental degradation is not the consequence of the use of a few exotic chemicals or the careless disposal of waste; but of 'normal' human activity.

A major political problem in bringing about changes in patterns and levels of consumption sufficient to guarantee the stability of the human environment is that the scientific evaluation of the consequences of continuing 'business as usual' is still uncertain. In the case of global warming it is likely to remain so until it is too late to take effective remedial action. The record appears to show that policy changes are possible if, as in the case of the ozone layer, there is a high degree of scientific certainty, and consensus, and abatement measures are not excessively costly. Any action to reduce carbon dioxide emissions, save forests and maintain biodiversity, or even to guarantee the phasing out of particular chemicals like CFCs, is ultimately confronted by the issue of global economic inequality. There is no question that the responsibility for current degradation of the environment rests squarely with a small minority of the world's population, located in developed, industrialized societies. Thus comparison of the energy and resource use of the developed and less developed worlds reveals that the calorie intake of American cattle is greater than that of the people of Asia and Africa. It is, therefore, hardly surprising that environmental questions and the 'development gap' between North and South have become inextricably linked in the politics of global environmental change. The nature of this connection, and indeed the diagnosis and possible solutions to global change problems, have been subject to fundamentally different interpretations.

## Approaches to Global Environmental Change: The Issue of Sustainability

A key distinction is between the orthodox view that solutions are available through the adaptation of human institutions (international cooperation, as will be argued below, is an important component of this) and radical interpretations which argue that the question of global change can only be addressed by an abandonment of current forms of socio-economic development and a levelling off of the growth trajectory. Failing this there may by some form of collapse after which the planet will adapt and survive but not humankind as we know it (Lovelock 1989). A relatively sanguine view of the latter possibility is associated with the 'deep green' philosophy of some environmentalists who have moved away from an 'anthropocentric' or human-centred view of the environment. Most analyses, however, still proceed on the basis that the essential task is to safeguard the human environment.

The most orthodox of these stress the importance of incorporating 'big science' (IPCC and the whole armoury of government funded global change research) into policy, and the development of 'win-win solutions' which will allow the continuation of growth along an environmentally sustainable path. The key concept here is 'sustainable development'. Coined in the mid-1980s by the Brundtland Commission, which was set up by the UN General Assembly to consider environment and development issues, and which was generally endorsed by governments at UNCED, 'sustainable development' is briefly defined as 'a process of change in which the exploitation of resources, the direction of investments, the orientation of technological development, and institutional change are all in harmony and enhance both current and future potential to meet human needs and aspirations' (Brundtland 1987:46).

The notion of sustainable development addresses the yawning gap between developed and less developed countries by affirming that the latter can develop, industrialize and take a productive place in the global economy without destroying the global environment. It also means, of course, that the North can maintain and improve its own standards of living. Opinions differ as to the changes that will be necessary and the degree of public and political understanding and will that are required.

Very often the core of the problem is viewed economically. At one extreme it is argued that there is little that could or should be done by governments if resource shortages occur, and that markets alone will provide (IEA 1994). Since the collapse of the Soviet 'alternative' model of planned development the notion that solutions must be found within the framework of an open market capitalist system has gained wide currency. Indeed it is explicitly stated in recent environmental agreements, including those emanating from the 1992 Earth Summit – for example the Preamble to the Framework Convention on Climate Change and the Rio Declaration itself. None the less, it is still widely argued that extensive national and international efforts are required to reform and regulate economic activity and utilization of the environment. This was the burden of the Brundtland report and of the recent successor to the 1970s 'Limits to Growth' computer simulation. Here it is argued that environmental overshoot and collapse is not inevitable if the right national and international policy directions for resource and energy use and population limitation are established now (Meadows et al. 1992).

Sustainable development, whether in market-led laissez faire or dirigiste mode, has considerable political attractions and served at UNCED to combine the environmental agenda of the North with the developmental requirements of southern governments. Radical political ecology, however, challenges its basic assumptions. From this perspective, existing models of development are seen as constituting the problem from which environmental consequences flow. These development models cannot be transformed through existing institutions into an environmentally friendly, sustainable version (Sachs 1993; *Ecologist* 1993). Thus, for radical ecologists, attempts to work within the 'sustainable development' framework on a global scale are positively harmful because they prioritize growth (as in the demands for additional development assistance at UNCED) which in turn fuels the engine of environmental destruction. The rhetoric of the Rio Declaration, and the accompanying policy recommendations contained in Agenda 21, stress the importance of local action and the rights of a virtuous trio of youth, women and indigenous peoples. In the radical view this will remain rhetoric, and malign rhetoric at that, because global action by governments will marginalize the very people in local communities who, left to their own devices and unconscripted into the global economy, might be capable of sustaining their own immediate ecosystems.

These broad approaches to the question of global environmental change provide the framework within which the more specific international politics of the environment has been conducted. They also provide a means, as will be discussed at the conclusion of this chapter, of evaluating the achievements and failures of international activity intended to address environmental issues and problems.

## International Cooperation and the Global Commons

As the Stockholm and Rio conferences demonstrate, the international political system provides a stage upon which governments and other actors can display (particularly to domestic publics) the extent of their environmental concern and good intentions. The 1992 Earth Summit was at the time the largest-scale diplomatic event ever held. Like Stockholm before it, the Rio Summit served to enunciate norms of environmental conduct. Many of these were stated in extraordinary detail in Agenda 21. This 600-page document was the fruit of two years of painstaking international negotiation in the 'Prepcom' for UNCED. Its forty chapters cover everything from 'making trade and environment mutually supportive' (chapter 2,B) to the role of local authorities in sustainable development (chapter 28) and managing fragile mountain ecosystems (chapter 13). Thus Agenda 21 provides a comprehensive set of guidelines which is truly global in scope (with the politically significant exception of Antarctica).[1] These guidelines do not, of course, have the binding force of international law, but progress towards their implementation will be discussed by a new United Nations body set up as a consequence of UNCED – the Commission for Sustainable Development.

Beyond exhortation, the principal focus of international environmental politics is the need to organize cooperation between states in coping with their mutual problems. This may be seen as the provision of 'governance without government'. It is a defining feature of the international system of sovereign states that there is no central government; no authority to regulate the use or misuse of the environment, to enforce standards and impose penalties. As has often been remarked, pollution does not recognize territorial boundaries and, as argued above, there are significant ways in which we may regard environmental problems as having global scope. There is, thus, a vital requirement for the exercise of 'government like functions' (we have used the term 'governance') through the cooperation of states.

In its simplest form this has involved agreement between two or more state governments on an issue of mutual interest. An early example is provided by the 1911 Convention for the Protection of Fur Seals signed between the United States, Canada and Russia. Transboundary atmospheric and water pollution issues have become increasingly significant in interstate politics as industrialization has proceeded. Negotiations on responsibility for and abatement of forms of pollution such as 'acid rain' have been particularly difficult because the costs and damage of pollution may arise hundreds of miles from its origin and within a different national jurisdiction (Carroll 1988, Part III). Bilateral and multilateral agreements – such as the Convention on

Long-Range Transboundary Air Pollution, signed by 32 European countries, the USA, Canada and the European Community in 1979 – have often been criticized for their ineffectiveness. Nevertheless they have encouraged serious collaborative research on environmental problems and, in the case of the Sofia Protocol to the Convention on Long-Range Transboundary Air Pollution, achieved real reductions in the levels of national emissions of pollutants (Sand 1992:132–5); indeed the scale of the development of international environmental law has been impressive.[2] There has been a parallel growth in international organization; whether in dedicated organizations such as UNEP or the commissions associated with the ozone 'regime' (see below), or through extension of the remit of existing organizations such as the World Meteorological Organization and the International Maritime Organization, and even the IMF and World Bank.

The scale of the attempt at international environmental governance is not in doubt, but its efficacy is. Many of the areas of global environmental concern have the characteristics of 'commons', that is to say they are not actually owned by anyone (they are not under sovereign jurisdiction) but are used by many. The global commons traditionally comprised the high seas and the deep sea bed. More recently Antarctica has been ascribed the status of a commons through a 1959 Treaty which placed territorial claims in abeyance. At about the same time it was possible to observe the opening up of a new commons in outer space and it is now recognized that the global atmosphere is also a commons.

Unrestricted use of such commons can, given current levels of exploitation, lead to ecological collapse. Discussion of the ways in which this can occur usually takes as its starting point the seminal article by Garret Hardin (1968) on the 'tragedy of the commons' (although the English philosopher David Hume had, as Hardin acknowledged, made the same essential points two centuries before). Hardin's analogy is with the medieval villager's common pasture. There is a short-run incentive for each villager to graze as many sheep as possible on the common pasture with the inevitable result that the pasture is eventually ruined by overgrazing. The structure of the 'tragedy of the commons' has many similarities with Mancur Olson's (1965) 'collective action' problem which posits that individuals have no incentive to pay for public goods from the enjoyment of which they cannot be excluded. Arguably a clean environment and pure air constitute such a public good. The solution to both these problems has traditionally been seen to lie with action by government, which may solve the overgrazing problem by legislating for 'enclosure'. This would involve the division of common land into private lots, with the assumption that individuals would then be motivated to tend their own property in a sustainable way. If the benefit to be derived from the commons is in the form of a public good, however, then governments may raise taxation to pay for its sustenance and use coercive measures against polluters.

The extent to which such analogies from the domestic political process are deemed to have relevance to international governance varies according to the perspective of the commentator. So, too, does assessment of the prospects for successful international cooperation. Here it is not too much of a caricature to say that the mainstream debate about international cooperation is polarized between neo-realists and liberal institutionalists (Milner 1992; Haas, Keohane and Levy 1993).

In the view of neo-realist analysts there are few incentives for co-operation among states. Rather they would be expected to behave self-interestedly in the manner of Hardin's medieval villagers; and in the international political system there is no overarching authority to restrain them or allocate property rights. Consequently governments have no incentive to prevent overfishing of the oceans or the emission of pollutants and cannot be expected to have much regard for the long-term consequences for the global environment. Lacking any basis for mutual cooperation, effective structures of rules and international organization can only be created and maintained by a hegemonic power – which may regarded as the functional equivalent of world government. As we noted in chapter two, advocates of the 'hegemonic stability thesis' argue that the United States did, in effect, play this role in designing and sustaining the institutions of international cooperation after the Second World War. However, the relative decline of the USA since the late 1960s places the future of multilateral international institutions in doubt. If this line of reasoning is accepted, then the future of the global environmental commons appears bleak.

Liberal institutionalists start, as would be supposed, from liberal rather than Hobbesian assumptions. They point to the evident possibility of international cooperation in managing the interdependence arising from mutual vulnerability to global environmental change. Perhaps the ultimate form of such interdependence is that associated with a common interest in the survival of global ecosystems. Institutions for international governance have been created and significantly determine and restrain national behaviour. They can provide international 'public goods' and they do not necessarily require 'hegemonic leadership'. This is essentially the international variant of the argument put forward by critics of Hardin's 'tragedy of the commons'. Ostrom (1990), Berkes (1989) and others have pointed out that the 'tragedy' is in fact not only historically inaccurate, but also refuted by evidence of the ability of communities to create effective institutions to govern local commons in a sustainable way without resort to enclosure or regulation by a coercive central government. This is encouraging for those who emphasize the possibility of international cooperation for the sustainable development of the global commons. Caution is in order, however. Whatever the rhetoric of 'international community', the sociology of the interstate system, with all its inequalities, political antagonisms and cultural diversity, is far removed from that of the small-scale communities which have managed in practice to refute Hardin's model of inevitable tragedy.

What does international cooperation on global environmental issues actually amount to? One way of investigating this is to pursue the idea of the global commons and the kind of governance functions that would be required for their sustainable management. These are essentially similar to those encountered in studies of small-scale commons (Ostrom 1990) but intrinsically much more difficult to organize. They include, first of all, the development of sets of collective rules and standards to allocate sustainable shares in common resources, or limit or prohibit forms of misuse and pollution. Such sets of rules and standards are commonly referred to as 'regimes'. Regimes denote the networks of norms, rules and decision-making procedures that coordinate behaviour in the international system (Krasner 1983). They include formal international law and are often administered by international organizations. Yet regimes also comprise informal understandings and practices. They are issue-specific, that is they 'govern' particular monetary, trade, pollution control or other activities. Liberal institutionalists see them as playing an important role in their own right through the way in which they structure the choices and behaviour of actors.

Despite the significance attributed to regime norms and rules, the 'collective action' problem identified by so many theorists suggests that it may be necessary to devise mechanisms for ensuring that participants keep to the rules and do not 'free ride' on the efforts of others. Otherwise, we must assume, users of common resources will not be prepared to limit their own activities in the ultimate collective interest unless they can be assured that others are doing likewise. Thus, critical functions of any commons regime are monitoring of behaviour and some form of rule enforcement.

Where sustainable management – and indeed the perception that a problem exists at all – rests upon scientific understanding, another key function will be the generation of knowledge and its evaluation and integration into the decision-making process. The final function will be essentially political, involving the making of unavoidable collective choices over the development of rules and their implementation.

## Rules and International Law

A primary outcome of international environmental negotiation is the production of rules and standards serving to coordinate international behaviour in the sustainable management of common resources. Such rules and standards may take the form of binding international legal instruments (treaties and conventions with their associated protocols) or they may be embodied in 'softer' forms of international law: recommendations and guidelines or merely 'understandings'. Here there is extensive evidence of international cooperation to preserve the global commons.

### *The oceans*

The oldest of the global commons are the oceans. Here the recent trend has been to 'enclose' great tracts of ocean sea-bed and fishery resources by the creation of 200-mile Exclusive Economic Zones (EEZs). This was an outcome of the prolonged deliberations of the Third United Nations Law of the Sea Conference.[3] Attempts had previously been made to manage fishery stocks on a regional basis by International Fisheries Commissions, but these were largely made redundant as key fishing grounds passed under national or European Community control. However evidence from the UN Food and Agriculture Organization (FAO) of continued overfishing and decline of stocks shows that the results of this 'enclosure' have been unimpressive, and probably worse than those obtained by the previous international commissions. In particular the FAO's evidence demonstrates the tendency for northern fishing fleets, having exhausted the stocks of northern waters, to overexploit southern fish stocks. This is of great significance due to the centrality of fish to the protein intake of many peoples of the South (Brown and Vidal 1994).

A marine resource which has always been treated on a global basis has been whales (or more correctly the fifty-eight species of cetaceans). By the conclusion of the 1946 International Convention for the Regulation of Whaling (ICRW) whale populations had already been subject, over the previous two centuries, to a series of spectacular commons tragedies where rapacious killing had not only made whole species of great whale virtually extinct but had decimated the associated whaling industries. This process continued until 1985, when a belated International Whaling Commission decision established a moratorium on all commercial whaling. The Commission itself was dominated by non-whaling countries and by a vociferous set of environmental NGOs who gave the whaling issue a high public profile. In 1994 the rules were revised to provide a southern ocean whale sanctuary but at the same time, controversially, to allow the resumption of the hunting of Minke whales (up to an agreed quota) by the Japanese and Norwegian industries.

The major area of international marine environmental cooperation involved the attempt to combat pollution. Very significant global rules have been developed under the 1972 London Convention on dumping and the 1973 and 1978 Conventions on Maritime Pollution (MARPOL). The former prohibits the dumping at sea of a range of toxic wastes and has recently, in 1993, been extended to cover low level radwaste (radioactive waste). MARPOL has been heavily involved with complex international standards and rules on tanker construction and operations designed, quite effectively, to reduce the incidence of maritime oil pollution.

### Antarctica

The arrangements for Antarctica are closely associated with but legally separate from those pertaining to the high seas. Antarctica is a commons by international design for, unlike the atmosphere or the deep oceans, it could realistically be appropriated by sovereign states. The original Antarctic Treaty – signed by an exclusive club of states with territorial or scientific interests in the continent (the Antarctic Treaty Consultative Parties, ATCPs) – was essentially designed to avoid a territorial struggle by putting aside such claims. In addition the intention was to isolate Antarctica – a valued site of international scientific cooperation – from Cold War competition and militarization. Thus the original treaty said nothing at all about the protection of the extremely fragile ecosystems of this 'last great wilderness on earth'.

Subsequently a dense network of environmental recommendations and rules has been established by the ATCPs. They include a large number of recommendations to preserve flora and fauna and to limit the impact of Antarctic scientific bases. Antarctic waters are regulated by the Convention on Antarctic Marine Living Resources, designed to control the exploitation of the fisheries of the Southern Ocean and the tiny but ubiquitous krill (collectively the largest biomass on earth) which is at the base of the short food chain. During the 1980s an unsuccessful attempt was made to provide a regulatory framework for future commercial exploitation of Antarctic mineral resources. The proposed convention was blocked by the defection of France and Australia and was replaced by the negotiation of an environmental protocol to the original Treaty (Madrid Protocol 1991). This provides for a fifty-year ban on mineral development alongside some of the most stringent environmental controls to be found in any international legislation. Significantly, these controls embody the precautionary principle – that action can, and indeed must, be taken to control a source of pollution even if there is at the time only inconclusive evidence of its damaging effects.

## The atmospheric commons

As was noted in the introduction to this chapter, the global atmospheric commons became the focus of international attention during the 1980s. Stratospheric ozone layer depletion through the action of man-made halogenated chemicals was first formally addressed in the Vienna Convention of 1985. This was a 'framework' convention which signalled a recognition by governments of the existence of the problem; and their intent to sponsor and share scientific research with a view to establishing international controls on the relevant chemicals. The latter were produced surprisingly quickly, albeit as the result of arduous negotiations, and embodied in the Montreal Protocol of 1987. This complex agreement set targets for the reduction of CFC production by national chemical industries and made special provisions for the developing world. In 1990 and again in 1992, at London and Copenhagen, the ozone regime was extended and tightened in the light of further scientific evidence about the causes and extent of ozone layer depletion. A complete phase-out of the main CFCs was advanced from the original target date of 2000 to 1996, although targets stretching well into the twenty-first century were agreed for a range of other ozone-depleting chemicals, the HCFCs and halons.

Although comparisons are often made between the ozone case and that of greenhouse gases and climate change, the scale and complexity of the regulatory problem arising from the attempt to moderate possible future climate change is hardly equivalent to the relatively simple matter of obtaining agreement on a specified and generally substitutable set of artificial chemicals, produced by a handful of manufacturers. There has been widespread disillusionment at the outcome of the attempt to erect an international climate change regime which would, in the first instance, attempt to limit future carbon dioxide emissions. From 1990 the UN General Assembly sponsored negotiations in the Intergovernmental Negotiating Committee (INC) for a climate change convention. The centrepiece was to have been a formal and binding commitment by the developed countries to reduce their carbon dioxide emissions to 1990 levels by the year 2000. In the event the United States government refused to accept such an obligation. The Framework Convention on Climate Change (FCCC) which was presented for signature at the Rio Conference and entered into force during 1994, was, in consequence, significantly watered down. The operative clause from Article 4 simply reads:

> Parties shall adopt . . . policies and take corresponding measures on the mitigation of climate change, by limiting anthropogenic emissions of

greenhouse gases and protecting and enhancing greenhouse gas sinks and reservoirs. These policies and measures will demonstrate that developed countries are taking the lead in modifying longer-term trends in anthropogenic emissions consistent with the objective of the Convention, recognizing that the return by the end of the present decade to earlier levels of anthropogenic emissions of carbon dioxide and other greenhouse gases not controlled by the Montreal Protocol would contribute much to such modification . . . (United Nations 1992, Article 4.1)

To compound this failure to negotiate binding targets for reduction of emissions, pre-UNCED negotiations failed to produce a related agreement on the preservation of forests, which constitute a 'sink' for greenhouse gases as well as the earth's major storehouse of biodiversity. A Convention on Biodiversity was eventually concluded at UNCED. This commits parties to taking national measures for the preservation of biodiversity and, significantly, establishes the sovereign rights of states over natural and genetic resources. The convention also contains clauses on technology access and transfer and was judged at the time by representatives of the United States to be a threat to its biotechnology business. The initial American refusal to sign has since been reversed by the Clinton administration.

## Monitoring, Compliance and Enforcement

The various rules mentioned above serve to coordinate national policies regarding the global commons. Adherence usually involves some immediate cost, whether in restrictions on fishing, modifications to tankers or emission reductions. In common with users of local commons, national governments will wish to ensure that their interests are protected through universal adherence to standards or rules. In some cases, notably that of the ozone regime, the international rules will be an extension of what were originally national regulations. Here, once the United States and other developed countries had – in the late 1970s – introduced domestic restrictions on the use of CFCs as aerosol propellants, there was pressure to internationalize the rules in order to provide a level commercial playing field.

Just as local commons regimes require some mechanism to ensure that individuals are not breaking the rules and taking excessive shares of a common resource, so the preservation of international environmental rules requires effective monitoring and compliance systems. The nature of the international system – legally composed of sovereign equals – does not allow for the kind of governmental enforcement possible at the local level. Insofar as it is possible to talk about enforcement at all, it would be 'horizontal enforcement'. This refers to an incentive to comply with rules deriving from the loss of reputation that would occur if a government or its subjects were to be found 'cheating'. Adherence to the rules is frequently based on reciprocity and this is well understood. Without assurances that others are in compliance, the agreements themselves will tend to unravel.

There is a strong parallel here with the extensive experience of international arms control where, in an atmosphere devoid of trust, agreements could only be sustained through rigorous monitoring and verification. The situation is not quite as extreme with international environmental regimes, but to be effective most rely heavily upon monitoring and information gathering activities. Thus one of the weaknesses of the whaling regime was the prolonged failure to implement an international observer scheme and the ease with which, it has now been publicly revealed, the Soviet Union was able not only to exploit loopholes in the agreement but to covertly flout its terms. The Antarctic regime has no centralized inspection mechanisms and parties are expected to report each other's behaviour. An understandable reluctance to do this has accentuated the role of private NGOs, and especially Greenpeace, in exposing breaches of the Antarctic and maritime pollution rules.

Recent attempts at regulating the atmospheric commons have placed great emphasis on 'transparency' and the continuous monitoring of compliance. Complex (but sometimes flawed) reporting procedures are part of the Montreal Protocol review process. The FCCC is essentially reliant upon an 'implementation review' procedure in which reports by governments on progress towards meeting the requirements of the convention are to be received and discussed by periodic conferences of the parties.

## Science and Policy

The international politics of the environment contains many of the traditional ingredients of interstate relations; the concern with national sovereignty and prestige, the furtherance of national economic and political interests and the pursuit of commercial advantage. There is, however, a significant added dimension in that the currency of negotiations is likely to be scientific evidence and prediction. This can give rise to novel problems of coping with highly abstruse technical material and integrating specialist advice into foreign policy-making procedures.

Scientific consensus is particularly important for the legitimation of international action to regulate the environmental commons. The obverse side of this coin is that a lack of conclusive information, or a disagreement between 'experts', frequently becomes an excuse for inaction. This happened regularly in the deliberations of the International Whaling Commission and similar problems have also beset the

Antarctic regime. The ozone regime presents the contrary case, where scientific consensus built an ever more powerful case for taking immediate action. The Vienna Convention and Montreal Protocol also provide an institutional model for the effective coupling of evolving scientific knowledge to policy. The initial convention provides a framework within which a continuing process of investigation and creation and adjustment of control measures can take place – a model which has been explicitly adopted elsewhere.

Although much of the influence of scientific advice derives from the belief that a scientific consensus represents objective knowledge to which political leaders must respond, it would be naive to suggest that the international scientific enterprise is depoliticized. Haas (1990; 1992) and others have proposed an explanation of regime creation based upon the influence of transnational knowledge-based networks or 'epistemic communities'. The members of such communities, it is argued, consciously use their position to set agendas, structure discussion and push for the adoption of international environmental agreements. As Haas's (1990) study of the Mediterranean Action Plan reveals, such communities may even achieve success on the basis of scientific estimates that later turn out to have been incorrect.

The most controversial area of current activity is 'global change' research which investigates the probability and ramifications of hypothesized climate change. The word 'hypothesized' is used because the 'enhanced greenhouse effect' remains only a well supported hypothesis, with all that implies for international action to regulate the global atmospheric commons. The scale of the associated international scientific enterprise is impressive indeed. Major funds, prestige and influence are at stake and it has a politics all of its own. The current international effort has at its apex the Intergovernmental Panel on Climate Change, set up by and reporting to the World Climate Conference, which brings together a high level group of international experts and is supposed to provide the best available advice concerning the likelihood of climate change. It was their report (Houghton 1990) which provided the stimulus to the FCCC negotiations through its warning of significant temperature and sea level rises over the next century if nothing is done to curb current and projected levels of greenhouse gas emissions. The IPCC is supported by and relates to a plethora of other agencies and international research programmes, such as the International Geosphere Biosphere Programme, the World Climate Research Programme, UNEP itself, the Global Environmental Monitoring System and the various bodies associated with the International Council of Scientific Unions (one of which is the Scientific Committee for Antarctic Research).

The sheer scale of this activity in international networking and research programmes is, in part, a testament to the progress of international cooperation in the second half of the twentieth century. It also demonstrates the significance of non-state actors in global environmental politics; whether these be NGOs such as Greenpeace involved in monitoring and lobbying activities, transnational business corporations such as DuPont engaged in the production of ozone-depleting chemicals, or environmental scientists whose predictions and recommendations inevitably influence government policy and whose continued research funding is dependent upon the identification of problems requiring investigation.

## International Organization

International organization is, according to Inis Claude's (1962) definition, essentially a process as well as a set of formal organizational structures. Both are highly significant in the politics of the global environmental commons. The complex organization that has developed to sustain, encourage and fund the range of collaborative scientific activities described above provides one instance. Organization is required to monitor and disseminate information and, above all, to provide a mechanism for the making of collective choices about regime rules and their implementation. Some sets of 'governance arrangements' for the global commons can survive with minimal levels of formal organization. The Antarctic Treaty System lacks even a dedicated secretariat and for many years relied upon meetings of the consultative parties, held at two-yearly intervals. Others have dedicated organizations like the International Whaling Commission or rely upon UNEP officials to service periodic meetings of the parties, as in the case of the ozone regime. The maritime pollution agreements rely upon the International Maritime Organization (IMO), which performs a wide range of other maritime functions as well.

Most activity, but not all, occurs within the dispersed and complex framework of the United Nations system. The majority of UN specialized agencies and programmes now have an environmental role. Some, like UNEP and the World Meteorological Organization, are centrally concerned. Others, particularly in the economic area (the IMF, the World Bank and UNCTAD), have only relatively recently become involved with environmental issues. Here the Global Environmental Facility of the World Bank has acquired particular significance as the primary funding agency for international environmental projects. Within the UN system there is now a major problem of coordination between all the involved agencies (Imber 1993).

International organizations continue to reflect the fact that their formal members are states, although particular secretariats and individuals such as Maurice Strong (Chairman of UNCED) or the ex-

Director General of UNEP, Mostafa Tolba, may be influential in their own right. There is also an increasing trend to grant observer rights on UN bodies to NGOs, a category that includes many well known environmental pressure groups. They have had influence, particularly in the development of the whaling regime, in the Antarctic and within the UNCED process (Princen and Finger 1994). In general, however, decision-making is still in the hands of government delegations usually operating under the UN rule of one state one vote, with the requirement of consensus for important issues. This does not always guarantee rapid action.

The need to operate within the framework of formal organizations also means that inter- and intra-organizational conflicts often intrude. One example is provided by the Antarctic Treaty Powers who have resolutely denied the right of the UN General Assembly to participate in the governance of Antarctica. Furthermore UNEP, which had successfully coordinated the ozone regime, was excluded from playing such a role in relation to the climate change negotiations, where the Intergovernmental Negotiating Committee was run by the UN General Assembly Secretariat. There may be elements of inter-organizational rivalry here, but deeper issues often lie behind organizational disputes. Frequently such issues have a North–South character. An example is provided by the Global Environmental Facility of the World Bank, which has been the subject of constant dispute. Thus Southern governments greatly prefer financial and other arrangements to be coordinated through UN agencies such as UNEP, which are subject to democratic voting procedures (that is one member one vote) and where they enjoy a substantial majority, rather than through organizations such as the World Bank which are dominated by developed countries. At present the Interim Ozone Fund is coordinated by UNEP; however the more recent Climate Change financial arrangements were made the responsibility of the World Bank's GEF.

## Intergovernmental Solutions to Global Problems?

The distinction between the global and the intergovernmental has great significance for the discussion of solutions to global environmental problems. The World Bank may call its environmental fund the Global Environmental Facility but it is actually an international fund run by an intergovernmental organization. UNCED may have been styled the Earth Summit and even hosted a 'global forum', but it was in reality a very large interstate diplomatic gathering at which non-state actors remained at the margin. Global environmental politics, despite the growing significance of NGOs, is still pre-eminently intergovernmental politics. The mainstream literature in international relations mirrors this. There is, for the most part, an assumption that interstate cooperation is desirable and could be efficacious in averting the 'commons tragedies' discussed above. The main arguments are about the effectiveness of and barriers to such cooperation.

There is, indeed, substantial evidence of the effectiveness of international cooperation. Particular achievements such as the reduction in levels of intentional oil pollution of the oceans following the implementation of the MARPOL, or the essential preservation of the Antarctic environment, bear witness to this. These examples have many more parallels at the regional level, where ecosystems have been protected and revived through concerted action; although the precise impact of, for example, the Mediterranean Action Plan is subject to dispute.

The effectiveness of international environmental regimes should not merely be seen in terms of the joint prohibition of undesirable behaviour, but also in terms of a more subtle alteration of national attitudes and legal codes. This is an area that has been subject to very little research and there is always the 'chicken and egg' question concerning the relationship between national and international influence. However, it is undeniable that the Convention on Trade in Endangered Species (CITES) has had a worldwide impact upon fashions related to animal products, and that the whaling moratorium has influenced worldwide attitudes to the killing of cetaceans. The relationship is subtle and reciprocal in ways which parallel that between the international and regional human rights regimes and the evolution of national attitudes and practices.

It is difficult to arrive at any clear conclusions on international activity and global change issues because the development of cooperation has been relatively recent. The ozone example may provide some optimistic evidence. Here there clearly has been an alteration in national policies, and CFC use has been progressively abandoned. Also, countries that might have developed substantial CFC-based industries (for example manufacture of refrigeration equipment by Indian and Chinese firms for huge potential markets) have joined the Montreal Protocol regime, which makes special provision for 'ozone friendly' technology transfer to developing countries. Nevertheless doubts remain as to the full implementation of the protocol and, even if all goes to plan, it will only be in the latter half of the next century that the ozone layer is fully restored and the regime may be judged completely effective.

## Problems of Implementation

One of the uncertainties still besetting the ozone regime, and a problem for international environmental agreements in general, concerns implementation. While such agreements are made between sovereign states, it is not state authorities themselves who are usually responsible for environmental degradation. It is individuals – firms within the state's jurisdiction or ships flying its flag or entering its ports – that are the ultimate object of international rules. Even if a state is technically in compliance with international agreements there is no guarantee that environmentally damaging behaviour will actually be changed. The continuance of such behaviour may, in rare cases, (for example the Soviet violations of the whaling regulations referred to earlier) be covertly sanctioned, but it is likely that state authorities may simply be incapable of either monitoring or controlling what is going on within their territories. This is now fully recognized in the negotiation of agreements and the FCCC, for example, goes to some lengths to ensure the provision of funding and assistance for governments in drawing up plans to fulfil their treaty obligations.

The problem of implementation is greatly complicated by the trend towards economic globalization, where ownership and production structures cross state boundaries. There are inherent temptations for globally oriented firms to locate environmentally damaging activities in 'dirt havens' – countries with lax regulations or with administrations either unwilling or unable to exercise control. One of the several unfortunate aspects of the preparatory stage of UNCED was undoubtedly the termination by the UN of its long-running programme on transnational corporations. The increasing significance of transnational economic activity in a global economy is, in fact, another reason to stress the importance of building international regimes with clear, commonly accepted and enforceable standards. In the absence of such provisions, irresponsible firms will continue to exploit differences in national environmental legislation.

An apparently unavoidable implication of concerted action through the UN 'family' of intergovernmental organizations is fragmentation (Imber 1993): there will be organizational rivalries and the missions and programmes of existing organizations will reflect previous priorities. Moreover, as Brundtland (1987:314) noted, the internal structure of governments can be a further impediment to effective implementation, in that environment ministries do not enjoy the same power and prestige as economic and finance ministries. Thus, while environmental problems may be conceived in 'holistic' global terms, the institutional responses are partial and fragmented.

This fragmentation is especially evident when one analyses responses to the conjunction between an increasingly globalized economy and global environmental change. Regimes and international organizations concerned, on the one hand, with economic management and, on the other, with environmental protection have until recently pulled in opposite directions, and arguably still do. Thus the

World Bank, with a mission to promote a particular kind of economic development, has frequently been criticized for funding projects such as the Trans-Amazonian Highway or the Indian Sardar Sarovar and Narmada Sagar dams, which sacrifice the environment to rather crude concepts of GNP growth. Similarly, the GATT world trade regime now under the auspices of the WHO (see below) exists to encourage the growth of international trade through the elimination of protectionism and discrimination. The resource implications of such encouragement, especially in terms of energy consumption and the pressure to alter patterns of agriculture and to indulge in deforestation in order to trade in global markets, appear to directly contradict the intentions of the Framework Climate Convention. The IMF can also be regarded as essentially part of the problem because its policies of 'structural adjustment' instruct governments to prioritize export-led economic stabilization, which all too often involves the depletion of environmental capital.

At a very basic level the problem is not institutional, but rooted in prevailing economic theory and politically determined growth imperatives. Environmental variables are rarely taken into account in compiling national income statistics or framing concepts of welfare. The *reductio ad absurdum* of this approach was provided by the celebrated memo of the Chief Economist of the World Bank in 1991. This concluded that the World Bank should be encouraging more migration of dirty industries to LDCs because, according to standard welfare measures, the costs of waste dumping there were much lower than in developed countries. Consequently underpopulated countries in Africa, for example, were vastly underpolluted. Therefore, 'the economic logic behind dumping a load of toxic waste in the lowest wage country is impeccable and we should face up to it'. The memo, it was later claimed, was written in a spirit of irony to draw attention to the limitations of conventional economic thought. One commentator characterized it as 'perfectly logical but totally insane'.[4]

The existing economic regimes and organizations, set up under very different circumstances at the end of the Second World War and responding to the growth and development priorities of the period, continue to embody an environmentally damaging – some would say disastrous – set of politico-economic ideas. The real question is whether the current fabric of international cooperation, of which the international economic regimes are a central part, is capable of reform in the interests of environmental effectiveness. As we suggested earlier, the reformist view is that it is. Agreements can be refined, means can be found to monitor and strengthen implementation. The establishment of the new World Trade Organization provides the opportunity to amend the thinking behind the GATT such that institutions which have been effective in implementing non-discrimination now enshrine the 'polluter pays principle'. Thus the management of markets could assist rather than contradict attempts to curtail global environmental change. The 'greening of GATT' is paralleled by the introduction of the GEF and 'green conditionality' by the World Bank.

Writing about the trade regime, a former senior member of the US Environment Protection Agency expresses the way in which economic and environmental interests can make common cause:

> Both sides of the trade and environment debate seek to improve the efficiency of resource use and to add to world-wide social welfare. Both free traders and environmentalists would like to deter one nation from irresponsibly shifting burdens to another or from one generation to the next. And both communities face a constant threat from special interests that seek to twist the policy process to their own advantage at the expense of the broader public good. Most importantly, policy choices are available that can make trade liberalization and environmental protection mutually compatible and minimize the extent of disputes. (Esty 1994:226)

The underlying assumption, as with the Hague Declaration, UNCED itself and the UN Commission for Sustainable Development, is that the development of international cooperation, especially in aligning environmental and economic regimes, still provides the answer to the question of global change. International institutions provide the necessary framework for the sustainable management of the globe.

## Radical Political Ecology

This supposedly reformist and managerial view of international co-operation has been subject to an increasing volume of radical criticism. The many hypocrisies and failings of UNCED presented an unmissable target for a diverse set of critics. Numbered amongst them are members of the conventional political left, grasping the connections between economic injustice, political oppression and environmental degradation; theorists of the postmodern condition, eco-feminists and green activists. Although their various analyses have many different points of departure they converge, significantly, on a number of common positions which either de-emphasize the significance of international cooperation or regard it as actively counter-productive.

At the heart of these perspectives is a critical view of the develop-ment of western society, with its emphasis on scientific manipulation, capitalist economic growth and (male) competitiveness. The global environmental crisis is regarded, not as a problem to be managed within the terms of existing scientific and economic theories and social and political institutions, but as their consequence. Hence the concept of 'sustainable development', as enunciated by Brundtland

and enthusiastically accepted by governments, is simply a politically useful contradiction in terms. At the same time the surrounding rhetoric of global interdependence and 'spaceship earth' is positively misleading because of its suggestion of a common fate and common responsibility (the Framework Climate Convention has a form of words which rather neatly alludes to 'common but differentiated responsibilities'). The reality is that ozone layer depletion, the build up of atmospheric carbon dioxide and even biodiversity loss and deforestation are directly attributable to a minority of the earth's population enjoying the unsustainable benefits of a consumerist lifestyle and dominating a highly unjust and unequal global economic structure.

Assuming a global perspective has another connotation: besides the neglect of fundamental inequalities, it denotes an unprecedented scientific and managerial hubris. As Sachs (1993:18) explains 'human arrogance has discovered the ultimate dominion – planet Earth'. International cooperation is deeply suspect. It sustains what is seen as the illusion of global management. And it reinforces trends towards ecological destruction (Middleton et al. 1993; Sachs 1993; Rich 1994) because it involves accommodation of the interests of national governments and major business corporations.

Thus, while the constructive role of free trade and a responsible corporate sector received much endorsement at UNCED, underlying assumptions about economic growth remained unquestioned. The dimension of global inequality was central to the proceedings, and reflected in the formal title of the Rio Earth Summit, however this particular agenda was set by the requirements of southern governments rather than their peoples. The essential line, here, was that the new environmental interdependence between North and South presented an opportunity to press for greater resource transfers from the former to the latter – for the kind of development that had been the subject of extensive international debate after the oil crisis of the 1970s. Hence a considerable amount of the conference's time at Rio was taken up with estimates of the concessional finances that would be required for sustainable development in the South, and inflated statements about national performances in aid giving. In the view of ecological radicals the extension of current aid arrangements, because they involve national development projects and in all probability the World Bank or other similar agencies, will merely exacerbate environmental problems.

The frequent conclusion is that the overarching structure of international economic and political institutions, and indeed the state itself, lies at the root of the problem. Ekins, for example, couples statehood with the damage wrought by scientific orthodoxy and the belief in economic development and growth. Sovereign statehood and, by implication, the international system, is both a recent and highly unfortunate development:

The results of endowing these awkward, artificial political entities with absolute power over the people within their boundaries has been disastrous for hundreds of millions of their citizens . . . many national governments have been supremely irresponsible in the conduct of their affairs: wasting their substance with massive arms spending, prestige projects and luxurious lifestyles; using those arms both to attack their neighbours and repress and torture their own citizens; ruthlessly enforcing the dominant development model on their poor people in order to finance their projects and lifestyles; and laying waste their natural environments. . . . The world over, in Sarawak, Brazil, India and many other countries – people who have lived largely free from outside interference for millennia are now feeling the oppressive, often genocidal impact of state power. (Ekins 1992:206)

Under these circumstances it is idle to expect any positive outcome from collaboration between such oppressive entities. Instead there is recourse to what has been called 'global civil society' (Rich 1994) or 'grassroots movements for global change' (Ekins 1992). Commons cannot be saved from tragedy at the international level, only local action will suffice.

In perhaps the most coherent critique of UNCED, the *Ecologist* (1993) argues that the history of modern economic development and statehood has been the history of the enclosure of commons and the destruction of those local communities and institutions that had sustained them. The discussion of global commons and global management at an international level actually detracts from local action for sustainability. At base, the degradation of the global environment presents a political problem of shifting power away from centralized national and international bureaucracies and back to local communities:

For those used to imposing their will and languages on others, or who see the environmental threats facing humanity as so overwhelming that only centralized decision-making by cliques of experts can meet the task in hand, the call for community control is at best a threat to their power and at worst a recipe for indecision and muddling through to ecological disaster. But the evidence is overwhelming that local level institutions in which power is limited and the common right to survival is the preoccupation of all, are the best means of repairing the damage done through enclosure. (*Ecologist* 1993:192)

## Conclusion

The different views of international cooperation are sharply divergent – perhaps excessively polarized. Although there is much force in the radical critique, it is one thing to argue that the scale of global change requires a complete reversal of the economic growth trajectory allied to a total overhaul of the international system, and quite another to contemplate it as practical politics. There is, amongst many radical critics, an evident yearning for a return to a pre-modern condition of ecological balance and community responsibility – in effect the obverse of Hobbes's view of the anarchic conditions preceding the development of the state. This paradise, if it ever existed, will not be regained. It is unlikely that the interstate system could be fundamentally transformed within the time-scale that matters for global environmental change (the time horizon of the IPCC suggests 30–100 years). Regulatory authority will still be in state hands and the logic of commons problems will require that agreements are formulated at the international level if any progress is to be made. Despite many failures and inadequacies there is evidence that international rules can be developed and implemented. It is surely unrealistic to dismiss this mass of, often unreported, international activity out of hand as some radical and indeed conservative (realist) critiques do.

However, it is also true that there are severe limits to what can be achieved in global terms at the intergovernmental level. Local action and the range of non-governmental organizations, strikingly described as 'global civil society' are of critical importance and may often be required to resist ill-advised governmental interventions. The mere existence of UNCED and evidence such as the strengthening of the whaling regime, seemingly unconnected to 'hard' national interests, also suggest that NGOs and more amorphous public opinion can have significant effects on the policies of governments. To use the terminology of the European Union it is not a matter of international co-operation or local community action but rather of subsidiarity: of establishing what is possible and appropriate at each level.

An essential challenge to international cooperation lies in the kind of development traced by critics, namely the breakdown of monolithic authorities, the pressure towards globalization of economic relations and the threats to the Bretton Woods organizations which are no longer capable of exercising their management functions (Rich 1994). It may well be the case that their centralized, development orientated policies have done incalculable harm in the past, but their removal leaves only the disciplines of the global market place, unrestrained by any regulatory power which might encourage or require environmentally responsible behaviour.

In the absence of a global authority, who is to conserve the global commons through the taxation of pollution, or ensure that harmful substances are banned? Who is to provide some basis for assessing whether rules are adhered to? Although 'scientism' may be decried, it is still the case that without large-scale investigation there is no way of being aware of a range of environmental threats, still less of understanding how they may be countered. Who is to fund and provide for this enterprise? Local communities have many virtuous qualities and many roles in sustaining their environment, but they cannot realistically organize the protection of the ozone layer or the scientific uses of Antarctica. In the end, despite many disappointments and failures, the politics of international cooperation is unavoidable.

## Notes

1  This is a consequence of the influence of the Antarctic Treaty Powers, who have resisted the intrusion of the UN General Assembly into the management of Antarctica which they regard as their exclusive responsibility.
2  There are now, for example, 16 international agreements on nature conservation, 23 global and regional marine pollution agreements, 14 on marine living resources, 24 on transboundary fresh water resources and 15 on hazardous substances and nuclear waste.
3  The Conference began in 1973 and concluded in 1982, having discussed the whole range of maritime legal issues. Most contentious was the argument about the deep sea-bed and the terms of a commons regime for the extraction of minerals. Eventually a complex set of arrangements was devised which made such minerals the common heritage of mankind and allowed for some redistribution of profits from mining to the international community as a whole. This was promptly rejected by the incoming Reagan administration, followed by other developed world governments. The 1982 Convention lay dormant until 1993 when sufficient ratifications were received for it to enter into force. Wholesale revisions of the sea-bed mining arrangements (Part XI) allowed developed countries to accede and the Convention became operative in November 1994. Long before then the 200-mile EEZ became customary international law as states simply extended their jurisdiction.
4  Larry Summers was the author of the memo, which was enthusiastically faxed around the world by the Washington office of Greenpeace (Rich 1994:246–9).

# 9

# Global Issues and the Challenge to Democratic Politics

## Mike Mannin

*So we say to our friends in the international community – thank you, thank you, thank you . . . after years of riotous living, the prodigal has returned.*
*Desmond Tutu, June 1994*

In a service at Westminster Abbey to mark the return of South Africa to the Commonwealth, Archbishop Tutu recounted his emotions during the first universal elections in May 1994 that were, for millions of his fellow South Africans, the expression of a personal freedom never before experienced. His reference to the international community and its part in the struggle for this freedom bore testament to the salience of external forces and actors in the democratization process. In fact external pressures were an integral factor in the delegitimation and eventual collapse of the apartheid system.

The role of global and transnational forces in transforming domestic politics has been the subject of a contemporary literature on democracy in global context (Held 1993; Huntington 1991; Pridham 1991). Several factors have contributed to this debate. Since the Second World War the decolonization process, the globalization of markets and capital and, more recently, the ending of the Cold War have been associated with theories and forecasts about democracy that transcend the traditional philosophical discourses on the subject.

During the twentieth century a series of democratic dilemmas has been identified. Questions have arisen concerning the universal potential of democracy compared with its western practice; the limits of its efficacy in liberal form; its use in the context of totalitarian systems; its applicability to mass society. These debates have in turn contributed to criticism that the term lacks focus in the analysis of governance (McLennan 1984). While the Second World War may have presented democracy, albeit temporarily, as a rallying cry against the forces of fascism, the post-war period did little to clarify these dilemmas. Democratic freedoms were neither universally recognized nor established in the context of Cold War rivalry.

The collapse of Keynesian-style economic management in the 1970s led to a virulent debate within established liberal democracies about state–individual relationships, the extent and direction of government involvement in the economy and forms of accountability appropriate to a new order of neo-liberalism personified in the 'ideologies' of Thatcherism and Reaganomics. In the late 1980s, when liberalization of the Soviet economy and accompanying *glasnost* led to the collapse of 'direct' democracy, the dominant model of market liberalism was rapidly exported to Central and Eastern Europe. Francis Fukuyama's (1992) assertion that liberal democracy in the context of market capitalism was the highest stage of political and economic development, provided a philosophical gloss to the 'evidence' of contemporary political changes, as states struggled to assert liberal capitalist values from the shell of socialist or communist systems.

This chapter examines the thesis, associated with post-Cold War liberal triumphalism, that we are witnessing the inevitable extension of a liberal market model of democratic government, beyond the developed, western states where it is most firmly established, to the former Soviet bloc and to the states of Latin America, Asia and Africa. Initially, however, we must attempt to define our key concepts.

## Democracy, Liberalism and Authoritarianism: Some Uncomfortable Interconnections

While it is not the task of this chapter to dwell on old philosophical arguments concerning the meaning of democracy, it is evident that the addition of a global dimension to investigation of democratic forms has shifted the ground on which these arguments take place without necessarily superseding the perennial debates. Indeed these have, in some cases, been heightened through discussion of the impacts of globalization (Zolo 1992).

Let us start with the assumption that democracy as a concept is universal. The term is certainly ubiquitous. Rule by the people for the people is a claim that has been made by the most bloody dictator as well as the most responsively engineered civic forum.[1] Throughout the Cold War period governing elites, in nearly all states, sought moral ascendency over internal opposition, or international legitimacy, by reference to the democratic nature of their processes of government. This could be expressed in terms of universal truths, rights and obligations borrowed from philosophical or historical sources. Whether those sources were Aristotelian, from Republican Rome, from states of nature or natural rights, there existed a universal justification for moral ascendancy or political expediency based on the concept of democracy. The problem for the term, however, is its very lack of universality or consistency when more carefully defined or when applied as a description of governance. The term has, in effect, a universal currency but not a common value, and here many of the old debates resurface.

At this point it might be helpful to list the characteristics of democracy that are, on face value, procedural in their content. First, democracy is taken to be a process by which the people exercise a command over decision-making machinery. In its purest form that command should be based on the right of individuals to gain equal access to decision-taking. Second, access should be available at any stage in the decision process and should result in unlimited control over the output of government. Third, inalienable rights of speech, assembly, movement and association are guaranteed by collective agreement. Collective agreement regarding individual rights both frees and binds the individual – in participation in and acceptance of the democratic process (Beetham 1993).

It has often been the struggle to achieve these rights that has produced universal claims of inalienability – the 'truths' of democracy that have shaped its definition in idealistic terms (Pennock 1979). In effect, procedural and idealistic definitions represent two sides of a coin rather than competing or divergent conceptions. Such divergence as exists emerges through emphasis on particular freedoms, or particular processes. Thus we take Beetham's point that 'Disputes about the meaning of democracy which purport to be conceptual arguments are really *about how much democracy* is either desirable or practical . . . or sustainable' (Beetham 1993:53). These disputes explain the existence of competing models of democracy and, even in the context of globalization, remain central to our discussion.

## Models of Democracy

With the list of democratic characteristics in mind, and with a concern to emphasize the debates that emerge when prioritization of those characteristics takes place, it may be worth conceptualizing democratic models using the quadrant of characteristics below.

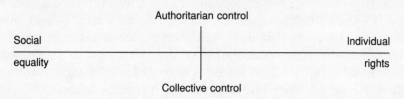

The horizontal axis represents the differentiation between social equality and individual rights; the vertical between collective access to decision making and authoritarian control of the decision process. The horizontal is concerned more with idealistic goals, the vertical with efficacy of democratic procedures. The organization of the state and the individual's relationship with the state are inevitably affected by the relationship between these different values.

In turn the ability of political actors to deliver desired democratic outcomes within the framework of the state is a function of the state's freedom both from internal opposition and external influence and challenge. Democratic outcomes are in part, therefore, affected by such factors as war, international or transnational political and economic relationships, or global phenomena such as population movements or environmental change.

From the characteristics outlined above, we would suggest four models of democracy appropriate to our analysis:

*authoritarian democracy* with its emphasis on popular will expressed through the personification of the state executive, with action and its approval by acclamation and/or direct election – a democracy of low intensity.

*direct democracy*, characterized by easy access for all citizens to the governmental process and binding collective decision-making with effective channels of accountability for public officials – a democracy of communitarianism or collective control.

*socialist democracy* that strives to create social equality by state planning and a large and complex yet deconcentrated system of administrative output and political accountability – a democracy of social justice.

*liberal democracy* with its stress on individual freedoms, on limited state activity, especially in the economy, and the representation of interests via elected public forums and group participation – a democracy founded on individualism.

Each of these models prioritizes different democratic characteristics; each views the state as a force to sustain its chosen prioritization, and each has varying perspectives towards external forces that could affect democratic priorities. The closer to the axis a state is seen to be, the greater its attempt to combine a range of democratic priorities; the further towards a pole, the greater its stress on a limited set of priorities.

Two points are worth recording here. First, the outer conceptual reaches of the quadrant may represent the limits to democracy as a working model. A position at an extreme is likely to produce opposition from dissatisfied, often excluded, political actors. Second, we should note the salience of the state to the achievement of democratic ideals and objectives. The state provides the most easily defensible space and the most easily recognized external borders for the practice of democracy; thus state sovereignty defines tangible limits to the responsibility of leaders. Yet it is the evident lack of state autonomy in the contemporary period that has bedeviled democratic theorists and practitioners alike.

In the present century increasing economic and financial globalization, and the globalization of ideas through information and media superhighways, has challenged the autonomy of the state. In consequence the ability of governments to prioritize democratic values has been undermined. But since governments differ in their prioritization of these values, it would be logical to conclude that their responses and attitudes to global pressures are varied. Why did Britain leave the Exchange Rate Mechanism after massive international currency pressures, while France survived? Why have most Middle Eastern countries remained obdurately authoritarian in their structures while Egypt and Tunisia have 'democratized' their political processes?

We may infer that states having democratic priorities and institutional arrangements sensitive to global pressures are inevitably more at the mercy of global forces than those whose institutional arrangements and policy priorities attempt to screen out external influences. We may hypothesize with regard to the four models of democracy that: *authoritarian democracy* may present a rigidity of institutional populist arrangements that allows it to resist/ignore international and global pressures, at least in the medium term. *Liberal democracy,* with a minimalist state, attempts to ride the international tides, so presenting the opportunity for maximizing state autonomy in a global environment. It is more problematic to envisage a state pursuing *socialist democracy* surviving the global flow of markets and ideas without the support of a socialist regional bloc; similarly the prioritization of *direct democratic* procedures with its emphasis on collective control and accountability would seem to leave a state vulnerable to the influence of global political and economic forces. In each of these cases the state's role is prioritized in different ways and, notwithstanding socio-economic factors, the mix of democratic ideals and procedures must be perceived as crucial to any analysis of the interaction between the processes of globalization and the procedures of liberal democracy.

This theme is explored in the following and subsequent sections on democracy in different political environments. First we examine the health of democracy in established liberal systems.

## Democracy, Globalization and Challenges to Established Liberal Systems

While the challenges to and responses of western liberal systems may not be uniquely different from those of states undergoing democratic transition or consolidation, it is essential that we test the triumphalist thesis of the 1980s in its own back yard. Since established liberal systems have a fundamental effect on the prospects for new democracies it follows that we need to understand the problems of the old.

What, then, can we identify as common features of western liberal systems in the later twentieth century? We can point to the existence of a civil society[2]: participation through citizenship, pluralist structures and processes and individual rights and duties within those processes. Additionally, a vital factor in maintaining the stability of western liberal democracies, at least until 1973, was a political economy of demand management and welfarism. Thus the search for a western, liberal political consensus to include labour, agricultural producers and middle income groupings led to both the welfarist output of governments and the development of interest groups and catch-all parties working within a system of representative government.

Keynesian-style economic management was vital for the sustenance of a consensual alliance which incorporated both agricultural and labour interests. The maintenance of both income and employment for diverse sectoral interests rested upon an interventionist state bureaucracy controlled by a politically sensitive executive. While the nature of such interventionism varied between the social Keynesianism of the French 'planned' economy and the fiscal Keynesianism of the United States, the anticipated outcome was the same: control of market fluctuations, full employment and some form of social protection via state or private provision.

The problem of government overload in the 1960s and 1970s has been superseded by the problem of state insolvency since 1973, and the post-war Keynesian model has largely been abandoned in favour of supply-led economic management. Consequently the benevolent welfarist state is replaced by a regulatory non-interventionist state with one eye on its budget deficit and another on its credit rating with the International Monetary Fund (IMF) or the European Commission.

### *The subordination of the nation-state?*

The resultant strains on decision-making and participatory processes have, in several cases, threatened the integrity of the state. Thus Canada, Belgium and Italy, where statehood was already stressed by uneasy historical, cultural or ethnic alliances, have recently experienced centripetal challenges driven, in part, by the impact of global economic forces. Conversely, other established democracies have responded to global economic challenges by turning to the 'protection' of elite centralism. This has manifested itself in the erosion of sub-national government autonomy, a decline in pluralist channels of participation and the reification of strong leadership as a solution to external economic threats and challenges. Britain, France and Germany displayed some or all of these characteristics during the 1980s. Even membership of the European Community – the most developed example of economic and political integration – may be interpreted as providing a framework shaped by and preserving the integrity of its members (Milward 1992).

Western liberal systems, then, have proved less resilient to external forces during the last fifteen years. Consequently a changed liberal paradigm has forced a re-evaluation of institutional and political processes, leading in some cases to a redefinition of the role of the state and its relationship with sub-national and international institutions.

The decline of welfarist liberalism and rise of its market-based variant is reflected, also, in the realignment of political parties seeking electoral survival in an increasingly unpredictable economic environment. The decline of socialist and social democratic parties and the rise of the neo-liberal right has, with the notable exception of Italy, been contained within existing party systems. This realignment has involved a general shift of established political parties towards the right, and the rise of nationalist and neo-fascist movements in France, Germany and Italy. In addition, support for environmental movements and the apathy of a confused electorate are manifestations of disappointment with the performance of traditional political leadership and processes in western liberal states. This has resulted both in startling electoral swings – Canada (1993), France (1993), Italy (1994) and in short-lived regimes (Denmark, New Zealand and Sweden) where neo-liberal solutions proved too painful for continuing electoral support.

Electoral dealignments may also be explained by factors associated with the new political environment of communication that has its roots in global transfers of technology and deregulation of communication networks. The ubiquity and speed of written and electronic broadcasting has altered the relationship between individuals and political systems in a number of ways. The information available to the individual is enhanced not only by the greater range of broadcasting networks available but also by the intensity of commentary, as networks, and channels within networks, battle for market shares (Keane 1991). The result is an organizational and ideological straitjacket of media presentation and image – the politics of soundbite and spin doctor.

We might conclude that the reduction of political messages to simple components dictated by the requirements of the communications industry has led inexorably towards a model of political leadership where presidential-style presentation of the political agenda has become the most efficient mode of communication. In this scenario, Thatcherism, Mitterandism and, more recently, Kohlism represent a convergence of political ideas and communication modes that may be redefining relationships between citizen and political actors towards a democratic process that bears little resemblance to the liberal representational forms of John Locke and J. S. Mill or the pluralist values of Robert Dahl.

Thus western liberal systems move into the twenty-first century with a nineteenth-century baggage of representational institutions and processes, overlaid by a sophisticated media-led model of limited but potentially authoritarian democracy. Under such conditions the genius of liberalism in western states, the civil society, is undermined by the over-zealous application of one of its most salient characteristics – the free market of communication.

### *Democracy, Italian style: some lessons in democratic practice*

We turn, now, to contemporary Italian politics as an example of a western system in democratic crisis. Italy has beckoned siren-like to our profession to come and explain its political contradictions, and remains a graveyard for academic prognosis. Yet Italy exemplifies a western liberal state in an advanced stage of reaction to many of the pressures, global and otherwise, discussed previously. We therefore find the call irresistible.

Italy has existed as a unified state since 1866 with a constitutional monarchy to 1922 followed by a period of fascism to 1943. After a period of bloody conflict partly civil in nature, Italy emerged after the Second World War with a constitution (1948) that reflected and contained such divergent historical forces as political Catholicism, Marxism, liberalism, nationalism, regionalism, republicanism and a muted but still present fascism. In consequence it is a masterpiece of obfuscation. This is manifest in such institutions as a uniquely powerful and privileged parliament, a limited executive, the availability of referenda, a constitutional court, regional government and, until 1993, a 'pure' form of proportional representation. This plethora of institutions is accompanied by a series of rights for the individual together with economic and social duties of government. The Italian constitution represents a mixture of the liberal and direct model, underpinned by constitutionally stated aims of social equality that would make it difficult to fit into any single quadrant of our diagram.

The post-war electoral success of both Christian Democracy (DC) and the Italian Communist Party (PCI) and the continuing representation of other long established parties – Liberals, Socialists, Republicans and Monarchists – was a testament to the representational genius of the constitution. It was also a recognition of the need for political compromise in order that the system survive. In the event, the dominance of the Christian Democrats was established from 1947 onwards and, throughout the first forty years of the Republic, the practice of Italian democracy was contained within a political settlement that allowed the emergence of '*partitocrazia*'. Thus, grafted on to Italy's constitutional democracy was a governmental coalition between political parties that divided state resources in relation to electoral strength. The electoral success of the DC coalition at national level, supported by the economic miracle of the 1950s and 1960s, was mirrored by considerable electoral success of the PCI and allies at local and regional level. The system of proportional representation contained electoral swings to the extent that, with some minor exceptions, the electoral players of 1947 were being dealt the same electoral hands in the 1980s.

The effect of this '*immobilismo*' may be briefly stated. The permanence of political elites created opportunities for elite control over public sector resources that was used to favour supporters. The growth of the public sector, conceived out of political necessity rather than social planning, brought with it inefficiency and opportunities for corruption through clientelistic relationships between citizens, politicians and administrators as well as a spiralling public debt. Economically unsound welfare expenditure was underpinned by an export-driven economy reliant on a flexible labour market and entrepreneurial skill. This, plus the inefficiency of revenue collection, allowed a black economy to emerge that sustained the profit margins of small firms and the wage levels of families. On these somewhat shaky foundations, the First Italian Republic survived until the late 1980s.

The demise of the post-war compact and the rise of Berlusconi (the media-mogal turned politician) can be attributed to a range of factors. From the mid-1970s Italian firms had experienced difficulties in maintaining export competitiveness. By the late 1980s the impact of global recession, compounded by the constraints of the European Community's programme for achievement of economic and monetary union, had seriously damaged the Italian economy. Poor economic performance fuelled growing political instability after 1989, when the end of the Cold War necessitated metamorphosis of parties of the left. In the case of the PCI, Gramscian ideological elasticity gave the opportunity of transformation, not without pain, to a Democratic Party of the left (PDS). This was assisted, in part, by the failure of the PSI to effectively claim the left of centre ground. Reported scandals spread to include PSI officials and leaders, and the delegitimization of both the

DC and PSI was evident from local and national opinion polls and elections during 1990–1. The 1992 national elections saw the emergence of the Northern League, a regionally based alliance critical of the extravagance of '*partitocrazia*'. This, coupled with a growing confidence among the junior magistracy to pursue Mafia and political scandals, fuelled public disenchantment with democratic processes. The problem for the electorate was, however, the lack of any new, positive focus for their allegiance.

Against a background of Mafia violence and financial scandals, the December 1993 local elections saw increased support for the autonomist Northern League and a resurgence of support for PDS, Verdi, (environmentalist) and other progressive parties, a growing support for the extreme right, and a collapse of the DC and PSI vote. With the expectation of a national election during 1994, and an anticipated victory for a PDS-led progressive left coalition, enter Silvio Berlusconi.

As head of Fininvest, Berlusconi controlled all Italy's commercial television networks, together with considerable financial, marketing and retail holdings. Consequently he had a particular interest in media deregulation and an anti-collectivist, anti-tax ethos that fitted one aspect of the political climate. By also presenting himself as a pro-Catholic, pro-family individualist he was able to delegitimate the new moderate reformist image of the PDS. He appeared to represent that miracle of political and economic rebirth that a substantial section of the Italian electorate earnestly sought.

Within the space of three months, and by utilizing the formidable resources of his business empire, he created a political movement demanding both public attention and alliances with other political elites. In particular his use of sophisticated marketing techniques, alongside a rapidly constructed grass roots organization run largely by young business and professional persons, brought both a new style to campaigning and a new cohort of political activists to Italian politics. The product was himself and the image was of a second coming – a second economic miracle.

Despite attempts to discredit both the man and message, the opposition Progressive Alliance lacked political technique or a rhetoric capable of countering the public suspension of disbelief engendered by the Forza Italia campaign. That disbelief was also held in abeyance as Berlusconi forged an alliance of seemingly absurd ideological reach – with Gianfranco Fini's neo-fascists in Southern Italy, and Bossi's Northern League, whose avowed aim was the creation of a confederal Italy. In the March 1994 elections, fought within a more majoritarian electoral system, Berlusconi's Freedom Alliance won 366 seats in the Chamber of Deputies out of 630, with the opposition Progressive Alliance gaining 213 seats (32 per cent). The reformed Christian

Democrats and their associates returned only 16 per cent of the vote (46 seats).

Berlusconi's personal victory was remarkable – perhaps unique in twentieth-century liberal democratic elections. Indeed his rise echoed that of Mussolini, a journalist whose image building was equally adept. The medium of television and the processes of marketing allowed access to the democratic process with immediate and breathtaking effects, which were subsequently characterized by President Mitterand as 'an approach to democracy we are not used to and which appears fearsome to me . . . There is a serious risk of perverting democracy' (*Guardian* 1994).

Subsequent events suggest significant dilemmas for Italian politics. Attempts to interfere with the public broadcasting system, the issue of Berlusconi's association with Fininvest; the investigation of his company's involvement in illegal payments to tax officers and the internecine warfare that emerged between the magistracy and Forza Italia over the *manni polite* (clean hands) campaign, cast doubt over the extent of commitment to reform presented during the election period. This, together with periodic and public disarray among coalition partners over fundamental economic and constitutional reform, led to Berlusconi's resignation in December 1994, underlining the fragility of the Italian Second Republic.

The implications of the Italian experience are various. In the face of media deregulation, older political values have been unable to compete with the message of market capitalism and are therefore generally in retreat (Woolacott 1994). Berlusconism represents the most extreme example of this phenomenon and Berlusconi himself is the first political entrepreneur to directly exploit the commercial values and associated media processes of the 'Third Capitalism'. In effect, Berlusconi attempted to move Italian democracy into the upper right quadrant of our diagram; to establish a new age of paternalist individualism.

There remain, however, other interpretations of the Berlusconi phenomenon that are even less optimistic for the health of democracy in Italy or in other western liberal states. Berlusconi's victory was shared with neo-fascists and with the regional, populist Northern League. The failure of Berlusconi to deliver the benefits of market liberalism to a disillusioned public seeking a radical break with its immediate past may well see a further decline in support for representative and pluralist processes. Berlusconi's replacement, Lamberto Dini, a banker at the head of a 'technocratic' government, offers no more than a respite before further political restructuring. Consequently, either an authoritarian right 'solution' or, alternatively, a break-up of the state with regionally varying consequences for democratic forms is possible. The logical outcome to the level of commercialization of the democratic process witnessed in Italy would be a significant devaluation of civil society and the processes of representative government.

Nevertheless several factors militate against any alarmist assessment of the impact of new political phenomena. Italians have had a varied democratic experience in the post-war period that shows, above all, a range and toleration of opinion within a broadly based constitutional framework. In addition, the subordination of state autonomy to external political and economic factors is evident in the case of Italy, as in other West European states. Hence, for example, governments in the 1990s are as constrained by the European Community's economic convergence regime as previous administrations. The change of government did not bring any marked alterations to economic policies already shaped by decisions taken externally and prior to Berlusconi's ascendency. In effect 'the road to (Italian) financial restoration was already decided and whoever won would make no difference' (Sidoti 1994).

In focusing on the Italian democratic process, we may be describing no more than a unique, idiosyncratic system whose vicissitudes hold no lessons for the future of democracy in other western liberal states. Conversely, observation of Italy's experience may provide us with some critical insights concerning the relevance of democratic theory and practice in a global context characterized by rapid economic and technological change. The somewhat different environments of newly established democracies are the subject of our next section.

## Democratic Change in the Global Context

Political systems undergoing transition from non-democratic to democratic forms of governance tend to lack the assumed infrastructure of democracy: a civil society with basic but shared expectations of political toleration, participation, and justice from a government with some degree of electoral accountability for its actions – and the associated superstructure of interest groups, parties, representative institutions and bureaucracy and civilianized military. Yet during the past few years, with bewildering speed and with the eyes of the international community upon them, previously authoritarian states are struggling to develop internally effective and externally recognized democratic forms.

The multi-causal dynamics of political change leading to democratization are identified by Huntington (1991). These include internal factors such as economic development, modern communications, evolving roles of political elites and changing social coalitions, cultural attitudes and values, all of which may account for different political outcomes in different countries. Moreover, external factors, be they global or regional in scope, have also contributed significantly to processes of change. The democratizations in Romania, East Germany or South Africa would not have taken place without external intervention – not, at least, at the time they did nor in the direction or pace that emerged.

## Democratization as a process

Since the 1980s democratic government, if measured in terms of elected regimes, has swept through countries of the Third, and more recently the Second World of Central and Eastern Europe (CEE). Latin America by 1986, experienced a 'special moment' in its history when all five Central American republics were ruled by elected governments (Berntzen 1993). Polls were held for the first time in Angola and Kuwait in 1992; Pakistan, Malawi, Yemen and Cambodia organized overdue and shaky elections in 1993; all CEE states and Russia had held at least two legislative elections by 1994; and with unparalleled symbolism for democratic idealists, South Africa also went peacefully through its first universal electoral hurdle in the same year. These and many other countries enjoyed that first experience of freedom celebrated by Archbishop Tutu's words at the start of this chapter.

Yet democracy is not a new process for the Third or Second World. Some of these transitions were re-democratizations; others, when carefully observed, looked little else than the continuation of previous authoritarian regimes with electoral trappings. In effect, while democratization implies a process, it does not guarantee an end product. Democratic governance may represent an end or an ideal form but, before that is reached, periods of transition and consolidation are necessary. If, therefore, democratization is a generic term to describe a general process, democratic transition may be specified as the period from collapse of an authoritarian system to the routinization of elite behaviour within a set of constitutional rules and democratic values. It will inevitably see the destruction of previous processes and institutions that are not compatible with democratic values. Democratic consolidation, longer than transition, involves the adjustment and routinization of new democratic processes and the internalization of those processes at elite and popular level (Pridham and Vanhanen 1994).

## Global influences on democratic transition and consolidation

Theoretical explanations of democratization have, until recently, underplayed the influence of external factors on states in the process of political change. It may be argued that previous waves of democratization, in the mid-nineteenth century or the first twenty-five years of this century, reflected domestic economic and political circumstances and/ or occurred as the result of military defeat. Thus democratic change occurs when ruling elites lose control of domestic economic resources and seek allies whose compensation is involvement in the political process, or where a period of internally or externally induced violence demands a re-legitimation of old political structures or the creation of more accessible new structures and processes.

During the past twenty-five years democratizations have taken place in the context of global economic pressures and a communications network that facilitates the global dissemination of ideas (Randall 1993). This suggests that explanations of democratization which fail to consider external influences are weak if not invalid. Thus a distinct, third wave of democratizations has led to a reassessment of democratic theory that is both eclectic in scope and universalistic in its pretensions to explain 'what amounts to one of the central current trends in global politics' (Munck 1994:335).

Huntington (1991), Przeworski (1991) and others produce perspectives that stress global economic and political factors which constitute preconditions or accelerators of democratic transition. The prospects for democratic consolidation are similarly examined in this global context, especially in terms of the impact of structural adjustment policies of the IMF and World Bank and the insistence on 'good governance' and democracy as a central aspect of aid and development policy (Leftwich 1993; Gills and Rocamora 1992; Knippers Black 1993). In effect the opportunities for gradualist democratization along paths shaped primarily by domestic socio-economic and political characteristics are curtailed by a range of explicit and implicit external imperatives. While domestic factors are an obvious and vital aspect of explanation or prognosis, they are now seen in terms of their relationship to external imperatives. Thus comparisons of democratizations in Southern Europe and Latin America or Central and Eastern Europe are increasingly expressed in terms of the different *conditionalities* imposed by external actors (Pridham and Vanhanem 1994). It is to these conditionalities; their nature, why they emerged and with what effects, that we now turn.

## Democratization and structural adjustment

We have earlier discussed the loose but universal application of the term democracy in the context of Cold War rivalries. During the period through to the late 1980s, although liberal democracy was a preferred condition, there was little evidence to suggest that western governments regarded issues such as free and fair elections or civil and individual rights as a primary condition for economic support or military or diplomatic protection. Neither did the World Bank or IMF show a serious commitment to promote democratic government. Indeed an authoritarian government of the right in Brazil, Argentina, Nicaragua, Zambia, the Philippines or Greece was seen as infinitely more conducive to western interests than a representative government critical of western values (Leftwich 1993).

Where democratic institutions and processes were encouraged it was at 'low intensity'; that is the lip service democracy of South Korea, Guatemala or Kuwait, where elected elites worked closely with supporting military agencies armed by, or with the acquiescence of, western governments. In such conditions, progressive or reformist movements could make little headway and were regarded as a disloyal opposition – and often a danger to continued western support (Gills and Rocamora 1992). Thus human rights violations coexisted with western aid programmes, trade links or military pacts. While such a paradox could be justified in terms of modernization theory (only after economic development reaches a certain level will political development to sustained democracy be attainable) democratic transition was inevitably impeded.

During the late 1970s and early 1980s a period of 'low intensity democracy' sprang from the growing confidence of the Carter and subsequent United States administrations that capitalism was winning the economic war against communism. By the mid-1980s the way was open for a free market crusade in the Third World. This was couched in terms of a 'Crusade for Democracy' (Ronald Reagan's phrase when addressing the British Parliament in 1982) but its principal emphasis was economic involving: 'intolerance of high public expenditure, debt servicing, privatisation and economic liberalisation, privatisation and public expenditure cuts promoted by the USA via the IMF, World Bank and Group of Seven industrialised countries' (Gills and Rocamora 1992:506). In this context democratic transition may be limited to forms of government that can best apply structural adjustment and accommodate social and political results that form 'a toxic cocktail of absolute decline' (Gills and Rocamora 1992:506).

Two factors, however, present a slightly more optimistic view. Firstly, the collapse of communism has removed the need for strategic advantage, which, in turn, has led to guarded US support for pro-democracy movements in Haiti, South Korea, Taiwan, Angola amongst others – a support that was previously withheld for fear that political disruption might ensue. Secondly, democratic transition has also come to the former Second World (Soviet bloc) with amazing rapidity. The major shift in economic and foreign policy of the Soviet Union produced conditions for transition that led to a contagion or demonstration effect throughout the region (Schmitter and Karl 1992). This has produced considerable optimism concerning democratization, particularly in Central and Eastern Europe (CEE). The following section concentrates on this region and its particular problems.

## Democratization in Central and Eastern Europe

The demolition of the Berlin Wall allowed a brief moment of euphoria for those whose horizons had been limited by the rigidities of Cold War politics. For Central and East Europeans hopes for better times were associated with the living standards of their western neighbours and their related social freedoms. In effect market liberalism, the dominant model of democracy in West Europe and the USA, was demanded both within and without the CEE as the replacement for authoritarian communism; and its implantation in weak but willing new partners was encouraged through direct and uninhibited international intervention.

The quinquennial anniversary of 'the fall' suggests a mixed assessment of the democratization process. Some form of democratic government has been established in over twenty states previously totalitarian in ideology and administration; associated political rights have been extended to new citizens, including freedom of movement. Internal markets are being developed and external markets actively sought. Most CEE states now play an active role in the Council of Europe and an independent role in the United Nations. Their already established legal sovereignty is now matched for the most part by an international political legitimacy. A superstructure of interest and party competition, together with varying forms of institutional representation, is evident within each of the states (save in the case of the former Yugoslavia and some of the successor republics of the Soviet Union) indicating some success in the transition to democracy (McFaul 1993; Pridham and Vanhanen 1994; Volten 1992; White et al. 1993).

The debit side of quinquennial assessment, however, depresses optimism. The paths of democratic transition have differed widely, and when examined separately CEE states appear to have reached varying stages of democratic consolidation. Thus Hungary, the Czech Republic, Poland and Slovenia enjoy, for different reasons, a degree of international confidence in their progress not yet extended to Slovakia, Bulgaria, Romania, the Ukraine or Albania. Progress towards establishment of a market economy varies, as is evident from widely different rates of inward capital investment between CEE states. In addition, the application of structural adjustment policies has resulted in economic and social strains and political reactions, including the re-emergence of reformed, ex-communist parties, some of which have enjoyed electoral success. The 1993 Polish and 1994 Hungarian legislative elections, for instance, produced swings to former communist parties. This, coupled with the emergence of extreme right sentiments based on ethno-nationalism, has created a less than optimistic climate for the establishment of civil societies in CEE states.

In effect, prospects for a smooth path to democratic consolidation in these states are a function of contemporary domestic factors that are inherently complicated, and external factors that inevitably interact with the economic and strategic interests of neighbouring states. What has emerged is a picture of established states struggling to develop the political process of liberal democracy in an environment of emergent and competing cultures associated with redefined nationalisms, re-found religiosity and ethnic particularism, coexisting within a framework of economic individualism.

Economic change has produced massive advantage for some but for many others increased deprivation has produced 'a nostalgia for communist comfort' (Denton and Mortimer 1994:25). While the continued existence of a communist sub-culture, represented by 'reformed' ex-communist elites, may present a brake to economic liberalization it may also play a significant factor in democratic consolidation, assisting relatively consensual transformation of elite attitudes. In this context of continuity and change, civil society itself needs only partial construction: while 'transformed' communist elites in CEE states may make life difficult for particular liberal market reformists, their return to the political arena is constrained within the developing liberal system and also contributes to its stability (Huntington 1991).

It is, however, to the external pressures on CEE democratic consolidation that we now turn, as a second and vital aspect of political change. The initial neo-liberal exhortations and interventions of western governments, IMF and World Bank showed little concern for the resulting problems of social adjustment (Leftwich 1993). More recently, with only a few CEE economies responding adequately to the rigour of the marketplace, the reaction of international actors has been more circumspect. Here it is the European Union (EU) that has emerged as 'the central body of post-Cold War Europe' (Hyde-Price 1994).[3]

At the G7 Paris Summit in 1989 it was decided that the EU should perform the role of broker in dealing with the painful decoupling of the CEE from the former Soviet Union. From 1989 Association Agreements (now termed European Agreements) were extended to most CEE countries, and a framework for joint decision taking was established. The effect, however, was to offer only partial access to the Single European Market, with notable restrictions to CEE access in such vital sectors as steel, agriculture and textiles and despite the almost free access of EU goods to CEE states. The pursuit of internationally applauded policies to control inflation and deficit expenditure in Hungary the Czech Republic, Slovakia, Poland and Slovenia leaves, in practice, only export-led opportunities for reflation and economic growth – hence the continued disappointment of CEE states with the guarded responses of the EU. Unwillingness to fully open markets has been accompanied by the confusing signal of agreement in principal for Polish, Romanian, Bulgarian, Czech, Slovak and Hungarian membership of the EU 'when circumstances permit'.

The ambivalence which has characterized the EU's relationship with the CEE states, coupled with the broader failure of western states to provide adequate financial support for the CEE transition process, raises the prospect of a crisis of ungovernability that will undermine any chance for EU membership in the foreseeable future. This raises, in turn

> the spectre of neo-authoritarianism amid resurgent nationalism and regionalism . . . with the current democratization of Eastern Europe and the former USSR [as] . . . a phase rather than a destination of history, with the end product being another form of authoritarianism, in this case, low intensity 'capitalism' (Gills and Rocamora 1992:514).

## Democratization in the Third World

In examining the impact of liberal democracy in CEE, little attempt was made to challenge the appropriateness of the concept to these societies, busy adjusting to its new demands, except insofar as the legacy of communist authoritarianism affected democratic consolidation. On a superficial level, liberal democracy was extended to a wider European 'home' and, as such, its values were not perceived as alien to the peoples it now encompasses. In turning to the experiences of non-western states, however, our starting point must be a consideration of claims for the ubiquity of liberal democracy that – however globally triumphant – remains conceptually of western genesis.

As we have already argued, liberal democracy is a particular variant of democracy. It is democracy qualified by a liberalism that reifies individualism, and hence the political, economic, social and moral rights of the individual over those of the community. Mores, laws, economic and political processes combine to preserve individual separateness and mutual respect for separateness. Government should maximize individual liberties rather than set out general frameworks for the good life. Liberal democracy, then, emphasizes the rights of the individual over the concept of community; a concept that, in many non-western societies, remains the preferred social paradigm.

There are many examples of community oriented polities in the non-western world; in the Middle East, South Asia and Africa. Whether the basis of this community orientation is religious or ethnic, uni-communal or multi-communal, the concept of individual freedom fits uneasily into an ethos of social solidarity and obligation to group mores, thus throwing into question such liberal values as religious toleration, gender equality and economic rights of market access. For Parekh 'the liberal principle of individuation and other liberal ideas are culturally and historically specific. As such, a political system based on them cannot claim universal validity' (1993:169).

This is not to dismiss the applicability of democracy per se. Direct democracy rests on a communitarian ethos, and as such may better fit the aspirations of non-western polities. The dilemma for liberal democrats is that the claims of communitarians to absorb only certain aspects of western values and to reject others, especially those associated with choice and individual rights, offend the application of liberalism itself. Some of the implications of this dilemma are explored in the following chapter.

For many non-western societies, economic dependence has brought subservience to external economic interests and political pressures, including demands for evidence of 'good governance', which have increasingly involved the introduction of liberal democratic procedures. The response to these demands has tended to be a minimalist democratic practice that has extended an uncertain and often marginal political choice. Thus, in Africa, single party regimes, the solution to ethnic conflicts of the 1960s and 1970s, have given way to neo-pluralist experiments that by 1990 had produced, according to one survey, only ten new liberal democratic states (Riley 1992).

A further problem for liberal democracy in a non-western context is associated with its secular ethos – and in particular a secular materialism that flies in the face of traditional religious movements. The Islamic Revolution of 1979, and the subsequent impact of Islamism, presents a further challenge to liberal triumphalism. Thus in Shiite thought democracy is associated with secularism and is, therefore, a transgression of God's law. Multi-party politics is erroneous and dangerous. 'Islam, it is argued, has a totality of view, exclusive of other beliefs, which militates against full participation in multi-party politics' (Deegan 1993:74). In consequence, the incompatibilities of Islamic and liberal philosophy, exacerbated by the growth of extremist movements, can be identified as a major threat to democratic freedoms. Nevertheless economic dependence, especially given the increasing uncertainty of oil markets, may place religious imperatives in a secondary position to economic inevitabilities. Radical Islamists present a challenge to political and economic reform in Islamic states but are themselves challenged by change and 'modernity'.

Democratization in non-western environments is shaped, therefore, by social and historical factors that on face value are not conducive to an easy transplant of liberal democratic values, though democracy of a direct or authoritarian variant, populist or con-associational in format,[4] seems less alien. The Philippines, Kenya, South Korea and Argentina have formal liberal representative procedures that are compromised by traditional elites whose power has been sustained despite the advent of electoral pluralism. Military presence, if not evident in the cabinet room, is only a short distance away in barracks and remains a threat to democratic consolidation. This is especially true in Central American 'democracies' such as Guatemala and El Salvador, and in the Philippines where 'the military actually gained more power as a direct consequence of democratic transition' (Gills and Rocamora 1992:515).

Throughout much of Latin America, the fragility of the democratization process is greatly exacerbated by massive external debt and associated structural adjustment policies which have impacted on already grotesque social inequalities through cuts in welfare services. Hence, in 1990 'three-quarters of the population was suffering from some degree or manifestation of malnutrition' (Knippers Black 1993:545). Despite the 1989 Brady Plan, which reduced foreign debt by one third, the debt service burden increased from 26 per cent (1990) to 30 per cent of GDP (1991). Consequently there remains a serious doubt over the region's ability to service its debt and sustain inward investment, and in 1992 the Inter-American Development Bank in its annual report wrote of the potential for social unrest due to unacceptably high unemployment levels, depressed incomes and a reduced commitment to social services (Gills and Rocamora 1992:508).

In consequence, the prospects for democratic consolidation remain bleak, as elites old and new seek to preserve dwindling economic privileges and contain social unrest. In order to sustain structural adjustment policies, reformers such as Menem of Argentina and Perez of Venezuela have been forced to initiate repressive action, hence further undermining the expectations of increasingly cynical electorates.

In these circumstances electoral processes serve, for the most part, to legitimate unreconstructed or partly transformed authoritarian elites whose overriding purpose is to preserve their own interests. The Paraguayan elections (1993) returned a party, the Colorandos, composed of the old military, economic and bureaucratic elites. The year before, Peru's elected President Alberto Fujimori dissolved congress and arrested several hundred members of the opposition. Neither country suffered any long-term international economic or political repercussions. In the absence of external support for the upholding of civil and social rights, however, this latest wave of democratic transitions has at best contributed to 'liberalization of authoritarian regimes rather than to an authentic democratization' (Berntzen 1993:603).

Compared with South America, many South East Asian countries enjoy a more economically secure base upon which to build processes of democratization. A coherent state-led objective of economic development, together with policies that attempt to contain social tensions, have allowed countries such as South Korea, Taiwan, Thailand, Malaysia and Indonesia to progress towards formal democracy on the back of economic growth. South Korea and Taiwan present good examples of moves towards democratic transition through a classical modernization process, with some evidence of the growth of pluralist organizations and the extension of government policy into social areas – some slight indication of a developing civil society.

When examined more carefully, however, even in the most successful Newly Industrializing Countries (NICs), democratization is closely entwined with still powerful and only semi-civilianized military elites. Thus Thailand has moved from civil democracy, military coup and back to civil democracy in the space of five years, Indonesia sustains its established ruling elite, legitimated by elections in 1992, and in South Korea civilianized military governments have existed since 1961. Nevertheless the region presents, for the most part, a potential for political stability – assisted by its considerable economic growth but served only by low intensity democracy and within the context of a continuing military presence.[5]

In Southern Asia, Pakistan moves between military rule and populist democracy. India, the world's largest democratic system, is suffering a range of centripetal pressures, including Hindu fundamentalism and regional secessionist movements. At the same time recent market liberalization has generated high levels of unemployment, particularly in the public sector, that may place considerable pressure on the federal structure. India has, however, the advantage of forty-six years of democratic practice that may well contain the strains on its established representative process.

It is in Africa that the prospects either for political stability or democratic consolidation look most bleak. Neither the brief experience of decolonizing democracy, when the trappings of western representation were used by the dominant elite as a means to gain access to the state apparatus, nor the subsequent emergence of socialist or capitalist one party states, has solved the lack of internal legitimacy affecting so many African states.

Throughout the Cold War years, with very few exceptions, the internal politics of African states attracted scant attention from the international community. African political elites, supported by Soviet or western aid and arms, were unaffected by the need to seek broad domestic political alliances and, with the exception of four cases – Botswana, The Gambia, Mauritius and Senegal – showed little inclination to develop liberal democracy in any meaningful form (Riley 1992).

The end of the Cold War also removed the strategic rationale for support of authoritarian regimes. The results are evident in the collapse of military dominated regimes in Angola, Ethiopia, Somalia, Zaire, Liberia and, more recently, Rwanda; and the 'pluralization' of politics in such countries as Tanzania, Kenya and Zambia. Western aid donors were, and are, in the position of demanding political conditionalities to aid programmes. Thus the World Bank in 1989 talked of a 'crisis of governance in Africa' that could only be rectified by establishing efficient public services and financial accountability in public affairs, an independent judicial system, representative institutions, a free press and pluralistic processes based on respect for human rights. Good governance is thus 'synonymous with sound development management'; implying a democratic, capitalist system, presided over by a minimal state (Leftwich 1993:610).

These sentiments have been reflected in the statements of most western governments, international and regional organizations and development agencies. Nevertheless the ability of African states to respond to political as well as economic conditionalities appears extremely limited. Their dependence on primary product exports in a declining and unstable world market undermines external credibility as well as reducing the ability to provide services necessary for the maintenance of popular support internally. This is not a new phenomenon. Africa's share of non-oil primary exports has fallen, since 1970, from 7 per cent to 4 per cent. The massive increases in oil prices between 1973 and 1980 seriously damaged the economies of African non-oil producing states; between 1965 and 1989 thirteen of twenty-one states with a declining Gross National Product (GNP) were African (Clapham 1993). This has served to increase dependence on the global economic institutions, resulting in the transformation of African states 'from Cold War pawns into irrelevant international clutter' (Decalo, S. quoted in Wiseman 1993:441).

As in the case of other regions, African states have experienced a spate of democratic transitions, especially since 1990, with pressure for multi-partism building from both within and without. But in the context of their domestic instability, economic weakness and international powerlessness, the movement from transition to consolidation seems impossible without a massive political and economic interjection from the West. In the short period since 1990 democratic transition has been either reversed or suspended in Nigeria, Gabon, Sierra Leone, Togo and Angola. More successful transitions, where opposition groups have replaced ruling authoritarian elites, are evident in Benin, Burundi, Cape Verde, Lesotho, Mali and Zambia. Thus the 'demonstration' effect of successful transition is considerably weaker in Africa than in Central and Eastern Europe or South East Asia. Consequently it is in this context that the South African elections of 1994, and their aftermath, may play a key role in establishing a more positive and optimistic perspective for African democratization.

## South Africa's Democratic Consolidation

South Africa shares with the rest of the continent the legacy of its artificial, imperial construction. Its development is, however, particularly complex, with a divided European heritage and its African and Coloured peoples similarly subject to internal divisions. These divisions were institutionalized through the post-Second World War apartheid system, which upheld the dominance of the white minority. Despite rhetorical condemnation of apartheid, the international community so generously praised by Archbishop Tutu in 1994, played a mixed role in implementing economic and political sanctions against the South African regime.[6]

The persistence of transnational anti-apartheid organizations and their success in sustaining international media interest was supportive but not decisive in the struggle to end apartheid. Of greater significance was the campaign to force British and American firms to disinvest during the mid-1980s, culminating in Chase Manhatten and Barclays well publicized decision to withdraw from their South African investment programme. For a variety of reasons, international investors lost confidence in the security of their South African investments, to the extent that, by 1986, South Africa had been practically excluded from world financial markets. The ensuing economic recession generated considerable pressure from South African business interests and the Dutch Reformed Church for the ending of apartheid. This coincided with increased external pressure, consequent upon the ending of the Cold War, creating a climate conducive to democratic transition. This contributed to the release from prison of Nelson Mandela in 1990, paving the way for South Africa's first universal elections in 1994.

While the pre-election period was not without violence between black communities, or secessionist threats from hardline whites, the elections in April 1994 were declared by a surfeit of international observers to be fair and largely free from violence and intimidation. The results provided the substantial victory (62.6 per cent) necessary for legitimation of an African National Congress government, and subsequently the Presidency of Nelson Mandela, but not the two thirds majority necessary to amend the recently agreed constitutional settlement and so endanger national reconciliation. Of equal significance, the National Party passed the 20 per cent barrier allowing it to argue strongly for its minority interests within a power sharing government, while Inkatha won control of Kwazulu Natal – a designer outcome for at least medium-term political stability.

South Africa's relative economic strength and the conciliatory policy positions adopted by both the National Party and ANC auger well for democratic consolidation (Munck 1994). Nevertheless, Zulu nationalism and the residual claims of the Afrikaner people may yet present a serious and potentially violent threat to the nation building process (Johnston 1994).

In this context the agency of Mandela and of De Klerk has played a significant part in the maintenance to date of positive attitudes towards national reconciliation among South Africans. This consolidation, watched so hopefully by the international community, may provide the necessary 'demonstration effect' to assist other African states struggling towards democratic transition. Nevertheless, South Africa may be perceived as a unique example of political change which consequently holds little reference for other African experiences.

More than any other part of the world Africa needs an optimum external environment to assist peaceful change. The pitiful condition of African economies gives little opportunity for economic policies that could maximise political support. According to Clapham (1993:437) African governments 'can only sit on the roller coaster and hope that the policies provided by western donors and creditors bring the necessary rewards before some jolt sends them flying.' In such circumstances, the Mandela factor can be of only ancillary relevance to democratization processes in Africa.

## Conclusions

The aims of this chapter were three-fold – to assess the global reach of liberal democracy and to test the post-Cold War triumphalist thesis in different contexts; to explore the concept of democracy in several of its forms and to relate these models to the globalization of ideas in the late twentieth century; and to examine some of the challenges to democracy.

### Only half a triumph?

We have observed liberal democracy in several situations and can note similar trends emerging in the immediate post-Cold War period. Some of these trends may pre-date the momentous events of the late 1980s but, when considered together, present an emergent paradigm within which globalization and democracy can be related. What emerges is a complex interconnection of externally induced change, and internal reaction to it, that contributes both to democratic transition and to established democratic practice in a sometimes positive, but often negative, manner.

In established liberal democracies, market-led solutions to the economic ills of Keynsian-style policy processes have met with a mixture of approval and resentment. While it may be too early to judge, the success of market-led economic and social policies looks somewhat patchy. History is, it seems, still in the making. What is evident is that established democracies, especially in West Europe, have utilized regional cooperation as a survival mechanism, with varying degrees of success, when faced with increased economic globalization.

External pressures have played a significant role in the democratization processes underway in Central and Eastern Europe. The task set by international rather than domestic imperatives – to democratize and to privatize at the same time – would seem impossible without further assistance from the European Union. However EU member states show no uniform position on this issue.

While the eventual establishment of western liberal or social democracies in most CEE countries looks at least a possibility, the prospects for democratic consolidation in South America and South Asia appear bleak. As market liberalization progresses in both regions, unemployment and declining public welfare services, exacerbated by a tradition of military intervention, suggest gloomy prospects for democracy except in its low intensity variant. It is probable that this will also be the dominant model in South East Asia, although the remarkable economic growth of the NICs could accommodate the development of more participatory and accountable democratic processes.

In the Middle East and North Africa, where cultural norms generate profound resentment of individualism, the destiny of political change is more closely identified with domestic than with external pressures. While global economic processes undoubtedly impact on these areas, the globalization of ideas concerning individual autonomy has only marginally influenced traditional communitarian values. Hence democracy remains contextualized by traditional values.

As already indicated, Sub-Saharan Africa is the gloomiest of regions to discuss, and the one most dependent on external political and economic forces. The negative impact of the liberal market model is most apparent in this region as a result, in particular, of externally imposed structural adjustment policies.

Pressures from international organizations such as the IMF, World Bank or G7 group have significantly affected the direction of political change in both established and emerging democracies. Social democracy in West Europe, socialist interventionism in CEE and redistributive social policies in some African and South American states have suffered the painful effects of structural adjustment, sometimes with disastrous results for democratic transition and consolidation. Indeed, for more weakly established democracies, the consequence is likely to be democratic reversal.

This ultimately places the ball firmly in the court of western governments to develop both a political conscience and a forum of accountability for 'unaccountable and unrepresentative governing institutions of the international system' (Gills and Rocamora 1992:521). This would involve recognition that the logic of economic globalization can produce a range of political responses, of which liberal democracy may not be the most appropriate; and that support may be needed for a range of variants – be they social, communitarian or individualist in ethos – if democracy is to develop and survive as a universally accepted phenomenon.

## A Polycentric Approach to Global Democracy

Recognition of a global dimension to democratic practice leads to consideration of a conceptual framework to include this dimension. This is no sterile exercise. The triumph of liberalism has brought mixed blessings to the world and little evidence that the future for millions of its inhabitants will be much improved. Indeed, given their patchy performance, there would seem to be an increased need to seek a moral justification for democratic forms of government. Can we therefore identity common parameters within which democratic values may be recognized; and processes by which those values might be globally applied?

For a framework to encompass universal democratic values we might consider the United Nations Declaration of Human Rights, which, in setting out a core of fundamental rights, provides 'a most valuable basis for a freely negotiated and constantly evolving consensus on universally valid principles of good government' (Parekh 1993:173). The application of universal rights, it is argued, rests ultimately on the legitimacy of international organizations that seek to apply, interpret and adapt them within the agreed framework of a cosmopolitan order (Held 1993; Archiburgi 1993).

Such an order might comprise, according to Held, overlapping spheres of influence structured around local, national, regional and international institutions. Through application of an agreed set of human rights within each of these levels of government, a formal link between the individual and a cosmopolitan order could be established. A reformed United Nations would need to play a major role here. Reforms might include establishment of an Assembly of the Peoples to represent citizens rather than states, modifications to Security Council membership and extending the jurisdiction of the International Court of Justice to cases between individuals and states (Archiburgi 1993).

These proposals, however, have considerable implications for state sovereignty, which remains a significant impediment to the development of supranational institutions. Clearly if a cosmopolitan order were to be established within a framework of universal rights it must be seen to complement rather than to challenge the role of the state.

It seems unlikely that such a global synergy will emerge in the foreseeable future. What seems more realistic is the development of regional organizations that match developing regional spheres of influence (Gills and Rocamora 1992). Regional organizations have the advantage of geographical, political, economic and historical-cultural linkages that may legitimize a supranational role. This could lead to their acceptance as superior units of democratic accountability within the context of a polycentric democracy, so avoiding the spatial implausibility of global solutions to parochial problems. If formal regional organizations are linked to globally recognized human rights this might form a practical and flexible connection between national autonomy and global community.

For Archiburgi (1993:314) 'The challenge of a cosmopolitan model is not substituting one power with another but in reducing the role of power in the political process while increasing the role of procedures.' Given the continuing debates centring around democratic ideals and outcomes, perhaps a partial regional framework for democratic practice is all that we can expect.

## Notes

1   Thus for Augusto Pinochet of Chile 'There has never been a dictatorship here. I am a democrat!' (*New Internationalist* September 1994:15).
2   A civil society may be 'viewed as a set of social organizations, outside of the state, which could be used to underpin the effective democratic order; trade unions, professional associations, the independent media and other social and economic groupings which help to integrate different sections of the community' (Wiseman 1993:439–49).
3   Hyde-Price also explores the role of the Council of Europe and the CSCE in providing international support for democratic transition in CEE.
4   Con-associational systems seek to draw deeply segmented polities together into a decision process, mainly through elite representation in grand coalitions (see Volten 1992, especially chapter three).
5   One consequence of the end of the Cold War has been a search for new markets for armaments, both by western and former eastern block manufacturers. Thus the scenario emerges where countries undergoing democratic transition – such as South Africa and the Czech Republic – are selling arms to states such as Zaire and Angola, thus increasing the likelihood of political destabilization in those countries.
6   Margaret Thatcher's very public admission of giving in 'just a little bit, a tiny bit' when questioned by the press about British support for tougher EC sanctions in 1986 illustrated the West's lack of commitment to South Africa's democratic transition in the context of economic and strategic interests.

# 10

# Universal Human Rights: Bringing People into Global Politics?

## Charlotte Bretherton

Since the Second World War there has developed a body of international law which establishes moral standards of governance and seeks to regulate the relationship between governments and their peoples. In providing the potential for direct links between the individual and global levels, the issues associated with human rights suggest the possibility of a universal civil society, hence presenting a unique challenge to state sovereignty and forming an important aspect of the globalization thesis. Human rights issues, in consequence, are highly controversial.

In its concluding section, the preceding chapter discussed the potential contribution of universal human rights to models of cosmopolitan democracy. This chapter takes up these issues, but focuses primarily upon the controversies surrounding human rights. These fall into three broad areas:

The scope of rights – whether or not there are fundamental human rights which have universal relevance irrespective of socio-cultural context.

The content of rights – whether or not fundamental human rights should be restricted to a minimal list of freedoms – from arbitrary imprisonment and execution, from torture and from slavery – or whether a range of factors essential to human survival, and to human dignity, should be included.

The protection of rights – how and by whom compliance with human rights provisions is to be monitored and ensured – and whether the rights of individuals can, or should, take precedence over the sovereignty of states.

These questions have been the subject of debate ever since human rights issues reached the global political agenda. Consequently, before embarking upon discussion of these controversies, it is necessary briefly to chart their emergence and development as an issue in global politics.

## Development of the Human Rights Agenda

Precedents for contemporary approaches to human rights date back to nineteenth-century campaigns for the abolition of slavery. Nevertheless, prior to the Second World War, the rights of individuals remained almost entirely a matter of domestic jurisdiction. International law was intended to regulate the conduct of interstate relations, in times both of peace and of war: reference to individuals was confined to rules governing the treatment of citizens of one state by the agents of another. In this scenario, which accords with realist interpretations of interstate relations, the state plays a benign role in relation to the individual, providing protection from the depredations of other states. Hence it was considered neither necessary nor appropriate, given the assumption of sovereign equality which underpins international law, to enunciate universal norms governing the relationship between the individual and the state: in a very real sense the individual was the property of the state. While rights and freedoms might be gained from or conceded by the state through a Bill of Rights, there was no possibility of recourse to an external authority should such rights be infringed or revoked.

In the period of optimism which followed the end of the First World War, liberal idealist commentators did emphasize the role of individuals in international affairs. It was believed that establishment of democratic principles of governance would enable the good sense of the principal victims of war, the people, to constrain the choices of elites, its perpetrators. In consequence the product of this idealist moment, the Covenant of the League of Nations, referred to the self-determination of peoples rather than the rights of individuals. Idealists believed that, in the democratic polities which were to be established, individual rights and freedoms would be assured. While contemporary liberal internationalists adopt a rather more pragmatic position than their inter-war forebears, the persistence of these themes is evident.

By the end of the Second World War it was clear both that idealist hopes for democratization had been premature, if not unfounded, and that individuals were very much in need of protection from their own states. While the excesses of Stalinism contributed to this conclusion, it was the genocidal massacre of Jews and Gypsies during the Holocaust which produced the moral outrage necessary for attempts to ensure that 'never again' would such horrors be perpetrated. Thus the Nuremberg War Crimes Trials of 1945–6 introduced into international law the concept of crimes against humanity. Indeed, by convicting Nazi officials for crimes against German citizens as well as in occupied territories, the trials implied reliance upon universal and inalienable rights deriving from natural law, and upon norms concerning the conduct of civilized societies embedded in the custom and practice of interstate relations. In the circumstances of 1945, the absence of substantial legal precedent did not impede prosecution of officials of an odious and vanquished regime. Nevertheless steps to ensure fuller codification of international humanitarian law began immediately.

The 1945 Charter of the United Nations affirmed, in its preamble, 'faith in fundamental human rights, in the dignity and worth of the human person, in the equal rights of men and women . . .' and in Article 1.3 included, among the purposes and principles of the organization, promotion of such rights and freedoms. The years immediately following witnessed considerable activity in building upon the Charter's provisions. Thus in 1946 the United Nations Commission on Human Rights was established and in 1948 the Convention on the Prevention and Punishment of the Crime of Genocide was opened for signature. In the same year the Universal Declaration of Human Rights was adopted unopposed by the United Nations General Assembly, albeit with eight abstentions: by the Soviet Union, Ukraine, Byelorussia, Czechoslovakia, Poland, Yugoslavia, Saudi Arabia and South Africa. Given the heightening tensions of this early Cold War period, the abstention of so many Eastern bloc countries is significant.

The Universal Declaration comprises thirty Articles and combines two broad categories of rights. Civil and political rights are covered by the first 21 Articles. Protection from arbitrary treatment by the state is a central aspect of these rights, but also included is the right to participate in the political process and, more controversially, the right to own property. A range of economic, social and cultural rights is included in the remaining Articles. These relate to the prosperity and dignity of human beings – including, for example, the right to a standard of living adequate to health and well being (Article 25) and the right to education (Article 26).

The drafting process of the Declaration was accompanied by deep divisions concerning both its content and status – between those who favoured a broad, aspirational and long-term approach intended to exert moral influence, and those who favoured a narrow specification of rights accompanied by binding obligations which would have immediate effect.[1] In the event, as we have seen, the Declaration reflected a broad approach to rights.

The status of the Universal Declaration is unique. It is not an international treaty requiring ratification but is simply a resolution of the General Assembly. Nevertheless the Declaration has been widely regarded as forming an appendix to the United Nations Charter, hence acquiring a status analogous to that of the Charter itself (Best 1990:4). In addition its architects anticipated that the Declaration would shortly be augmented by a more binding covenant; an expectation that was thwarted, at least temporarily, by the rapidly changing political environment of the post-war period.

As we saw in the case of security issues (chapter six), the development of the United Nations' role was severely inhibited by the onset of the Cold War. Since human rights issues were subordinated within the Charter to security issues, it is perhaps unsurprising that, after the initial flurry of activity, progress on human rights was remarkable mainly for its leisurely pace. Thus, from 1948 onwards, the Commission on Human Rights degenerated into a locus for Cold War political and ideological confrontation focused around the two broad categories of rights – civil and social – contained in the Universal Declaration. The right to freedom of information – not conspicuously present in Soviet society – was the issue most frequently discussed in a Commission dominated by the West in the early years. Conversely Soviet representatives attempted, whenever possible, to prioritize issues of racial discrimination in the United States and unemployment generally in the West (Donnelly 1993:8).

These difficulties were exacerbated by expanding membership of the UN as a result of decolonization. Western domination of the United Nations system was resented by representatives of newly independent states. They had played no part in the formulation of the Universal Declaration of Human Rights and, in consequence, questioned its universality. In particular the Commission's focus on civil and political rights was considered, not without justification, to prioritize a liberal capitalist agenda: it was economic, social and cultural rights which accorded most closely with the needs and interests of Third World countries. Here Soviet bloc and Third World representatives made common cause, and by the mid 1960s western domination of the United Nations system had ended. As a consequence, although deep divisions concerning the meaning of rights persisted throughout the Cold War and beyond, the human rights agenda gained fresh impetus and a changed focus – exemplified by the formulation, and opening for signature in 1965, of the International Convention on the Elimination of All Forms of Racial Discrimination.

In 1966, after eighteen years delay, codification of the fundamental rights included in the Universal Declaration was finally completed. However there emerged not a single covenant, as had originally been intended, but two – the International Covenant on Civil and Political Rights and the International Covenant on Economic, Social and Cultural Rights – reflecting the failure of the Commission to agree, despite years of debate, on the relative status of these rights. The Covenants came into effect in 1976 and, together with the Universal Declaration, are collectively referred to as the International Bill of Rights.[2]

Production of these comprehensive documents marked the end of the initial period of UN standard-setting in the area of rights, which should have been accompanied by attention to monitoring and compliance. However, the persistence of the Cold War ensured that human rights issues remained both the subject of ideological contention and subordinate to strategic interests: indeed it was the failure to develop even rudimentary monitoring and compliance procedures that prompted the creation of Amnesty International in 1961.

Despite the difficulties of the Cold War period, human rights issues were not absent from the global agenda. The intervening years saw the formulation of a number of Conventions intended to focus attention upon and elaborate or extend existing rights. They include the following – the figures in brackets indicate ratifications as at 1st June 1994:

Convention on the Elimination of All Forms of Discrimination against Women, 1979 (133)

Convention against Torture and Other Cruel, Inhuman or Degrading Treatment or Punishment, 1984 (82)

Convention on the Rights of the Child, 1989 (159)

Convention on the Protection of the Rights of All Migrant Workers and Their Families, 1990 (2). Entry into force dependent upon acceptance by at least twenty states.

The pattern of ratifications is interesting. Relatively few governments, it seems, are prepared to make public their unwillingness to respect and protect the rights of women and children. A total of 174 states has ratified one or several human rights instruments but six new states and four others – Brunei, Malaysia, Singapore and Saudi Arabia – have ratified none.

The generally low level of ratifications in Asia and the Middle East is indicative, in part, of rejection of the universality of human rights norms. A further indication of this rejection is provided by the development of regional human rights regimes serving Europe, Africa and Latin America.[3] In two of these cases, the normative basis of the regime differs in emphasis from the Universal Declaration, with the European Convention prioritizing individual freedoms and the African Convention emphasizing the rights and responsibilities of peoples. This difference reflects contrasting perceptions of the individual, and of society–state relationships, and highlights the practical implications of philosophical debates about universality.

## Are Human Rights Universal?

To enjoy universal status, rights must be applicable to all persons at all times. Thus universal human rights cannot be made contingent upon citizenship or some other qualification, they do not have to be earned and they cannot be renounced; they accrue to all human beings simply as a consequence of being human and their basis is moral rather than political. Ultimately, then, human rights imply an evaluation of the intrinsic and equal worth of all human beings; which sets them apart from, and above, other species. Article 1 of the Universal Declaration clearly reflects this view:

> All human beings are born free and equal in dignity and rights. They are endowed with reason and conscience and should act towards one another in a spirit of brotherhood.

These propositions are grounded in a philosophical tradition, dating back to Plato, which identifies the capacity for reflection, for rational action and for the assumption of moral responsibility as essential characteristics of human beings (or perhaps of male human beings); providing 'a special added ingredient which puts them in a different category than the brutes', upon which mutual respect is based (Rorty 1993:115).

It is not difficult to identify a number of problems with this optimistic view of human nature. Followers of Nietzsche would present the counter-claim that human beings, far from having superior characteristics, are an unusually nasty type of animal. Contemporary environmental thought, from the very different perspective of ecological holism, also rejects the dualistic separation of the human and natural worlds. Marxists see human nature as neither universal nor fixed, but contingent upon material conditions. And feminists would point out that all these perspectives are products of the masculine imagination and, hence, essentially gendered.

Since there can be no agreement on what is essentially human, upon which a universal concept of rights might be founded, is there any point in posing the question? One contemporary approach to this dilemma is to deny the validity of the question; to reject essentialist approaches to human nature as an aspect of western ideological domination and to emphasize, instead, relativism, diversity and difference. This is an important contribution to the development of ideas, reminding us that modern political ideologies – whether they be liberal, socialist or nationalist – have overwhelmingly reflected the interests, observations or experience of white, privileged, western males. Accepting contemporary relativism would involve, also, denial of the existence of universal human rights.

Before discussing alternative approaches to the dilemma of universality, let us consider some implications of its denial. Proceeding from the assumption, which has so far only been implicit, that human rights matter and ought to be protected, we discuss two areas – cultural relativism and women's rights – which exemplify distinct problems associated with the universality of rights.

### Cultural relativism

This concept implies that moral values cannot be universal, rather they are culturally specific; embedded in the norms, beliefs and customs of particular societies. To demonstrate that this is, indeed, the case, we need look no further than our second problem area – women's rights. Here a very clear example of the impact of diverging cultural norms is provided by the issue of reproductive rights, and in particular the right to abortion. Moreover, insofar as the rights of the foetus are pitted against the rights of women, this issue also raises culture-specific judgements about what constitutes a human being.

Acknowledgement that moral values can be both culturally specific and highly contested should not, however, lead us to abandon our search for the universal. Rather, by examining some practical implications of arguments based on cultural relativism, we must attempt to separate genuine moral dilemmas from manipulation by governments.

Since the end of the Cold War, it has been argued, the case for cultural relativism has declined (Donnelly 1993; Thakur 1994b). Notions of 'three worlds' of rights – western emphasis upon civil and political rights; socialist emphasis upon economic and social rights and Third World emphasis upon peoples' rights to development – are unhelpful caricatures and should be abandoned. Social and economic rights are considered important in many western states, particularly in Scandinavia, while the collapse of the Soviet bloc demonstrated that civil and political rights were valued by the peoples of Central and Eastern Europe if not by their governments. The Third World, however, is still with us, and a closer examination is warranted of claims emanating from some regions of the Third World to a different concept of rights.

We noted above the existence of the African Charter on Human and Peoples' Rights. This reflects what has been considered a specifically African concept of human rights, developed from the norms of traditional African societies and based upon two important principles – communitarianism, which rejects the individualism of the western model, and decision-making through consensual procedures, which obviates the need for competitive elections. These principles are central to claims of cultural relativism and have relevance beyond Africa: we will devote some attention to each.

In communitarian models full status as a human being, or 'personhood', does not inhere in the individual but is acquired through group membership, and through fulfilment of a range of obligations to the group. Human rights, in consequence, are contingent upon status: non-members of the group, or those who fail to fulfil their social obligations, such as barren women, may be considered less than human (Howard 1989:133). However in Africa and elsewhere the consequences of treating others as less than human are evident – they provide a powerful argument against cultural relativism.

Claims to consensual decision-making are based upon the practices of small-scale, traditional societies. While there is some debate concerning the extent to which such societies ever existed, there is much evidence to suggest that translation of consensual procedures from the village to the state level is a myth used to legitimate repressive, single party regimes. Moreover, given the multi-ethnic character of many African states, there are considerable tensions between notions of communitarianism and the consensus-seeking state.

Rhoda Howard has concluded (ibid.:136) that there is not an African concept of human rights and that cultural relativist claims all too often conceal widespread and systematic abuse of human rights. It must be emphasized, nevertheless, that the economic and other problems facing African governments, which have been highlighted in several previous chapters, pose insurmountable difficulties in honouring aspects of human rights, particularly economic and social rights.

In the context of South-East Asia too, Bilahari Kausikan, a spokesperson for the Singaporean Foreign Ministry, advances claims for consensual governance as a culture-specific concept. He also emphasizes 'the realities of exercising authority in heterogeneous, unevenly modernized, and imperfectly integrated societies' in which 'Good government may well require, among other things, detention without trial, curbs on press freedoms . . . and draconian laws to break the power of entrenched interests' (Kausikan 1993:38). Since Singapore suffers from fewer problems than most Third World countries we might conclude, with human rights activist Aryeh Neier, that Kausikan's concern is not to protect cultural traditions but 'to delegitimize international efforts to address the abuses that particularly characterize his own government and its regional allies' (Neier 1993:51).

The impact of cultural relativism continues to be evident in the United Nations system. The Group of 77 (G77) caucus of Third World states enjoys considerable voting strength and is prepared to use it.[4] In 1992, for example, G77 succeeded in blocking publication of information concerning human rights in future editions of the annual UNDP Human Development Report and regularly defeats resolutions condemning the human rights record of China. Moreover the June 1993 World Conference on Human Rights, convened to review and strengthen global human rights mechanisms, almost foundered as a result of attempts by representatives of Asian countries, in particular the Chinese delegation, to reject universal concepts of rights. Nevertheless the Conference did make progress in some areas – notably women's rights.

## Women's rights

As we have seen, there are areas of overlap between cultural relativism and women's rights. For example violations of women's human rights arising from norms and practices associated with marriage and sexual behaviour – such as brideprice, dowry and ritual genital mutilation – are culture-specific and are defended as traditional practices constitutive of group membership. These practices, however, are manifestations of a much broader relativism; that is the universal ascription of inferior status to women. This global phenomenon, the extent of which was formally documented for the first time during the 1975–85 United Nations Decade for Women (UN 1991), reflects the assumption that women are not fully adult or, indeed, are not fully human. This assumption is explicit, in many countries, in laws governing property ownership and inheritance, as well as other areas. Consider, for example, legislation in Pakistan to the effect that evidence provided by two women is equal to that of one man, and that compensation for the life of a murdered woman should be half that of a man (Ashworth 1985:146).

Consideration of women's rights as a special category within the human rights lexicon is justified on two grounds. First, norms and values concerning the attribution and content of rights reflect the experience and interests of men. In consequence they are far from universal; in many important respects human rights are men's rights. The principal difficulty lies in their focus, which is almost exclusively upon the relationship between individuals and the state. Thus a major objective of human rights is to protect the individual from cruel and arbitrary treatment by the state. While this is an important, and evidently necessary, function of human rights, it is not in the public sphere of individual–state relationships that women are most in danger, but in the private sphere of domestic relationships. Such arguments apply equally to children and, particularly in western societies, the elderly. Nevertheless it is upon issues affecting women that we focus; and evidence of violence against women is not difficult to find:

Violence against women is the most pervasive abuse of human rights. It exists in various forms in everyday life in all societies. In Mexico a woman is raped every nine minutes. An estimated 1,000 women are burned alive each year in dowry-related incidents in the state of Gujarat alone, in India. One in ten Canadian women are abused or battered by their husbands or partners (Kerr 1993:4).

Sadly this sample from the catalogue of abuse against women does not exhaust the matter. Most societies exhibit a preference for the birth of sons – in Britain, for example, the birth of a prince has merited a twenty-one gun salute, a princess only ten. In regions where son preference is strong, and poverty endemic, there is much evidence of intentional neglect and infanticide of female infants (Ashworth 1985:147). Thus, as UNICEF has pointed out, respect for human rights is 'likely to depend on the one cruel chromosome' (Kerr 1993:3).

The first argument for according special status to women's rights is based upon their exclusion from traditional concepts of human rights; the second argument is not. In every aspect of human rights covered by the Universal Declaration there are widespread violations involving women, many of which are gender specific.

The area of social and economic rights is fundamental to women. Here there are very significant differences between women, especially between the developed and developing worlds, in areas such as access to adequate living standards and to education. Nevertheless in every country of the world woman-headed households constitute the poorest group, nowhere is the entitlement (Article 23 of the Universal Declaration) to 'equal pay for equal work' even approximated, and women's exclusion from ownership of wealth is a global phenomenon.[5] Moreover economic dependence contributes to the diminution of women's social status and reduces their ability to escape violent and abusive relationships. Barrington Moore Jr includes, among the 'universal causes of unhappiness' requiring remedy, 'the exactions of ruthless authorities who carry off the fruits of prolonged labour' (cited in Howard 1989:132). He was apparently unaware that this reference to slavery corresponds with the routine experience of a majority of the world's women.

Commitment to honouring women's economic and social rights would involve fundamentally challenging existing economic structures and patterns of privilege. In consequence, while such rights have been the subject of periodic expressions of commitment, it is civil and political rights which have been the principal focus of the Commission on Human Rights. It might be supposed that in the public sphere of civil and political rights the principal victims of rights violations would be men. However media publicity concerning use of mass rape as an instrument of war in Bosnia–Herzegovina from 1992 and in Rwanda in 1994 has drawn attention to a pervasive phenomenon. In 1991 Amnesty International (AI) published a report detailing gross human rights violations against women prisoners of conscience. While many such women are community leaders or political activists whose treatment, while reprehensible, is analogous to that of men similarly involved in peaceful dissent, others are specifically targeted because of their vulnerability rather than their actions: 'young women who can easily be sexually abused or humiliated, frightened mothers who will do anything to protect their children, pregnant women who are fearful for their unborn babies . . .' (AI 1991:1).

Moreover women prisoners are much more likely than men to be sexually abused and raped while in captivity; only women suffer the trauma of impregnation by their captors. Should they escape, women refugees experience particular difficulty in convincing immigration officials of their right to asylum in cases where they fear persecution of a sexual or gender specific nature (Robertson 1994:2). Finally, women comprise the overwhelming majority of the world's refugees. The UN High Commissioner for Refugees has described their experiences thus: 'Rape, abduction, sexual harassment, physical violence and the not infrequent obligation to grant "sexual favours" in return for documentation and/or goods remains a distressing reality for many women refugees' (cited in AI 1991:48).

Despite the extensive violation of women's human rights, and in particular the pervasive and persistent nature of domestic violence against women, this issue was first raised at the UN Commission on Human Rights only in 1984, towards the end of the first UN Decade for Women (Ashworth 1985:151). This period saw inclusion of a gender dimension in many UN policy areas, reflecting extension to the global level of feminist arguments concerning the inadequacy of protections for women which operate only in the civil, or public sphere. Since 1984 women's rights issues have attained increasing prominence at UN forums, and at the 1993 World Conference on Human Rights the principle that women's rights are human rights was formally accepted. As a consequence a Special Rapporteur on Violence against Women was appointed in April 1994. These gestures at least acknowledge that a problem exists.

## A Universal Concept of Rights?

Through emphasizing the cultural specificity of moral values, cultural relativism denies the possibility of universal rights. According to this view, human rights as presently formulated are the product of an individualistic, western philosophical tradition which is inappropriate to non-western cultures: consequently attempts to impose such rights globally are an aspect of western hegemony. While there is some validity in this contention, it is all too frequently used by repressive regimes to deflect attention from their excesses. Moreover, cultural relativism in its extreme form defines boundaries between what is human and what is not; it is the logic of 'the gallant and honourable Serb who sees Muslims as circumcised dogs' (Rorty 1993:124).

While we do not deny the significance of cultural values, nor seek to minimize cultural differences, we believe that a universal concept of rights is both necessary and achievable. This view also informs the arguments about women's rights outlined above. In common with cultural relativists, feminist perspectives deny the universality of human rights as currently formulated. However, feminists emphasize the gender specific nature of human rights, urging a truly universal concept of human rights, into which women's rights are fully incorporated. Such a concept requires a basis, however. Given the difficulty in establishing an ontological foundation for claims of universality – in that human nature can be shown neither to be essentially rational nor essentially evil – we adopt an alternative approach which links arguments concerning human frailty and human sympathy.

Bryan Turner proposes the universality of 'human frailty and the precariousness of institutions' as the basis of a theory of human rights (1993:179). He contends that human beings are frail, and hence vulnerable, as a result of poor environmental adaptation: in consequence they have sought protection through the construction of social institutions, latterly the state. However this arrangement is inadequate for two reasons. First, the contemporary state is incapable of protecting citizens from the impacts of globalization; second, the state does not protect all citizens equally. For many individuals and social groups the state is a principal source of harm; for others the state has failed to extend protection to the area of greatest vulnerability – the domestic sphere.

Turner's anthropological perspective can be augmented by the philosophical arguments of Richard Rorty (1993). Rorty contends that human beings are characterized, not by rationality or irrationality, but by the capacity for sympathy. In effect, awareness of our own frailty generates consciousness of the frailty of others; and our capacity to imagine the suffering of others enables us to sympathize with their hunger, pain or loss. Thus the anger I have experienced while researching this chapter is based on my imagining another woman's pain as my pain, her children's suffering as my children's suffering.

In consequence, the basis upon which we claim the universality of human rights is thus: Human beings are highly vulnerable to harm and are aware both of their own frailty and that of others. The institutions constructed to protect human beings at the level of the state are inadequate, and there is a need to develop and strengthen global human rights institutions. Our capacity to sympathize with the suffering of others is necessary to such development. Sadly, however, the generalization of this capacity beyond the family or local community, across divisions of ethnicity, race and gender, remains problematic. It is inhibited by a number of factors, among which conditions of economic and social deprivation are prominent – for contemplation of the universality of rights is surely a preoccupation of the relatively privileged. This brings us to our second major issue; what should be the content of a universal concept of human rights?

## The Content of Human Rights

Debates about the content of rights largely reflect ideological preferences, as evidenced by inclusion of the right to own property – an economic right – among the civil and political rights of the Universal Declaration. Principally at issue is the scope and focus of the human rights agenda; in consequence our discussion focuses upon two broad approaches – minimalist and comprehensive.

Minimalists emphasize the significance of a core of rights, to be considered either in isolation, as the totality of entitlement, or as the apex of a hierarchy of rights. This core of rights is typically restricted to the most basic civil and political rights – freedom from arbitrary arrest and imprisonment, from punishment without due process of law, from torture, disappearances and enslavement – and it is this core which has been the principal focus of attention, both within the United Nations system and from human rights organizations. Indeed an even more minimal core of rights is implied by the derogation provisions of the UN Covenant on Civil Political Rights, which permit suspension, in periods of public emergency, of all rights save those to life and freedom from torture.

The minimalist approach is frequently justified on the grounds of practicality, that is the enhanced potential for achieving a limited number of the most fundamental rights; whereas an expanded concept of rights hinders their achievement because 'the relatively small neat set of rights that can be realized suffers from being mixed up with the great gaseous mass of those that can not' (Best 1990:17). However the contention that there is confusion about the status of 'core' rights, some of which are in any case non-derogable, is contradicted by the considerable efforts made by governments to deny or conceal their contravention. Indeed the norms prohibiting cruel and arbitrary treatment of citizens are almost universally accepted, albeit far from universally respected.

A variation on the minimalist theme is suggested by the philosopher, John Rawls (1993:71), who sees respect for human rights as 'a necessary condition of a regime's legitimacy and of the decency of its legal order'. Attempts to universally establish an expansive concept of human rights would be met by two sets of difficulties, however: the unavailability, in some societies, of the material conditions necessary for implementation of such rights; and the existence, in others, of ordering principles which render such rights inappropriate. The solution to the first set of difficulties is clear – 'each society now burdened by unfavourable conditions should be raised to, or assisted toward, conditions that make a well ordered society possible' (ibid.:75). The second set of difficulties echoes our discussion of cultural relativism, with particular reference to hierarchical societies ordered, for example, according to religious principles. Here Rawls invokes the liberal tradition of tolerance. He argues that, provided the organizing principles of hierarchical societies are accepted domestically as legitimate, it would be wrong to attempt to impose rights based on the principle of equality. Consequently universal conceptions of rights should not be expanded beyond the minimalist core. Where societies are characterized by, for example, 'the subjection of women abetted by unreasonable religion' (ibid.:77) liberals may express disapproval but should not urge acceptance of the alien principle of equal rights.

Rawls' reiteration of the classical liberal position is interesting in that it exposes the contradictions inherent in contemporary liberal attempts to conflate human rights with democracy, to which we shall return. However, by failing to acknowledge that the subjection of women is a characteristic of *all* societies, Rawls exposes, also, the central contradiction of the minimalist approach: the core protections, in failing to address violence against women of epidemic proportions, or to protect the rights of children and the elderly or infirm, fail also to meet the criterion of universality.

Advocates of an inclusive concept of human rights regard freedom and social justice as inseparable. Rene Cassin, the French socialist who played a pivotal role in framing the Universal Declaration, put it succinctly – 'The right to eat is a human right without which all others are nugatory; and to talk of "the right to life" without it is humbug' (cited in Best 1990:17). Conversely, prioritization of economic and social rights at the expense of civil and political rights – however justified this might appear to be – can all too easily be used in attempts to legitate repression.

Acceptance of arguments for an inclusive concept of human rights, however, does not solve the problem of what should be included. One approach to this dilemma, which immediately gives rise to a contingent dilemma, is to attempt directly to relate human rights to the basic requirements of human survival and human dignity. Thus Donnelly (1993:196) defines human rights as 'the social and political guarantees necessary to protect individuals from the standard threats to human dignity posed by the modern state and modern markets.' This definition is useful in that it clearly links the political and economic aspects of rights, and reminds us that policies and agents of the state pose by no means the only threat to those rights. Nevertheless it fails adequately to encompass the rights of women and other excluded groups; nor does it help to resolve our contingent dilemma: what are the basic needs of human beings for which corresponding rights may be formulated?

A useful starting point for consideration of an inclusive concept of human rights is provided by the three documents comprising the International Bill of Rights. While some commentators urge acceptance of these instruments, as formulated, on the grounds that they already have wide currency (Donnelly 1993; Thakur 1994b), others adopt a more critical stance. Johan Galtung has attempted systematically to assess the degree of correspondence between basic human needs and the rights contained in the International Bill. He advocates a needs-based approach to rights, but rejects a narrow focus on survival/subsistence needs 'for which a well-organized prison would do' in favour of an approach which emphasizes human development, the realization of human potential (Galtung 1994:125).

Galtung begins by developing a typology of needs based on the distinction between material and non-material needs.[6] Material needs are for survival – involving safety from violence; and well-being – involving access to clean air, food, water, clothing, shelter, health care. Non-material needs are for freedom – involving the absence of repression; and identity – which gives meaning to existence. Galtung then proceeds to compare and contrast the needs he has identified with the rights accorded by the International Bill of Rights. While there is a large degree of correspondence between needs and rights, there are several areas where needs have no corresponding right and, conversely, where rights have no corresponding, universal need. This approach enables us to transcend the traditional distinction between civil and political and social, economic and cultural rights and identify key areas where there is poor correspondence between rights and needs. It allows us, also, to leave behind some of the old controversies while highlighting contemporary, and equally controversial, debates concerning omissions from and interpretation of the United Nations instruments.

Among the category of rights without corresponding needs are the provisions of the following three articles of the Universal Declaration:

Article 16, which provides protection for families, based on heterosexual relationships, as 'the natural and fundamental group unit of society'.

Article 17, which establishes the right of 'everyone' to own property. In practice, while such ownership is not a basic need, its universal application would have interesting redistributive effects in favour of, for example, the majority of women who are excluded from property ownership.

Article 21, which establishes the right to political participation and corresponds with the need for freedom from repression. This article, however, moves beyond a needs-based approach by stipulating that participation should be achieved through 'periodic and genuine elections'.

These Articles evidently seek to universalize a particular model of social, economic and political relationships, and the provisions concerning political participation and property ownership, in particular, have been much invoked since the end of the Cold War. These rights, which form part of the civil and political provisions, are increasingly regarded as subsuming all other civil and political rights. Consequently their prioritization, and their interpretation as necessitating economic liberalization and government according to the principles of liberal democracy, represents an obfuscation of the human rights agenda never achieved through attempts to prioritize social and economic rights. As we saw in the previous chapter, the introduction of low intensity, 'lip service' democracy provides scant protection for human rights.

A further, highly controversial area where rights have been accorded without adequate foundation in need, and where interpretation is crucially important, is the right to self-determination of peoples. Although absent from the Universal Declaration, this right was established by Article 1 of the Covenant on Economic, Social and Cultural Rights. This departure from the language of individual rights was included at the insistence of the Third World bloc and was intended to delegitimize colonialism. Subsequently, however, many of its proponents have had cause to reflect upon the precise meaning of self-determination, and of a people. We have argued, in chapter six, that recourse to this right is unlikely to result in the success of a large number of secessionist movements. Nevertheless the right is available and has evidently been the subject of renewed interest, since the end of the Cold War.

The response, within the UN system, has been to refocus attention on minority rights, an issue which had been moribund since 1977. Thus, in 1992, the General Assembly adopted a Declaration on the Rights of Persons Belonging to National, Ethnic, Religious and Linguistic Minorities. However, the provisions of this Declaration are considered totally inadequate as an articulation of minority rights (Farer and Gaer 1993:293).

The second area where rights and needs fail to coincide – needs without a corresponding right – frequently reflect issues which have emerged, or attained significance, relatively recently; gay and lesbian rights for example. A further set of 'new' needs is associated with environmental degradation and pollution: corresponding rights would include access to clean air and water and a living and working environment free from harmful pollutants.

Efforts to remedy omissions from the human rights agenda have been criticized on the grounds that they lack criteria and, echoing the minimalist view above, that their effect is to draw attention from, or dilute, existing provisions. Nevertheless there is a strong case for invoking the criterion of basic human need in respect of, for example, the environmental rights suggested above, particularly as this would involve recognition that human needs can, and do, change as a result of changing circumstances. The need for protection from the effects of ozone depletion, for example, was formally addressed only in 1985 (see chapter eight).

The issue of women's rights also reflects poor correspondence between needs and rights, but in a different way. Here the issue is not to remedy omissions but to adapt and strengthen existing human rights instruments to ensure their inclusiveness. Indeed it is essential that women's rights are incorporated into the mainstream rights provisions: the enumeration of additional, and separate, rights for women would all too easily result in their marginalization. The concept of mainstreaming was accepted at the 1993 World Conference on Human Rights and has since attracted a great deal of rhetorical support. As the UN Secretary-General has argued, 'The international community has passed resolutions. It has issued declarations. There have been studies and surveys. The basic facts are well known. Now is the time for action' (Boutros-Ghali 1994:5).

The Secretary-General's statement raises issues of monitoring and compliance, which bring us to the last of the three questions posed at the start of this chapter: is there any point in attempting to clarify or expand concepts of rights if there is no means of ensuring that progress is made towards their implementation?

## Protection of Rights: Standard-Setting, Monitoring and Compliance

In its 1994 Report, Amnesty International detailed grave abuses of human rights in 151 countries. These refer, of course, only to areas within the remit of AI – abuses actively perpetrated by agents of governments or by armed opposition groups, and to capital punishment in all circumstances. Significant, and horrific, as these abuses are, they are inevitably less numerous than those arising from neglect. Whether through lack of commitment or capacity, inadequate resources or incompetence, or some combination of all four, governments everywhere fail to protect the basic human rights of their citizens. In some regions, nevertheless, progress has been made in complying with human rights provisions: consequently we shall discuss ways in which such progress can be encouraged as well as mechanisms for monitoring compliance. A number of areas are considered – the UN machinery; the role of states, individually or as parties to *ad hoc* groupings or regional arrangements; and the role of non-governmental organizations (NGOs). The relationship between these various state and non-state actors and individuals, in whom human rights inhere, may be conceptualized in terms of three competing models.

The realist, state-centric model emphasizes the primacy, and sovereignty, of states. Hence, for realists, the rights of individuals are a matter of domestic jurisdiction and the role of intergovernmental organizations and NGOs is, at best, advisory. In terms of interstate relationships, the exigencies of sovereignty prohibit interference in the domestic affairs of other states, while foreign policy should be informed by self-interest rather than considerations of morality. Hence decisions to provide financial assistance, or indeed torture equipment, should be based upon the single criterion of advantage to the supplier.

A modification of the realist view is provided by the internationalist model (Donnelly 1993:31). Here states continue to occupy a central role and retain primary responsibility for individual rights. Nevertheless their actions are influenced, and to some extent modified, by an evolving consensus on human rights norms. Intergovernmental organizations and NGOs are capable of playing a significant role, and in some circumstances do so, but their capacity for effective action remains conditional upon the cooperation of states. Thus the influence of the UN Commission on Human Rights or of Amnesty International is considerably greater in Canada than in China or, indeed, the United Kingdom.

The third model might be labelled cosmopolitan (Donnelly op. cit.). Here the individual is at the centre of analysis, and a direct relationship is posited between individuals and intergovernmental organizations and NGOs. Thus the primacy of the state in global politics is increasingly challenged, both from below and above, to the extent that the development of a global civil society is presaged. Cosmopolitans would emphasize the development of the UN human rights machinery since the end of the Cold War as well as the proliferation in number, and growth in membership, of human rights and other NGOs during the same period.[7]

The usefulness of these models lies in their ability to conceptualize the roles of the various actors involved in human rights protection, and the record of action – involving standard-setting, monitoring and compliance – to promote and protect these rights.

## The human rights machinery of the United Nations

The UN General Assembly and its subsidiary, the Commission on Human Rights, occupy the apex of a 'lush institutional ensemble . . .

composed mainly of commissions and one sub-commission, committees both regular and special, working groups and special
rapporteurs' (Farer and Gaer 1993:257). The proliferation of bodies
concerned with human rights is associated, in part, with the development of the various UN instruments, but also reflects a pragmatic
response to Cold War blockages in committees: in the climate of the
Cold War, in order to make progress, it was the practice to create
alternative bodies. In consequence there is inevitably duplication and
overlap and here, as elsewhere in the UN system, there is scope for
reform and rationalization in the interests of efficiency. Coordination
on human rights issues is provided through biennial meetings of committee chairs and by the Centre for Human Rights at Geneva, which
services most of the UN human rights bodies.[8]

As evidenced by the numerous human rights instruments produced,
this complex UN machinery has achieved an impressive record in
human rights standard-setting. Progress in the areas of monitoring and
compliance has been less impressive, but has nevertheless been evident.

At its initial meeting in 1947 the Commission on Human Rights was
faced with numerous complaints of human rights violations. It decided
not even to read them, stating in its report: 'The Commission recognizes that it has no power to take any action in regard to any complaints
concerning human rights.' This 'crippling act of self-denial' ensured
the impotence of the Commission for the next twenty years (Farer
and Gaer 1993:272). In 1967, at the insistence of the growing Third
World bloc (which had intended the provision to apply only to colonial territories and South Africa) the Commission was empowered to
examine complaints of human rights violations. This provided, for the
first time, a direct link between individuals, NGOs and the United
Nations.

Since 1967 the Commission has established a variety of procedures
for dealing with complaints, typically through creation of investigatory
working groups. These are routinely attended by NGO representatives,
who report on human rights violations, and some proceedings are
made public. Nevertheless governments make strenuous efforts, sometimes successfully, to prevent public discussion of their human rights
records (Farer and Gaer 1993:278). In recent years the Commission
has attempted to circumvent obstruction by uncooperative governments by considering human rights violations on a global, thematic
basis rather than country by country. In 1980, for example, a Working
Group on Enforced or Involuntary Disappearances was established
which takes up complaints directly with governments. By 1990 it had
investigated more than 19,000 disappearances, successfully locating
disappeared persons in approximately 10 per cent of cases. Other
thematic areas include arbitrary executions and torture, where special
rapporteurs have 'aggressively pursued their mandates' investigating

and publicizing abuses widely (Donnelly 1993:62). Consequently, while the activities of the Commission and its subsidiary bodies continue to be constrained by pressure from member governments, notably that of the People's Republic of China, considerable progress has been made since the inauspicious start in 1947.

In addition to the Commission, specialized committees have been established in connection with each of the human rights conventions. The differing structures, procedures and powers of these committees inevitably reflect the political priorities of member governments: here it is instructive to contrast those of the Committees on the Elimination of Racial Discrimination (CERD) and of Discrimination Against Women (CEDAW). Thus CERD, which is supported by G77 countries, was established fourteen years earlier and meets three times a year, whereas CEDAW meets only once. CEDAW is not permitted to receive communications from individuals and, unlike any other UN human rights organization, meets in Vienna. It is also chronically underfunded, hence lacking both the time and resources necessary for effectiveness (Kerr 1993:5–6). The concessions gained by women lobbyists at the 1993 World Conference must be viewed in this context. Moreover the status of CEDAW reflects that of the Convention on Discrimination against Women itself, which is subject to more reservations by the parties than any other human rights convention.

The issue of reservations by states party to the various human rights instruments reminds us of their voluntary nature. The UN is an intergovernmental organization and has neither powers nor resources beyond those granted by its members. Consequently the organization's compliance role is limited to moral suasion and threats of public revelations of human rights violations – except in very exceptional circumstances where the Security Council has authorized action.[9] Nevertheless the fact that most governments are highly sensitive about such revelations is indicative of considerable success in standard-setting; the core human rights norms, at least, are well established and governments are anxious to maintain their reputation in this respect. In consequence monitoring of compliance is crucial.

In recent years the capacity and willingness of UN bodies to monitor implementation of human rights provisions has gradually increased. This capacity should be further enhanced, and the profile of human rights issues generally raised, as a result of the appointment in February 1994 of the first High Commissioner for Human Rights. Nevertheless the UN bodies depend very heavily, in their monitoring role, upon the information provided by human rights NGOs. In recent years there has been increasingly close cooperation between UN bodies and NGOs – symbolized, perhaps, by an early initiative of the new High Commissioner; the establishment in May 1994 of a 24-hour 'hot-line' for reporting human rights violations requiring urgent action.

## The role of non-governmental organizations

NGOs, by their nature, focus upon a narrow range of issues. Frequently, also, their operations are local or regional in scope. They represent, therefore, particular interests or constituencies and cannot claim the universality necessary for full participation in the process of standard-setting. Only the United Nations, with almost universal membership, has the capacity and authority to generate universal norms. Nevertheless NGOs make an important contribution to standard-setting by raising, and pursuing, issues of interpretation or omission. Some of these areas – environmental issues and women's rights – are discussed above. In such cases issues are pursued by an *ad hoc* coalition of NGOs, not all of which focus primarily upon human rights issues, while advocacy at the UN level is accompanied by consciousness-raising and activism at grassroots level. This is significant both in providing links between local communities and the UN system and in focusing upon the broad agenda of human rights. Nevertheless it is in the narrower sphere of gross violations of civil and political rights that the contribution of NGOs is best known, and here their role is primarily in monitoring and, through publicizing violations, contributing to pressures for compliance.

There is a large number of human rights NGOs operating in most regions of the world. Some of these are relatively small and narrowly focused, for example the Mothers of the Plaza de Mayo in Argentina. This group was founded in 1977, during a period of terrible repression, by a small group of women attempting to trace their disappeared children. Their weekly vigil generated a movement of some 5,000 women whose persistence became a symbol of resistance. This group, together with other NGOs, was also an important source of information to the United Nations, supplying accurate lists of disappearances which were used to counter the denials of the Argentine government (Donnelly 1993:50).[10]

The largest human rights NGO is Amnesty International, which was founded in 1961 following a letter to the *Observer* newspaper and now has branches worldwide (see note 7). Amnesty has established a reputation for integrity and neutrality through the scrupulousness of its reporting procedures and its policy of giving equal focus to human rights violations in different regions of the world. In precluding activists from investigative and lobbying activities in their own countries the objectivity of the organization is also enhanced. As Ramesh Thakur has argued (1994b:149), 'Who is going to believe China's protestations that AI is a tool of western capitalism, when AI has a long and proud record of opposing the use of the death penalty in the United States and investigating human rights abuses in Northern Ireland?'

AI is based on individual membership and has a substantial income from subscriptions and donations, much of which is devoted to consciousness-raising activities. While its principal targets are governments responsible for human rights violations, which its members lobby directly, the organization also regularly activates the UN human rights procedures by appearing as a complainant. In consequence Amnesty, together with many other NGOs, plays an important role in linking individuals, the holders of rights, and the UN rights bodies. Moreover its high-profile monitoring and compliance activities complement and augment UN efforts. NGOs such as Amnesty are very much less inhibited than the UN by pressure and protestations from governments.

### States, groups of states and regional organizations

States are both the subjects of international law and, through membership of intergovernmental organizations, its formulators. In terms of standard-setting, while many of the specialized UN human rights bodies are comprised of international lawyers and other experts, government representatives dominate the principal decision-making bodies. Nevertheless no government can be assured that its preferences will be reflected in outcomes. In common with the General Assembly itself, the Commission on Human Rights is numerically dominated by G77 countries, whose representatives have tended to exercise powers of veto rather than initiation. This latter role has been assumed by an *ad hoc* coalition of states, prominent among which have been the governments of Canada, Costa Rica and the Netherlands (Donnelly 1993:61–2). Consequently standard-setting can be seen as the outcome of intergovernmental bargaining; the resultant human rights provisions are the property of the universal organization.

While most states participate in the standard-setting and monitoring procedures of the UN, their compliance records are somewhat mixed. Human rights legislation strikes at the heart of state sovereignty and ratification of the various UN covenants is, in consequence, voluntary. While some states have ratified all the covenants presently in force, many have not: the relationship between ratification and compliance is, in any event, tenuous. Nevertheless states parties are required to produce reports on their compliance record, which are publicly examined, while protocols to the covenants permit public examination of complaints from individuals. While these latter are optional, and have been ratified by only 72 states (as at 1 June 1994), they represent a major development in the relationship between individuals, states and the global political system. These procedures, however, are considerably weaker than those associated with the regional human rights regime in Europe.

Formulated under the aegis of the Council of Europe, the European Convention for the Protection of Human Rights and Fundamental Freedoms, together with its associated procedures and institutions, is regarded as an exceptionally robust human rights regime (Best 1990; Donnelly 1993). The European Commission on Human Rights receives and investigates complaints from individuals and, where these are upheld, passes them on to the European Court of Human Rights for adjudication. Decisions are binding on governments that have accepted the compulsory jurisdiction of the Court; Turkey and Malta have not. Hence even in this case the abrogation of sovereignty, although real, is voluntary. Moreover it is alleged that the court is sensitive to the interests of governments which have accepted its jurisdiction – for example its verdict that the United Kingdom was not guilty of torture despite having found the treatment of prisoners in Northern Ireland to be 'degrading and inhuman' (Stack 1992:147).

The uneven and problematic record of compliance by individual states is echoed in the efforts of governments, unilaterally or multilaterally, to encourage compliance by others. In recent years, and more particularly since the end of the Cold War, human rights issues have attained greater prominence in foreign policy. From the early 1970s the governments of the Nordic countries, the Netherlands and Canada – known collectively as the 'like-minded countries' – have affirmed their commitment to prioritizing aid and trade links with countries emphasizing both economic and social and civil and political rights. They have subsequently suspended relations with various countries on the grounds of human rights violations (Donnelly 1993:127). The European Community has also increasingly emphasized human rights in its foreign policy, and the 1990 Fourth Lomé Convention between the Community and the African, Caribbean and Pacific (ACP) countries includes an article reflecting the broad agenda of the International Bill of Human Rights. The subsequent cessation of aid to Sudan on human rights grounds is said by the ACP vice-president to have 'caused a lot of concern within the ACP Group' (Simmonds 1991:53). Subsequently the European Community has tended to follow the United States government, in common with the IMF and the World Bank, in emphasizing democratization – a wholly inadequate synonym for human rights, as we have argued.

While human rights conditionality clauses in aid and trade agreements may have positive impact, they give rise to a number of problems – not least accusations from their targets of arrogant and unwarranted interference. To be effective, such policies would need to be accompanied by debt forgiveness and to be pursued, and coordinated, by a large number of donor countries, intergovernmental organizations such as the World Bank and the IMF, and development agencies. They would also need to inform the investment policies of the corporate sector. Moreover assistance with implementation and monitoring of progress in complex areas such as economic and social rights or women's rights is extremely difficult, with the result that release of a few political prisoners is likely be accepted as evidence of good intent. Furthermore the cessation of relations, if conditionality is not met, also brings the end of political leverage. Consequently the 'like-minded countries' have preferred, where possible, to support and encourage respect for human rights through working in partnership rather than by using the threat of sanctions (McAllister 1993). At present, however, such policies remain isolated examples of good practice. The greatest impediment to human rights conditionality is the prospect of negative impacts upon those who impose it: in consequence outrage at human rights violations is likely to be louder and more sustained in the case of violations in Sudan than in Indonesia or China.

## *The three models re-considered*

At the start of this section we briefly outlined three models – realist, internationalist and cosmopolitan – which focus attention on different aspects of the human rights protection mechanisms. Inevitably none encapsulates the complex and highly differentiated arrangements which exist; indeed it is the function of models to highlight what is significant at the expense of what is not.

Features of the realist model are apparent, in that states clearly play a significant role and many continue, with impunity, to exhibit contempt for the human rights of their citizens. Nevertheless, domestic and foreign policy decisions are influenced by pressure from external and internal sources, moral considerations are not uncommon in foreign policy, and NGOs both at the domestic and global levels are increasingly active – in accordance with the internationalist model. Finally we can see some evidence for the cosmopolitan model, albeit tentative and uneven, in the increasing ability of individuals, whether or not through the mediation of NGOs, to make representations to UN bodies concerning the human rights record of their governments.

An optimistic interpretation would see the three models as representing phases through which human rights protection is progressing. Thus the realist model encapsulates the relative inactivity of the Cold War period; the internationalist model approximates most closely to the contemporary phase; and the cosmopolitan model suggests, perhaps, movement towards a universal, authoritative human rights regime as the basis of a cosmopolitan civil society.

# Conclusion

This chapter addressed three questions concerning human rights. First we considered whether there could be a universal concept of human rights and, if so, on what basis. We concluded that there could, and should, be such a concept, based on the related premises of human frailty and human sympathy. However, existing concepts of civil and political rights are not universal because their focus upon protection from the state excludes the pervasive phenomenon of domestic violence. Consequently a truly universal concept of human rights must extend protection to women, children and others who are vulnerable to violence or neglect in the domestic sphere.

Next we discussed what might be the content of our universal concept, examining both minimalist and inclusive approaches. We found to be invalid the contention that extension of rights beyond a core of civil and political rights distracts attention from that core; indeed these 'core' rights have been and remain the primary focus of attention and are universally recognized, although far from universally respected. We expressed concern, however, that the contemporary practice of some western governments to subsume human rights within the concept of democracy raises precisely the dangers identified by minimalists.

In arguing for an inclusive concept of rights we advocated a needs-based approach which takes account of both material and non-material needs and facilitates the enumeration of new rights as new needs emerge, for example in relation to environmental issues. Clearly this can, and does, generate controversy, but we are unimpressed by arguments that the human rights agenda should not be further politicized. The routine declaration of entrenched positions which has too frequently characterized intergovernmental meetings should be challenged by genuine debate about the content of rights, with full participation by NGOs representing divergent interests and regions. Human rights issues provide an important focus for political engagement on a range of concerns which directly impinge upon people's everyday lives: they should be discussed widely.

Finally we considered the procedures and actors involved in the protection of rights, and found that success in standard-setting has not been matched by equal progress in monitoring and compliance. The record of states, both in complying with human rights norms and in encouraging the compliance of others, remains extremely patchy and nowhere are human rights fully respected. UN monitoring procedures have been enhanced, however, and are complemented by increasingly effective cooperation between UN bodies and NGOs. Particularly encouraging is the development of mechanisms facilitating access by individuals to the UN rights bodies, and of urgent action procedures which enable rapid follow-up of complaints. Nevertheless a great deal more needs to be done in strengthening monitoring procedures and compliance mechanisms.

Weak and imperfect as the universal rights regime may remain, progress has been made. Human rights issues do bring people into global politics, in particular the poorest and most vulnerable people, for whom recognition of fundamental rights is crucial. A disproportionate number of such people are women. Human rights matter, and their advocacy requires both perseverance and courage.

## Notes

1  The deliberations of the Commission are discussed by Best (1990) who uses Foreign Office sources to demonstrate that the British representative was the principal exponent of the latter view. Indeed it is clear that exasperation with the Commission's proceedings was instrumental in convincing the British Government of the need for a European Convention more narrowly focused on civil and political rights.

2  As at 1 June 1994 the Covenant on Civil and Political Rights had been ratified by 127 states, the Covenant on Economic, Social and Cultural Rights by 129. The Convention on the Elimination of all forms of Racial Discrimination (CERD) had 139 ratifications by that date.

3  These regional regimes comprise:

> The European Convention for the Protection of Human Rights and Fundamental Freedoms, opened for signature in 1950 and associated with the Council of Europe.

> The American Convention on Human Rights, opened for signature in 1969 and associated with the Organization of American States.

> The African Charter on Human and People's Rights, opened for signature in 1981 and associated with the Organization of African Unity.

4  See, for example, the predominance of G77 members at the Commission on Human Rights, where the 53 seats are allocated as follows:

| | |
|---|---|
| Africa | 15 |
| Asia | 12 |
| Central/South America | 11 |
| CEE | 5 |
| West Europe and Others (USA, Canada, Australia, New Zealand) | 10 |

5  It is estimated that women own only 1 per cent of land, property and financial resources and receive only 10 per cent of earned income despite contributing 16 of every 24 hours worked (UN 1991, *The World's Women: 1970–1990 Trends and Statistics*).

6  Galtung's principal distinction, reflecting his structuralist approach to analysis, is between actor-dependent and structure-dependent factors. This distinction has the greatest significance for the consideration of how needs are to be met, in that actors are subject to admonition or prosecution and can be replaced, whereas structural change requires a fundamental reordering of patterns of wealth and power.

7  The UN World Conference on Human Rights in June 1993 was attended by more than 3,000 representatives of 813 NGOs, outnumbering the 2,100 government representatives present. As at December 1993 Amnesty International alone had more than 1,100,000 members in 150 countries and 4,349 formally registered local groups, plus several thousand informal groups in more than 80 countries.

8  Farer and Gaer (1993) provide a clear outline of the structure and functions of the principal UN bodies concerned with human rights, including a helpful diagram on pages 258–9.

9  Notable, here, is the operation of sanctions against the apartheid regime in South Africa. Recent cases where the Security Council has authorized action associated with human rights issues are discussed in chapter six under the heading of humanitarian intervention.

10 Subsequently the Grandmothers of the Plaza de Mayo was formed. This group continues its attempts to trace the more than 800 babies known to have been born to disappeared women and sold to childless families (Donnelly 1993:48).

# References

Adams, B. 1993: The UN, World Conferences and Women's Rights. In J. Kerr (ed.), *Ours by Right: Women's Rights as Human Rights*, London: Zed Books, 115–18.

Adams, N. 1993: *Worlds Apart: The North–South Divide and the International System*. London: Zed Books.

Adedeji, A. (ed.) 1993: *Africa Within the World: Dispossession and Dependence*. London: Zed Books.

Ajami, F. 1993: The Summoning. *Foreign Affairs*, September/October, 2–9.

Akehurst, M. 1984: Humanitarian Intervention. In H. Bull (ed.), *Intervention in World Politics*, Oxford: Oxford University Press, 341–58.

Allen, C., Baylies, C. and Szeftel, M. 1992: Surviving Democracy? *Review of African Political Economy*, 54, 3–10.

Allen, T. and Thomas, A. (eds) 1992: *Poverty and Development in the 1990s*. Oxford: Oxford University Press.

Amin, S. 1991: The Real Stakes in the Gulf War. In D. Broad and L. Foster (eds), *The New World Order and the Third World*, Montreal: Black Rose Books, 69–78.

Amin, S. 1993: The Challenge of Globalization: Delinking. In The South Centre (ed.), *Facing the Challenge: Responses to the Report of the South Commission*, London: Zed Books, 132–8.

Amnesty International 1991: *Women in the Front Line: Human Rights Violations Against Women*. London: AI Publications.

Amnesty International 1994: *Report 1994*. London: AI Publications.

Anderson, B. 1991: *Imagined Communities: Reflections on the Origins and Spread of Nationalism*. London: Verso.

Anderson, V. 1991: *Alternative Economic Indicators*. London: Routledge.

Archiburgi, D. 1993: The Reform of the UN and Cosmopolitan Democracy: a critical review. *Journal of Peace Research*, 30(3), 301–15.

Arend, A. C. and Beck, J. R. 1993: *International Law and the use of Force*. London: Routledge.

Armstrong, P., Glyn, A. and Harrison, J. 1991: *Capitalism Since 1945*. Oxford: Blackwell.

Arrighi, G. 1991: World Income Inequalities and the Future of Socialism. *New Left Review*, 189, 39–65.

Ascherson, N. 1994a: An urban spectre with a suit and a laptop is haunting Europe. *Independent on Sunday*, 15.5.94.

Ascherson, N. 1994b: The better past was not a fantasy, and we can come good again. *Independent on Sunday*, 12.6.94.

Ashworth, G. 1985: Women are not half human: an overview of women's rights. *Third World Affairs*, 145–55.

Baird, V. 1994: Lethal Lies: the Arms Trade. *New Internationalist*, 261, November, 4–7.

Bachrach, P. and Baratz, M. 1962: The Two Faces of Power. *American Political Science Review*, 56.

Bauer, P. 1984: *Equality, the Third World and Economic Delusion*. London: Methuen.

Bayart, J-F. 1991: Finishing with the Idea of the Third World: The Concept of the Political Trajectory. In J. Manor (ed.), *Rethinking Third World Politics*, London: Longman, 51–71.

Bayliss, J. and Rengger, N. (eds) 1992: *Dilemmas of World Politics: International Issues in a Changing World*. Oxford: Clarendon Press.

Beetham, D. 1993: Liberal Democracy and the Limits of Democratisation. In D. Held (ed.), *Prospects for Democracy*, Oxford: Blackwell, 55–74.

Bellamy, C. 1994: Russian top brass ponder Nato invitation. *Independent*, 18.1.94.

Bello, W. 1994: *Dark Victory: The United States, Structural Adjustment and Global Poverty*. London: Pluto Press.

Berdal, M. 1993: Peacekeeping in Europe. *Adelphi Paper*, 284. London: IISS/Brasseys.

Bernard, M. 1994: Post-Fordism, Transnational Production and the changing Global Political Economy. In R. Stubbs and G. R. D. Underhill (eds), *Political Economy and the Changing Global Order*, Basingstoke: Macmillan 216–29.

Berkes, F. (ed.) 1989: *Common Property Resources: Ecology and Community-Based Sustainable Development*. London: Belhaven.

Berntzen, E. 1993: Democratic Consolidation in Central America: a qualitative comparative approach. *Third World Quarterly*, 14(3), 589–604.

Beschorner, N. 1992/3: Water and Instability in the Middle East. *Adelphi Paper*, 273, Winter. London: IISS/Brasseys.

Best, G. 1990: Whatever Happened to Human Rights? *Review of International Studies*, 16, 3–18.

Black, I. 1993: Studied calm greets new military order. *Guardian*, 6.11.93.

Boonekamp, C. F. J. 1990: Voluntary Export Restraints. In P. King (ed.), *International Economics and International Economic Policy*, New York: McGraw Hill, 23–33.

Boulding, K. E. 1977: Twelve Friendly Quarrels with Johan Galtung. *Journal of Peace Research*, XIV(1), 75–86.

Boutros-Ghali, B. 1992: *An Agenda for Peace. Preventitive Diplomacy, Peace-making and Peace-keeping.* New York: United Nations.

Boutros-Ghali, B. 1993a: *Report of the Secretary-General on the Work of the Organization*, September. Geneva: United Nations.

Boutros-Ghali, B. 1993b: Empowering the United Nations. *Foreign Affairs*, Winter 1992/93, 89–102.

Boutros-Ghali, B. 1994: *Address on the occasion of International Women's Day, 8th March*, SG/SM/94/33. Geneva: United Nations.

Bradshaw, M. J. and Lynne, N. J. 1994: After the Soviet Union: The post-Soviet states in the world system. *Professional Geographer*, 46(4), 439–49.

Brandt, W. 1980: *North South*. London: Pan Books.

Braudel, F. 1981: *Civilisation and Capitalism, 15th–18th Centuries (3 vols)*. New York: Harper and Row.

Brenton, T. 1994: *The Greening of Machiavelli: The Evolution of International Environmental Politics*. London: RIIA/Earthscan.

Bridge, A. 1994: Kozyrev raises spectre of resurgent Russia. *Independent*, 24.2.94.

Brown, P. and Vidal, J. 1994: Catastrophe threatens world's Fisheries as stocks fall, *Guardian*, 12.3.94.

Brundtland, G. H. 1987: Chairman, World Commission on Environment and Development. *Our Common Future*. Oxford: Oxford University Press.

Brunt, R. 1989: The Politics of Identity. In S. Hall and M. Jaques, *New Times: The Changing Face of Politics in the 1990s*, London: Lawrence and Wishart, 150–9.

Bull, H. (ed.) 1984: *Intervention in World Politics*. Oxford: Oxford University Press.

Bullock, A. and Stallybrass, D. (eds) 1977: *The Fontana Dictionary of Modern Thought*. London: Fontana/Collins.

Burk, K. 1991: The International Environment. In A. Graham and A. Seldon (eds), *Government and Economies in the Postwar World*, London: Routledge, 9–29.

Burton, J. W. 1972: *World Society*. Cambridge: Cambridge University Press.

Buzan, B. 1991a: *People, States and Fear*, second edition. Hemel Hempstead: Harvester Wheatsheaf.

Buzan, B. 1991b: New patterns of global security in the twenty- first century. *International Affairs*, 67(3), 431–51.

Buzan, B., Jones, C. and Little, R. 1993: *The Logic of Anarchy: Neorealism and Structural Realism*. New York: Columbia University Press.

Carr, E. H. 1939: *The Twenty Years Crisis 1919–1939*. London: Macmillan.

Carroll, J. E. (ed.) 1988: *International Environmental Diplomacy*. Cambridge: Cambridge University Press.

Castles, S. and Miller, M. 1993: *The Age of Migration: International Population Movements in the Modern World*. London: Macmillan.

Chacholiades, M. 1990: *International Economics*. New York: McGraw Hill.

Chapman, G. 1992: TV: The World Next Door. *Intermedia*, January/February, 20(1), 30–3.

Chowdhury, A. and Islam, I. 1993: *The Newly Industrialising Countries of the Third World*. Hemel Hempstead: Harvester Wheatsheaf.

Christian Aid, (undated): *Who Runs the World?* London: Christian Aid.

Clapham, C. 1993: Democratisation in Africa: Obstacles and prospects. *Third World Quarterly*, 14(3), 423–38.

Claude, I. L. Jnr 1962: *Power and International Relations*. New York: Random House.

Clay, J. W. 1989: Epilogue: The ethnic future of nations. *Third World Quarterly*, 11(4), October, 223–33.

Colman, D. and Nixson, F. 1986: *Economics of Change in Less Developed Countries*, Oxford: Philip Allan.

Connaughton, R. 1992: Military Intervention and UN peacekeeping. In N. S. Rodley (ed.), *To Loose the Bands of Wickedness: International Intervention in Defence of Human Rights*, London: Brasseys, 165–97.

Connor, W. 1993: Beyond Reason: The nature of the ethnonational bond. *Ethnic and Racial Studies*, 16(3), July, 373–89.

Corbridge, S. 1994: *Debt and Development*. Oxford: Blackwell.

Cox, R. 1981: Social Forces, States and World Orders: Beyond International Relations Theory. *Millenium: Journal of International Studies*, 10, 127–55.

Cox, R. 1983: Gramsci, Hegemony and International Relations: An Essay in Method. *Millenium: Journal of International Studies*, 12(2), 162–75.

Dalton, G. 1974: *Economic Systems and Society*. Harmondsworth: Penguin.

Damrosch, L. F. and Scheffer, D. F. (eds) 1991: *Law and Force in the New International Order*. Colorado: Westview Press.

Daniel, P. 1991: Editorial: Foreign Investment Revisited. *IDS Bulletin*, 22(1), 1–6.

Deegan, H. 1993: *The Middle East and Problems of Democracy*. Buckingham: Open University Press.

Denton, N. and Mortimer, L. 1994: Nostalgia for communist comfort. *Financial Times*, 5 May.

Dessler, D. 1989: What's at Stake in The Agent Structure Debate. *International Organization*, 43, Summer, 441–74.

Deudney, D. 1990: The Case Against Linking Environmental Degradation and National Security. *Millenium: Journal of International Studies*, 19(3), 461–76.

Deudney, D. and Ikenkerry, G. J. 1994: After the Long War. *Foreign Policy*, 94, Spring, 21–35.

Dicken, P. 1992: *Global Shift*. London: Paul Chapman Publishing.

Donnelly, J. 1993: *International Human Rights*. Oxford: Westview Press.

Donnelly, M. 1994: The Political Economy of Japanese Trade. In R. Stubbs and G. R. D. Underhill (eds), *Political Economy and the Changing Global Order*, Basingstoke: Macmillan, 485–96.

Dunn, J. 1994: The Dilemma of Humanitarian Intervention: The Executive Power of the Law of Nations, After God. *Government and Opposition*, 29(2), 248–61.

Dunning, J. H. 1988: *Explaining International Production*. London: Unwin Hyman.

Eckersley, R. 1992: *Environmentalism and Political Theory: Toward an Ecocentric Approach*. London: UCL Press.

Ecologist, The 1993: *Whose Common Future? Reclaiming the Commons*. London: Earthscan.

Edwards, C. 1985: *The Fragmented World*. London: Methuen.

Ekins, P. 1992: *A New World Order: Grassroots Movements for Global Change*. London: Routledge.

Enloe, G. 1988: *Does Khaki Become You? The Militarization of Women's Lives*. London: Pandora.

Enloe, G. 1989: *Bananas, Beaches and Bases*. London: Pandora.

Enloe, G. 1993: *The Morning After: Sexual Politics at the End of the Cold War*. Berkeley: University of California.

Entessar, N. 1989: The Kurdish Mosaic of Discord. *Third World Quarterly*, 11(4), 83–100.

Esty, D. C. 1994: *Greening the GATT: Trade, Environment and the Future*. Washington, DC: Institute for International Economics.

Eyal, J. 1993: Russia's covert colonialism. *Independent*, 16.11.93.

Eyal, J. 1994: Letting Russia draw the line. *Independent*, 21.2.94.

Falk, R. 1993: Democratising, Internationalising and Globalising: A Collage of Blurred Images. *Third World Quarterly*, 13(4), 627–40.

Farer, J. and Gaer, F. 1993: The UN and Human Rights: At the End of the Beginning. In A. Roberts and B. Kingsbury (eds), *United Nations Divided World*, second edition, Oxford: Oxford University Press, 240–96.

Friedman, M. 1968: The Case for Flexible Exchange Rates. In R. E. Caves and H. G. Johnson (eds), *Readings in International Economics*, London: Allen and Unwin, 413–37.

Fukuyama, F. 1989: The End of History. *The National Interest*, Summer, 3–18.

Fukuyama, F. 1992: *The End of History and the Last Man*. London: Hamish Hamilton.

Fukuyama, F. 1994: The mystery deepens: the persistence and fragility of civil society. *The Times Literary Supplement*, 4778, 28.10.94, 3.

Galtung, J. 1969: Violence, Peace and Peace Research. *Journal of Peace Research*, 3, 167–89.

Galtung, J. 1971: A Structural Theory of Imperialism. *Journal of Peace Research*, 13(2), 81–94.

Galtung, J. 1981: A Structural Theory of Imperialism: Ten Years After. *Millenium: Journal of International Studies*, 9(3), 183–96.

Galtung, J. 1990: Cultural Violence. *Journal of Peace Research*, 27(3), 291–305.

Galtung, J. 1994: *Human Rights in Another Key*. Cambridge: Polity Press.

GATT, 1987: *International Trade 1986–87*. Geneva: GATT.

Gellner, E. 1983: *Nations and Nationalism*. Oxford: Blackwell.

Gellner, E. 1991: Nationalism and Politics in Eastern Europe. *New Left Review*, 189, September/October, 127–32.

George, S. 1992: *The Debt Boomerang: How Third World Debt Harms Us All*. London: Pluto Press.

George, S. 1993: Uses and Abuses of African Debt. In A. Adedeji (ed.), *Africa within the World: Beyond Dispossession and Dependence*, London: Zed Books, 59–72.

Ghai, D. and Hewitt de Alcántara, C. 1990: The Crisis of the 1980s in Sub-Saharan Africa, Latin America and the Caribbean: Economic Impact, Social Change and Political Implications. *Development and Change*, 21(3), 389–426.

Giddens, A. 1990: *The Consequences of Modernity*. Cambridge: Polity Press.

Gill, S. (ed.) 1993: *Gramsci, historical materialism and international relations*. Cambridge Studies in International Relations 26. Cambridge: Cambridge University Press.

Gill, S. and Law, D. 1993: Global Hegemony and the Structural Power of Capital. In S. Gill (ed.), *Gramsci, historical materialism and international relations*, Cambridge: Cambridge University Press, 93–124.

Gills, B. and Rocamora, J. 1992: Low Intensity Democracy. *Third World Quarterly*, 13(3), 501–24.

Gilpin, R. 1975: *U.S. Power and the Multinational Corporation*. New York: Basic Books.

Gilpin, R. 1981: *War and Change in World Politics*. Cambridge: Cambridge University Press.

Goldgeier, J. M. and McFaul, M. 1992: A tale of two worlds: core and periphery in the post-Cold War era. *International Organization*, 42(2), Spring, 467–91.

Gore, A. 1994: Forging a new Athenian Age of democracy. *Intermedia*, May, 22(2), 4–6.

Goulding, M. 1993: The Evolution of United Nations Peacekeeping. *International Affairs*, 69(3), 451–64.

Grant, R. and Newland, K. (eds) 1991: *Gender and International Relations*. Buckingham: Open University Press.

Gray, C. 1994: Global Security and Economic Well-Being: A Strategic Perspective. *Political Studies*, 42(1), March, 25–39.

Greenaway, D. 1983: *International Trade Policy*. Basingstoke: Macmillan.

Griffiths, S. I. 1993: Nationalism and Ethnic Conflict: Threats to European Security. *SIPRI Research Report No. 5*. Oxford, Oxford University Press.

Grifin, K. 1991: Foreign Aid After the Cold War. *Development and Change*, 22(4), 645–85.

Grimwade, N. 1989: *International Trade*. London: Routledge.

Grosby, S. 1994: The verdict of history: the inexpungeable tie of primordiality. *Ethnic and Racial Studies*, 17(1), January, 164–71.

Haas, P. M. 1990: *Saving the Mediterranean: The Politics of International Environmental Cooperation*. New York: Columbia University Press.

Haas, P. 1992: Introduction: epistemic communities and international policy coordination. *International Organization*, 46(1), Winter, 1–36.

Haas, P. M., Keohane, R. D. and Levy, M. A. (eds) 1993: *Institutions for the Earth: Sources of Effective International Environmental Protection*. Cambridge MA: MIT Press.

Hall, S. and Jacques, M. 1989: *New Times: The Changing Face of Politics in the 1990s*. London: Lawrence and Wishart.

Hall, S. 1989: The Meaning of New Times. In S. Hall and M. Jacques, *New*

*Times: The Changing Face of Politics in the 1990s*, London: Lawrence and Wishart, 116–34.

Halliday, F. 1986: *The Making of the Second Cold War*, second edition. London: Verso.

Halliday, F. 1990: The Ends of Cold War. *New Left Review*, 180, 5–23.

Hardin, G. 1968: The Tragedy of the Commons. *Science*, 162, 1243–8.

Harris, N. 1986: *The End of the Third World: Newly Industrializing Countries and the Decline of an Ideology*. Harmondsworth: Penguin.

Hartman, C. and Vilanova, P. 1992: *Paradigms Lost: The Post Cold War Era*, London: Pluto Press.

Held, D. (ed.) 1993: *Prospects for Democracy*. Cambridge: Polity Press.

Held, D. 1993: Democracy: From City-States to Cosmopolitan Order? In D. Held (ed.), *Prospects for Democracy*, Cambridge: Polity Press, 13–52.

Helleiner, E. 1994: From Bretton Woods to Global Finance: A World Turned Upside Down. In R. Stubbs and G. R. D. Underhill (eds), *Political Economy and the Changing Global Order*, Basingstoke: Macmillan, 163–75.

Herman, E. 1992: US Sponsorship of International Terrorism. In D. Broad and L. Foster (eds), *The New World Order and The Third World*, Montreal: Black Rose Books, 17–40.

Herz, J. H. 1950: Idealist internationalism and the security dilemma. *World Politics*, 2, 157–80.

Hewitt, A. (ed.) 1994: *Crisis or Transition in Foreign Aid?*. London: Overseas Development Institute.

Higgins, A. 1994: Moscow asserts its authority over former empire. *Independent*, 13.1.94.

Higgins, R. 1993: The United Nations and Former Yugoslavia. *International Affairs*, 69(3), 465–83.

Hildyard, N. 1993: Foxes in Charge of the Chickens. In W. Sachs (ed.), *Global Ecology: A New Arena of Political Conflict*, London: Zed Books, 22–35.

Hirschman, A. 1990: Es un Desastre para el Tercer Mundo el Fin de la Guerra Fria? *Pensamiento Iberoamericano*, 18, 175–81.

Hobbelink, H. 1991: *Biotechnology and the Future of World Agriculture*. London: Zed Books.

Hobsbawm, E. J. 1990: *Nations and Nationalism Since 1780: Programme, Myth and Reality*. Cambridge: Canto.

Hobsbawm, E. J. 1992: Nationalism and Ethnicity. *Intermedia*, 20(4–5), 13–15.

Hollis, M. and Smith, S. 1991: *Explaining and Understanding International Relations*. Oxford: Clarendon.

Holsti, K. J. 1991: *Peace and War: armed conflicts and international order 1648–1989*. Cambridge: Cambridge University Press.

Hough, J. F. and Fainsod, M. 1979: *How the Soviet Union is Governed*. Cambridge, Mass. and London: Harvard University Press.

Houghton, J. T. et al. (eds) 1990: *Climate Change, the IPCC Scientific Assessment: Report Prepared for IPCC by Working Group 1*. Cambridge: Cambridge University Press.

Houghton, J. 1991: Scientific Assessment of Climate Change: Summary of the IPCC Working Group 1 Report. In J. Jager and H. L. Ferguson (eds), *Climate Change: Science, Impacts and Policy: Proceedings of the Second World Climate Conference*, Cambridge: Cambridge University Press, 23–45.

Howard, R. 1989: Is there an African concept of human rights? *Global Politics*, Block V. Milton Keynes: Open University, 131–43.

Huntington, S. P. 1991: *The Third Wave: Democratization in the Late Twentieth Century*. Norman, Oklahoma: University of Oklahoma Press.

Huntington, S. P. 1993a: The Clash of Civilizations. *Foreign Affairs*, Summer, 22–49.

Huntington, S. P. 1993b: Why International Primacy Matters. *International Security*, 17(4), 68–83.

Hyde-Price, A. 1994: Democratization in Eastern Europe – the external dimension. In G. Pridham and T. Vanhanen (eds), *Democratization in Eastern Europe – domestic and international perspectives*, London: Routledge, 220–52.

Ihonvbere, J. O. 1994: The 'irrelevant' state, ethnicity and the quest for nationhood in Africa. *Ethnic and Racial Studies*, 17(1), January, 42–60.

IISS 1994: *The Military Balance 1994–1995*. London: Brasseys.

Imber, M. 1993: Too Many Cooks? The post-Rio reform of the UN. *International Affairs*, 69(1), 55–70.

IMF, 1991: *World Economic Outlook*, Washington: IMF.

IMF, 1992: *World Economic Outlook*. Washington: IMF.

Institute of Economic Affairs, 1994: *Global Warming: Apocalypse or Hot Air?* London: IEA.

James, A. 1990: *Peacekeeping in International Politics*. London: Macmillan/IISS.

Jeffries, I. 1993: *Socialist Economies and the Transition to the Market: A Guide*. London: Routledge.

Jenkins, R. 1987: *Transnational Corporations and Uneven Development*. London: Methuen.

Jervis, R. 1991/92: The Future of World Politics: Will it Resemble its Past? *International Security*, 16(3), Winter, 39–73.

Jervis, R. 1993: International Primacy: Is the Game Worth the Candle? *International Security*, 17(4), Spring, 52–67.

Johnston, A. 1994: South Africa – the election and the transition process. *Third World Quarterly*, 15(2), 187–204.

Kausikan, B. 1993: Asia's Different Standard. *Foriegn Policy*, 92, Fall, 24–41.

Keane, J. 1991: *The Media and Democracy*. Cambridge: Polity Press.

Kegley, C. W. and Wittkopf, E. R. 1993: *World Politics: Trends and Transformation (4th edition)*. New York: St Martins Press.

Kennedy, P. 1988: *The Rise and Fall of the Great Powers: Economic Change and Military Conflict from 1500 to 2000*. London: Unwin Hyman.

Kenwood, A. G. and Lougheed, A. L. 1992: *The Growth of the International Economy*. London: Routledge.

Keohane, R. O. 1984: *After Hegemony: Cooperation and Discord in World Political Economy*. New Jersey: Princeton University Press.

Keohane, R. O. and Nye, J. S. 1977: *Power and Interdependence: World Politics in Transition*. Boston: Little, Brown and Company.

Kerr, J. (ed.) 1993: *Ours By Right: Women's Rights as Human Rights*. London: Zed Books.

Kessel, J. 1994: Realistic new attitudes reduce threat of water wars. *Guardian*, 25.7.94.

Khor Kok Peng, M. 1992: *The Future of North–South Relations: Conflict or Cooperation?* Penang: Third World Network.

Kindelberger, C. 1981: Dominance and leadership in the international economy. *International Studies Quarterly*, 25(3), June, 242–54.

Klatt, M. 1994: Russians in the 'Near Abroad'. *RFE/RL Research Report*, 3(32), 19.8.94, 35.

Knippers Black, J. 1993: Elections and other Trivial Pursuits – Latin America and the New World Order. *Third World Quarterly*, 14(3), 545–72.

Kober, S. 1990: Idealpolitik. *Foreign Policy*, 79, Summer, 3–24.

Krasner, S. 1985: *Structural Conflict: The Third World Against Global Liberalism*. Berkeley: University of California Press.

Krasner, S. D. (ed.) 1983: *International Regimes*. Ithaca: Cornell University Press.

Krugman, P. R. and Obstfeld, M. 1994: *International Economics*. New York: Harper Collins.

Lang, T. and Hines, C. 1993: *The New Protectionism*. New York: The New Press.

Layne, C. 1993: The Unipolar Illusion: Why New Great Powers Will Rise. *International Security*, 17(4), 5–51.

Lebow, R. N. 1994: The long peace, the end of the cold war, and the failure of realism. *International Organization*, 48(2), Spring, 249–77.

Leftwich, A. 1993: Governance, Democracy and Development in the Third World. *Third World Quarterly*, 14(3), 605–24.

Lenin, V. I. 1965: *Imperialism the Highest Stage of Capitalism*. Peking: Foreign Languages Press.

Lipietz, A. 1992: After Rio: A New Relationship between North and South? *Studies in Political Economy*, 41, 57–72.

Lipton, M. and Maxwell, S. 1992: *The New Poverty Agenda: An Overview*. Brighton: Institute of Development Studies.

Lloyd, J. 1994: How to make a market. *London Review of Books*, 16(21), 10.11.94, 29–32.

Loescher, G. 1992: Refugee Movements and International Security. *Adelphi Papers*, 268, Summer. London: Brasseys/IISS.

Lovelock, J. 1989: *The Ages of Gaia: A biography of our living earth*. Oxford: Oxford University Press.

Lukes, S. 1974: *Power: A Radical View*. London: Macmillan.

Mahbub ul Haq 1995: Whatever Happened to the Peace Dividend? *Our Planet*, 7(1), 8–10.

Matthews, K. 1993: *The Gulf Conflict and International Relations*. London: Routledge.

Mayall, J. 1991: Non-intervention, self-determination and the 'new world order'. *International Affairs*, 67(3), 421–9.

Mazrui, A. A. 1990: *Cultural Forces in World Politics*. London: James Currey.

McAllister, E. 1993: Aid Conditionality as a Lever for Women's Equality: Help or Hindrance? In J. Kerr (ed.), *Ours by Right: Women's Rights as Human Rights*, London: Zed Books, 106–14.

McFaul, M. 1993: *Post-communist Politics – Democratic Prospects in Russia and Eastern Europe*. Washington: Centre for Strategic and International Studies.

McLennan, G. 1984: Capitalist state or democratic polity. Recent developments in Marxist and pluralist theory. In G. McLennan, D. Held and S. Hall (eds), *The Idea of the Modern State*, Milton Keynes: Open University Press, 80–109.

Maitland, D. 1984: *The Missing Link*. Geneva: ITU.

Meadows, D. H. et al. 1972: *Beyond the Limits: Global Collapse or Sustainable Development?* London: Earthscan.

Mearsheimer, J. J. 1990: Back to the Future: Instability in Europe after the Cold War. *International Security*, 15(1), 5–56.

Meier, G. and Seers, D. (eds) 1984: *Pioneers in Development*. New York: Oxford University Press.

Merridale, C. 1991: Perestroika and political pluralism: past and present prospects. In C. Merridale and C. Ward (eds), *Perestroika: the Historical Perspective*, London: Edward Arnold.

Middleton, N., O'Keefe, P. and Moyo, S. 1993: *Tears of the Crocodile: From Rio to Reality in the Developing World*. London: Pluto Press.

Milner, C. and Greenaway, D. 1979: *An Introduction to International Economics*. Harlow: Longman.

Milner, H. 1992: International Theories of Co-operation Among Nations: Strengths and Weaknesses. *World Politics*, 44(3), April, 466–9.

Milward, A. 1992: *The European Rescue of the Nation State*. Berkeley: University of California Press.

Moghadam, V. M. 1993: *Modernizing Women: Gender and Social Change in the Middle East*. Boulder: Lynne Reiner.

Mohanty, C. 1986: Under Western Eyes: Feminist Scholarship and Colonial Discourses. *Feminist Review*, 30, 61–88.

Monimart, M. 1991: Women in the Fight Against Desertification. In S. Sontheimer (ed.), *Women in Third World Development*, Colorado: Westview, 32–64.

Moore, M. (ed.) 1993: Good Government? *IDS Bulletin*, 24(1).

Morgenthau, H. J. 1967: *Politics among Nations: The Struggle for Power and Peace*, 4th edn. New York: Knopf.

Morphet, S. 1990: Resolutions and vetoes in the UN Security Council: their relevance and significance. *Review of International Studies*, 16, 341–59.

Morse, E. L. 1976: *Modernization and the Transformation of International Relations*. New York: Free Press.

Munck, G. L. 1994: Democratic Transitions in Comparative Perspective. *Comparative Politics*, 26(3), 335–73.

Munck, R. 1994: South Africa – the great economic debate. *Third World Quarterly*, 15(2), 205–18.

Murphy, C. N. 1994: *International Organisation and Industrial Change: Global Governance Since 1850*. Colorado: Lynne Reiner.

Murphy, C. N. and Tooze, R. (eds) 1991: *The New International Political Economy*. Colorado: Lynne Reiner.

Myers, N. 1989: Environment and Security. *Foreign Policy*, 74, Spring, 23–41.

Myerson, A. R. 1992: *International Herald Tribune*, 28.9.92.

Nairn, T. 1977: *The Break-up of Britain*. London: New Left Books.

NATO 1991: *Rome Declaration on Peace and Cooperation*. Press Communiqué S–1 86, 8 November. Brussels: NATO.

Nederveen Pieterse, J. 1994: Globalization as Hybridization. *International Sociology*, 9(2), 161–84.

Neier, A. 1993: Asia's Unacceptable Standard. *Foreign Policy*, 92, Fall, 42–51.

O'Brien, R. 1992: *Global Financial Integration: The End of Geography*. London: Routledge/RIIA.

ODI 1988: *Commodity Prices: Investing in Decline?* Briefing Paper, March. London: Overseas Development Institute.

OECD, 1992: *Globalisation of Industrial Activities*. Paris: OECD.

OECD, 1994: *OECD Economic Surveys: Korea*. Paris: OECD.

O'Loughlin, J. 1986: World-Power Competition and Local Conflicts in the Third World. In R. J. Johnson and P. J. Taylor (eds), *A World in Crisis? Geographical Perspectives*, Oxford: Blackwell, 231–68.

Olson, M. 1965: *The Logic of Collective Action: Public Goods and the Theory of Groups*. Cambridge MA.: Harvard University Press.

Ostrom, E. 1990: *Governing the Commons: The evolution of institutions for collective action*. Cambridge: Cambridge University Press.

Parekh, B. 1993: The Cultural Particularity of Liberal Democracy. In D. Held (ed.), *Prospects for Democracy*, Cambridge: Polity Press, 156–76.

Pennock, J. R. 1979: *Democratic Political Theory*. New Jersey: Princeton University Press.

Pick, H. 1992: Exiling our empathy. *Guardian*, 8.11.92.

Peterson, V. S. (ed.) 1992: *Gendered States*. Colorado: Lynne Reiner.

Ponton, G. 1994: *The Soviet Era: From Lenin to Yeltsin*. Oxford and Cambridge Mass.: Blackwell.

Pridham, G. (ed.) 1991: *Encouraging Democracy: The International Context of Regime Transition in Southern Europe*. Leicester: Leicester University Press.

Pridham, G. and Vanhanen, T. 1994: *Democratization in Eastern Europe – domestic and international perspectives*. London: Routledge.

Princen, T. and Finger, M. 1994: *Environmental NGOs in World Politics: Linking the Local and the Global*. London and New York: Routledge.

Pringle, P. and Torday, P. 1992: $10 billion aid for Russia. *Independent*, 13.3.92.

Przeworski, A. 1991: *Democracy and the Market: Political and Economic Reforms in Eastern Europe and Latin America*. Cambridge: Cambridge University Press.

Qadir, S., Clapham, C. and Gills, B. 1993: Sustainable Democracy: Formalism vs Substance. *Third World Quarterly*, 14(3), 415–22.

Quarrie, J. (ed.) 1992: *Earth Summit 1992*. London: Regency Press.

Radice, H. 1984: The National Economy – A Keynesian Myth? *Capital and Class*, 22, 11–23.

Ramsay, R. 1984: UNCTAD's failures: the rich get richer. *International Organization*, 38(2), 387–97.

Randall, V. 1993: The Media and Democratization in the Third World. *Third World Quarterly*, 14(3), 625–46.

Rawls, J. 1993: The Law of Peoples. In S. Shute and S. Hurley (eds), *On Human Rights: The Oxford Amnesty Lectures 1993*, New York: Basic Books, 41–82.

Remnick, D. 1994: Getting Russia right. *New York Review of Books*, 41(15), 22.9.94, 22–6.

Rich, B. 1994: *Mortgaging the Earth: The World Bank, Environmental Impoverishment and the Crisis of Development*. London: Earthscan.

Riley, S. 1992: Democratic pressure of political adjustment: democratic politics and political choice in Africa. *Third World Quarterly*, 13(3), 539–52.

Rivlin, B. 1992: Regional Arrangement and the UN System for Collective Security and Conflict Resolution: A New Road Ahead? *International Relations*, XI(2), August, 95–110.

Roberts, A. 1993a: The United Nations and International Security. *Survival*, 35(2), 3–30.

Roberts, A. 1993b: Humanitarian War: military intervention and human rights. *International Affairs*, 69(3), 429–49.

Roberts, A. and Kingsbury, B. (eds) 1993: *United Nations, Divided World*. Oxford: Oxford University Press.

Robertson, C. 1994: UN is failing to address abuses against women. *Amnesty*, 68, July/August, 2.

Robertson, R. 1992: *Globalization: Social Theory and Global Culture*. London: Sage Publications.

Robock, S. H. and Simmonds, K. 1989: *International Business and Multinational Enterprises*, Boston, Mass.: Irwin.

Rodley, N. S. (ed.) 1992: *To Loose the Bands of Wickedness: International Intervention in Defence of Human Rights*. London: Brasseys.

Rorty, R. 1993: Human Rights, Rationality and Sentimentality. In S. Shute and S. Hurley (eds), *On Human Rights: The Oxford Amnesty Lectures 1993*, New York: Basic Books, 111–34.

Rubinstein, R. A. 1993: Cultural Aspects of Peacekeeping: Notes on the Substance of Symbols. *Millenium: Journal of International Studies*, 22(3), 547–62.

Russia and the Successor States Briefing Service, vol. 3, no. 1, February 1995: 2.

Sachs, J. 1994: The bank that foreclosed on Russia. *Independent*, 26.1.94.

Sachs, W. (ed.) 1992: *The Development Dictionary: A Guide to Knowledge as Power*. London: Zed Books.

Sachs, W. (ed.) 1993: *Global Ecology: A New Arena of Political Conflict*. London and New Jersey: Zed Books.

Sakharov, A. 1990: *Memoirs*. London: Macmillan.

Salame, G. 1993: Islam and the West. *Foreign Policy*, Spring, 22–37.

Samudavanija, C-A. 1991: The Three-dimensional State. In J. Manor (ed.), *Rethinking Third World Politics*, London: Longman, 15–23.

Sand, P. H. (ed.) 1992: *The Effectiveness of International Environmental Agreements: A Survey of Existing Legal Instruments.* Cambridge: UNCED, Grotius.

Scammell, W. M. 1986: *Solzhenitsyn: a Biography.* London: Paladin.

Scammell, W. M. 1987: *The Stability of the International Monetary System.* Basingstoke: Macmillan.

Schmitter, P. and Karl, T. 1992: The types of democracy emerging in Southern and Eastern Europe, and South and Central America. In P. Volten (ed.), *Bound to Change: Consolidating Democracy in East Central Europe,* New York: Westview Press, 42–68.

Schopflin, G. 1993: Culture and identity in post-communist Europe. In S. White, J. Batt and P. Lewis (eds), *Developments in East European Politics,* Basingstoke: Macmillan, 28–32.

Sedgemoor, B. and Skinner, D. 1987: *The City Big Bang 2000.* London: Campaign Group of Labour MPs.

Senjur, M. 1992: The Viability of Economic Development of a Small State Seperating from a Larger One. *Development and International Cooperation,* VIII(14–15), 5–21.

Shakhmazarov, G. 1988: Governability of the World. *International Affairs (Moscow),* 3, March, 16–24.

Shaw, M. 1994: Forcing the World to Work. *New Statesman,* 26.8.94, 22–3.

Shaw, T. M. and Inegbedion, E. J. 1994: The Marginalisation of Africa in the New World (Dis)Order. In R. Stubbs and G. R. D. Underhill (eds), *Political Economy and the Changing Global Order,* Basingstoke: Macmillan, 390–403.

Shehadi, K. S. 1993: Ethnic Self-Determination and the Break-up of States. *Adelphi Paper 283,* London: IISS/Brasseys.

Shiva, V. 1989: *Women, Ecology, Development.* London: World Books.

Shuman, M. 1994: *Towards a Global Village: International Community Development Initiatives.* London: Pluto Press.

Shute, S. and Hurley, S. 1993: *On Human Rights: The Oxford Amnesty Lectures 1993.* New York: Basic Books.

Sidoti, F. 1994: The Significance of the Italian Elections. *Government and Opposition,* 2, 332–47.

Simmonds, E. 1991: Early dialogue necessary with human rights violaters. *The Courier,* 128, August, 52–3.

Singer, H. W. and Ansari, J. A. 1988: *Rich and Poor Countries.* London: Unwin Hyman.

Singham, A. W. and Hune, S. 1986: *Non-Alignment in an Age of Alignments.* London: Zed Books.

Sklair, L. 1991: *Sociology of the Global System: Social Change in Global Perspective.* Hemel Hempstead: Harvester Wheatsheaf.

Skolnikoff, E. B. 1993: *The Elusive Transformation: Science, Technology and the Evolution of International Politics.* Princeton, NJ: Princeton University Press.

Smith, A. 1992: Is there a global culture? *Intermedia,* 20(4–5), August/September, 11–12.

Smith, D. 1994: Just War, Clausewitz and Sarajevo. *Journal of Peace Research,* 31(2), 136–42.

Smith, G. B. 1992: *Soviet Politics: Struggling with Change,* second edition. Basingstoke: Macmillan.

Smith, M., Little, R. and Shackleton, M. (eds) 1981: *Persectives on World Politics*. London: Croom Helm.

Smith, S. 1993: The Environment on the Periphery of International Relations: An Explanation. *Environmental Politics*, 2(4), 28–45.

Snowdon, B., Vane, H. and Wynarczyk, P. 1994: *A Modern Guide to Macroeconomics*. Aldershot: Edward Elgar.

Sodersten, B. 1980: *International Economics*, second edition. Basingstoke: Macmillan.

Sodersten, B. and Reed, G. 1994: *International Economics*, third edition. Basingstoke: Macmillan.

Sontheimer, S. (ed.) 1991: *Women in Third World Development*. Colorado: Westview.

Sørensen, G. 1993: Political Conditionality. *The European Journal of Development Research*, Special Edition, 5(1).

Stack, J. F. Jnr. 1992: Judicial Policy-Making and the Evolving Protection of Human Rights: The European Court of Human Rights in Comparative Perspective. *West European Politics*, Special Edition, 137–55.

Starr, J. R. 1991: Water Wars. *Foreign Policy*, 82, Spring, 17–36.

Stockholm International Peace Research Institute 1994: *SIPRI Yearbook*. Oxford: Oxford University Press.

Stone, N. 1994: Brothers in and out of arms. *Guardian*, 23.2.94.

Stopford, J. and Strange, S. 1991: *Rival States, Rival Firms: Competition for World Market Shares*. Cambridge: Cambridge University Press.

Strange, S. 1987: The persistent myth of lost hegemony. *International Organization*, 41(4), Autumn, 551–74.

Strange, S. 1988: *States and Markets: An Introduction to International Political Economy*. London: Pinter.

Strange, S. 1991: An Eclectic Approach. In C. R. Murphy and R. Tooze (eds), *The New International Political Economy*, Colorado: Lynne Reiner, 11–32.

Strange, S. 1994: Rethinking Structural Change in the International Political Economy. In R. Stubbs and G. D. R. Underhill (eds), *Political Economy and the Changing Global Order*, Basingstoke: Macmillan, 103–15.

Suny, R. 1991: Incomplete Revolution. National Movements and the Collapse of the Soviet Empire. *New Left Review*, 189, September/October, 111–25.

Svetlicic, M. 1993: Globalisation, Economic Integration and Political Disintegration. *Development and International Cooperation*, IX(16), 99–118.

Tan, G. 1993: The Next NICs of Asia. *Third World Quarterly*, 14(1), 57–73.

Taylor, A. J. P. 1954: *The Struggle for Mastery in Europe 1848–1918*. Oxford: Clarendon Press.

Taylor, P. J. 1986: The World System Project. In R. J. Johnson and P. J. Taylor (eds), *A World in Crisis: Geographical Perspectives*, Oxford: Blackwell, 37–54.

Thakur, R. 1994a: From Peacekeeping to Peace Enforcement: the UN Operation in Somalia. *The Journal of Modern African Studies*, 32(3), 387–410.

Thakur, R. 1994b: Human Rights: Amnesty International and the United Nations. *Journal of Peace Research*, 31(2), 143–60.

Thirlwall, A. P. 1994: *Growth and Development*. Basingstoke: Macmillan.

Tickner, J. A. 1991: Hans Morganthau's principles of political realism: a feminist reformulation. In R. Grant and K. Newland (eds), *Gender and International Relations*, Buckingham: Open University Press, 27–40.

Tisdall, S. 1994: Turn back and you face collapse, US tells Russia. *Guardian*, 25.1.94.

Toye, J. 1993: *Dilemmas of Development: Reflections on the Counter-Revolution in Development Economics*, second edition. Oxford: Blackwell.

Triffin, R. 1960: *Gold and the Dollar Crisis*. New Haven: Yale University Press.

Triffin, R. 1989: The International Monetary System and the Paper-Exchange Standard. In O. F. Hamouda, R. Rowley and B. M. Wolf (eds), *The Future of the International Monetary System*, Aldershot: Edward Elgar, 161–93.

Turner, B. S. (ed.) 1993: *Citizenship and Social Theory*. London: Sage.

Turner, B. S. 1993: Outline of a theory of human rights. In B. S. Turner (ed.), *Citizenship and Social Theory*, London: Sage, 162–90.

UNCTAD 1993: *Trade and Development Report 1993*. New York: United Nations.

United Nations, 1987: *Yearbook of the United Nations*. New York: United Nations.

United Nations, 1990: *Global Outlook 2000*. New York: United Nations.

United Nations 1991: *The World's Women: 1970–1990 Trends and Statistics*. New York: United Nations.

United Nations 1992: *Framework Convention on Climate Change*. A/AC.237/18 (Part II Add.1), 15 May 1992. Rio de Janeiro: UNGA.

United Nations Development Programme 1994: *Human Development Report 1994*. New York: Oxford University Press.

Usborne, D. 1992: Nixon corners Bush over aid to Russia. *Independent*, 13.3.92.

Van Evera, S. 1990/91: Primed for Peace: Europe after the Cold War. *International Security*, 15(3), Winter, 7–57.

Vogler, J. 1993: Security and Global Environmental Change. *Conflict Processes*, 1(2), 15–23.

Volten, P. M. E. (ed.) 1992: *Bound to Change: Consolidating Democracy in East Central Europe*. New York: Institute for East–West Studies.

Walker R. 1993: *Inside/Outside*. Cambridge: Cambridge University Press.

Wallensteen, P. and Axell, R. 1993: Armed Conflict at the End of the Cold War, 1989–92. *Journal of Peace Research*, 30(3), 331–46.

Wallerstein, I. 1974: *The Modern World System 1: Capitalist Agriculture and the Origins of the European–World Economy in the Sixteenth Century*. New York: Academic Press.

Wallerstein, I. 1991: *Geopolitics and Geoculture: Essays on the Changing World System*. Cambridge: Cambridge University Press.

Walton, J. and Seddon, D. 1994: *Free Markets and Food Riots: The Politics of Global Adjustment*. Oxford: Blackwell.

Waltz, K. 1979: *Theory of International Politics*. Reading, Mass.: Addison-Wesley.

Waltz, K. 1993: The Emerging Structure of International Politics. *International Security*, 18(2) Fall, 44–79.

Walzer, M. 1980: *Just and Unjust Wars*. Harmondsworth: Penguin.

Warren, B. 1980: *Imperialism: Pioneer of Capitalism*. London: Verso.

Waterman, P. 1993: *Globalization, Civil Society, Solidarity: Politics and Ethics of a World Both Real and Universal*. The Hague: Institute of Social Studies Working Paper no. 147.

Watkins, K. 1992: *Fixing the Rules: North–South Issues in International Trade and the GATT Uruguay Round*. London: Catholic Institute for International Relations.

Watkins, K. 1994: GATT: a Victory for the North. *Review of African Political Economy*, 59, 60–6.

Wendt, A. 1987: The Agent–Structure Problem in International Relations Theory. *International Organization*, 41.

White, S. 1977: Political socialization in the USSR: a study in failure? *Studies in Comparative Communism*, 10(3), Autumn, 328–42.

White, S. 1979: *Political Culture and Soviet Politics*. London: Macmillan.

White, S. 1993: Eastern Europe after communism. In S. White, J. Batt and P. Lewis (eds), *Developments in East European Politics*, Basingstoke: Macmillan, 2–15.

White, S., Batt, J. and Lewis, P. (eds) 1993: *Developments in East European Politics*. Basingstoke: Macmillan.

Willets, P. (ed.) 1995: *We the People: The Influence of Non-Governmental Organisations at the United Nations*. London: Christopher Hurst.

Williams, M. 1993: Re-articulating the Third World Coalition: The Role of the Environmental Agenda. *Third World Quarterly*, 14(1), 7–29.

Williamson, J. and Milner, C. 1991: *The World Economy*. New York: Harvester Wheatsheaf.

Winsbury, R. 1994: Who will pay for the Global Village? Funding the Buenos Aries Declaration, *Intermedia*, June/July, 22(3), 23–31.

Wiseman, J. 1993: Democracy and the new pluralism in Africa. *Third World Quarterly*, 14(3), 589–604.

Wolfers, A. 1962: *Discord and Collaboration*. Baltimore: Johns Hopkins University Press.

Woolacott 1994: Italy brainwashed by soft soap and hard sell. *Guardian*, 30.5.94, 24.

World Bank 1993: *World Development Report 1993*. New York: Oxford University Press.

World Bank 1994: *World Development Report 1994*. New York: Oxford University Press.

Young, S., McDermott, M. and Dunlop, S. 1991: The Challenge of the Single Market. In B. Burgenmeier and J. L. Mucchielli (eds), *Multinationals and Europe 1992*, London: Routledge, 3–21.

Zolo, D. 1992: *Democracy and Complexity – a realistic approach*. Oxford: Blackwell.

# List of Abbreviations

| | |
|---|---|
| ACP | African, Caribbean and Pacific Countries |
| AI | Amnesty International |
| ANC | African National Congress |
| APEC | Asia–Pacific Economic Cooperation |
| ATCP | Antarctic Treaty Consultative Party |
| CDI | Community-based Development Initiatives |
| CEDAW | Committee on the Elimination of all forms of Discrimination Against Women (also Convention) |
| CEE | Central and East European Countries |
| CEMA | Council for Mutal Economic Assistance |
| CERD | Committee on the Elimination of all forms of Racial Discrimination (also Convention) |
| CFC | Chlorofluorocarbon |
| CIS | Commonwealth of Independent States |
| CITES | Convention on Trade in Endangered Species |
| COMECON | Council for Mutual Economic Assistance |
| CPSU | Communist Party of the Soviet Union |
| CSCE | Conference on Security and Cooperation in Europe |
| EC | European Community |
| EEZ | Economic Exclusion Zone |
| EFTA | European Free Trade Association |
| ERM | Exchange Rate Mechanism |
| EU | European Union |
| FAO | Food and Agriculture Organization |
| FCCC | Framework Convention on Climate Change |
| FDI | Foreign Direct Investment |
| GATT | General Agreement on Tariffs and Trade |
| GDP | Gross Domestic Product |
| GEF | Global Environmental Facility |

| | |
|---|---|
| GNP | Gross National Product |
| ICRW | International Convention for the Regulation of Whaling |
| IISS | International Institute of Strategic Studies |
| IMF | International Monetary Fund |
| IMO | International Maritime Organization |
| INMARSAT | International Maritime Satellite Organization |
| IPCC | Intergovernmental Panel on Climate Change |
| ITO | International Trade Organization |
| LDC | Less Developed Country |
| LLDC | Least Developed Country |
| MARPOL | Conventions on Maritime Pollution |
| NACC | North Atlantic Cooperation Council |
| NAFTA | North American Free Trade Area |
| NAM | Non-Aligned Movement |
| NATO | North Atlantic Treaty Organization |
| NIC | Newly Industrializing Country |
| NIEO | New International Economic Order |
| NGO | Non-Governmental Organization |
| NTB | Non-tariff Trade Barrier |
| OAS | Organization of American States |
| ODA | Overseas Development Assistance |
| OECD | Organization for Economic Co-operation and Development |
| OPEC | Organization of Petroleum Exporting Countries |
| OSCE | Organization for Security and Cooperation in Europe |
| PPPD($) | Purchasing Power Parity Dollar ($) |
| SAL | Structural Adjustment Loan |
| TRIMs | Trade Related Investment Measures |
| TRIPs | Trade Related Intellectual Property Rights |
| TNC | Transnational Corporation |
| UNCED | United Nations Conference on the Environment and Development |
| UNCHE | United Nations Conference on the Human Environment |
| UNCTAD | United Nations Commission for Trade and Development |
| UNDP | United Nations Development Programme |
| UNEP | United Nations Environment Programme |
| UNHCR | United Nations High Commissioner for Refugees |
| UNICEF | United Nations Children's Fund |
| UNPROFOR II | United Nations Protection Force II |
| VERs | Voluntary Export Restraints |
| WEU | Western European Union |

# Index